PAMELA COLMAN SMITH

TAROT ARTIST

PAMELA COLMAN SMITH

TAROT ARTIST

~THE PIOUS PIXIE~

DAWN ROBINSON-WALSH

FONTHILL

First published in Great Britain in 2020 by Fonthill Media.
This edition published in 2026 by
Fonthill
An imprint of
Pen & Sword Books Ltd
Yorkshire – Philadelphia

ISBN 978-1-03615-651-0

A CIP catalogue record for this book is available from the British Library.

MIX
Paper | Supporting responsible forestry
FSC® C013604

The Publisher's authorised representative in the EU for product safety is
Authorised Rep Compliance Ltd., Ground Floor, 71 Lower Baggot Street, Dublin D02 P593, Ireland.
www.arccompliance.com

For a complete list of Pen & Sword titles please contact

PEN & SWORD BOOKS LIMITED
47 Church Street, Barnsley, South Yorkshire, S70 2AS, England
E-mail: enquiries@pen-and-sword.co.uk
Website: www.pen-and-sword.co.uk
or
PEN AND SWORD BOOKS
1950 Lawrence Road, Havertown, PA 19083, USA
E-mail: uspen-and-sword@casematepublishers.com
Website: www.penandswordbooks.com

Acknowledgements

This was a project born of my burning desire to know more about a woman I encountered writing my book, *Secret Bude*. Exploring Pamela's life was, at times, all-consuming. Her story requires a team of researchers and a limitless budget, but this is the work of one person; therefore, any errors of interpretation are mine alone.

Pamela's later life, which unfolds in stunningly dramatic Cornwall, particularly entranced me but I soon realised I could not understand her end without knowing more about her beginning and her transitions. Pamela had so many labels attached to her; it was surprising but gratifying to find no conclusive evidence for most of them.

Gratitude and thanks are very much due to:

The wonderful gentleman introduced by the late Barbara Alexander, the late Tony Edwards, the only person I met who knew Miss Smith. Pamela's errand boy in Bude, Tony's oral recollections helped immensely.

Aptly named Sister Benignus is the keeper of the Diocesan Archives for the Catholic Church. She provided me with what felt like a breakthrough in uncovering a collection of letters from Pamela to the then Bishop of Plymouth (with few responses). She was happy to let me see and use them. These convinced me my hunch about Pamela's devotion to Catholicism and sense of mission was correct.

Lynne Holehouse, the talented Bude artist who gave me space to write in her delightful studio, also created a unique artistic representation of Pamela, whose image watched over me as I sat writing and editing. A version is included in this book.

At the eleventh hour, Angie Hodges of the Catholic History Society visited Parc Garland, yielding amazing photographs of Pamela's home as it is now, including one of her chapel. I am immensely grateful to Angie and her husband, Phil Hodges, for their invaluable help, and to Hayley White, for our discussion of Parc Garland. When I visited, it was derelict.

Susanna Dark's intuitive tarot classes in Bude helped to spark my interest. Lorraine Puerto-Terron of The Bencoolen Inn, the site of Pamela's flat, was delightfully helpful. Jackie and Brian Adams who knew Father du Moulin-Brown, Pamela's priest, were an informative delight.

Ray Boyd kindly provided me with old photographs and information, especially of the Strand, to help me gain a feel for my beloved Bude in the 1940s when Pamela lived in the town.

Thanks also indeed to Darren Jones for his splendid image of Pamela with her toy theatre, to the National Trust for photos from Smallhythe, to the Royal Shakespeare Company for the image from Stratford, to the LSE's Women's History Collection for images that made me realise what a huge movement Women's Suffrage was, and to my mother-in-law, Dorothy Walsh, who lent me an original copy of Ellen Terry's memoirs containing some of Pamela's artwork.

Susannah Mayor, curator for the National Trust at Ellen Terry's Smallhythe home in Kent, was hugely helpful and informative, showing me incredible unpublished full-colour artwork of Pamela's. There are many others who took time to assist, including academics Melissa Boyd Parsons, Professor Katharine Cockin, Professor Kathleen Pyne, Mary Greer, The Catholic History Society, artist Jane Mackay for her insights on synaesthesia, and Susan O'Keeffe from the Yeats Society.

To my publisher, Fonthill Media, for having faith in my book and providing helpful guidance.

Last but very much not least, my good friends who have listened to me for what feels like years talking endlessly about Pamela, accompanying me on visits, helping with my research, answering questions, debating ideas, and listening to my incessant chatter: I thank you all.

CONTENTS

1
The Pious Pixie

Pixie painted, Pixie was pious, and Pixie died a pauper. An artistic career cut short by a curious religious devotion, she was a woman of little or no interest after 1920, though she lived until 1951. That is tarot artist Pamela Colman Smith's succinct life story, or is it?

Pamela, the notable creator of the world's best-selling tarot deck, was considered by many to be an extraordinary biracial, lesbian, mystical, synaesthete artist, whose main life achievement was her artwork for a deck of cards. So many labels attached attempting to define and categorise her as 'different' are overwhelming, yet in her early thirties, she grew mindful and found her faith, fully embracing the beliefs and rituals of the comforting Catholic Church. Contemporaries, if they cared at all, felt her change of mindset deleterious to her character and career, as she rose to fresh personal challenges embracing her new life in Cornwall through a faith that made her happier.

It is early summer 2017 when a group of enthusiastic (mainly American and female) visitors arrive by coach in Bude, Cornwall. They halt at the historic landmark Falcon Hotel, its gleaming white façade accentuated by bursts of radiant light. Beautifully situated alongside Bude's unique, choppy sea canal, the chill breeze hastens in from the harbour warmed only a little by the sun. The Falcon, built by Bude's benefactor, Sir Thomas Acland, has welcomed visitors for over two centuries, overlooked by the hillside parish church he also commissioned, part of the fabric of the unassuming coastal town where Pamela Colman Smith, known by some as 'Pixie', died aged seventy-three.

Journeying that day from Silvanus Trevail's gothic Camelot Hotel, originally created on the rugged Cornish coast as a railway terminus accommodation for those using the planned branch line from Camelford, the visitors travel to Bude from Tintagel, a place known for its Arthurian lore. As they stepped from the bus, making their way along the shady lane to the church, carrying their divining rods and pendulums to communicate with the spirit world, they visited Pamela's burial ground, paying their considerable respects to give their thanks to her memory. It is extraordinary how on their journey to uncover magical and mystical Britain, visiting towns like Glastonbury, they chose on this indecisive weather day to visit the small coastal town of Bude, nestled just inside the Duchy of Cornwall, to see the rather ordinary burial ground of the rather extraordinary Pamela.

I was invited by eminent tarot blogger, writer, and teacher, Mary Greer, to show the group St Michael's and All Angels churchyard, highly visible throughout Bude, given its prominent hillside position. The bells mournfully mark the passing of the hours, a poignant reminder of Pixie's hidden slumber. The church (built in 1834–5) is of a High Anglican persuasion but offers an ecumenical Bude burial ground for all Christian denominations, as it did for Pixie Pamela. Built by the Welsh architect, George Wightwick, gifted to the local people by their benefactor, the graveyard contains the remains of many mariners who died off the treacherous wreckers' coast fringing Bude; some were mere children, others adults, but among their number lies Miss Pamela Colman Smith, known anonymously in Bude as Miss Smith.

It is an unusual churchyard, for there are no crows cawing. By contrast, St Michael's is extremely tranquil, with melodic birdsong; it is a place at peace with itself, benignly guarding the canal.

The exact spot of Pamela's forever resting place is not known, much to the frustration of its seekers, but how much does it really matter? She was granted a pauper's burial, close to the silent woodland at the edge of the churchyard, marked at best by a wooden cross now long since decayed. This followed her minimal funeral service within the church, presided over by her Catholic parish priest, Father du Moulin Browne, who surely knew this devoted member of his flock very well. It seemed we were close to the spot as pendulums rhythmically swayed and Bude's special visitors intuited the psychic energy at this emotional, spiritual occasion. People believe in Pamela, wanting her to have the credit she deserves but never received, for her largely anonymised yet vital work in creating the Rider-Waite-Smith (previously Rider-Waite) tarot deck in 1909. They also want a grave, a site to visit. We are all fascinated by this vibrant, creative woman, yet some are even more intrigued by her conversion to Catholicism, which lasted from pre-1911 until the end of her days in 1951. Author Mary Greer wrote of the Bude visit on her blog:

> It was one of the highlights ... a group of Tarot enthusiasts we brought dowsing rods, a pendulum and a medium with us ... where the outer corner of the old churchyard seemed to yield a very positive response to our asking for her grave ... one of the participants dropped her pendulum in that spot and heard it hit the ground, but no amount of searching through the grass turned it up. When we got back to the bus the driver asked if anyone had left a pendulum in the bus, and there it was! So, that night at the Camelot Castle Hotel bar we used the pendulum to ask Pixie whether she had returned the

pendulum to the bus—Yes!—and if we had found her burial site, along with many more questions. Nothing scientific and definitive in all this, but ... our little foray into her mystery.[1]

Author Susan Wands, one of the visitors, noted in a 2018 podcast how she felt closer to Pamela in the bar of the Camelot Hotel than in the churchyard, feeling Pixie's legacy tells us to live life authentically, rather than seek out her grave.[2] Pamela liked a drink, so she would have enjoyed the gathering at the Camelot. As for paying homage to her in the churchyard, she would have undoubtedly caricatured the situation, as she did so many others, although she would perhaps have been secretly touched and pleased by the impromptu service in her honour.

The group expressed acute surprise that beautiful Bude, now a friendly family seaside and surfing resort known for its environmental vision, has no lasting memorial to Pamela, who died relatively unknown within the town having lived here for her latter unremarkable years, and in her beloved Cornwall for around thirty years altogether. Surprisingly, few people in the town know much about her. There is no blue plaque, no museum, no ostentatious display—indeed, no display at all. Bude has some old, long-established families who co-exist alongside a relatively transient population. People here come and go, as Pamela herself did. Did Bude just happen to be her final resting place or did she actively choose to be here? That is one of her many mysteries.

In 2018, another group followed the same journey. Linda Marson of Global Spiritual Studies, whose pendulum was the one previously lost during the 2017 visit, said:

> Magic happened today—I went around the graveyard testing my pendulum response at places I knew she was not buried (e.g., at gravestones). Then when I went to the spot from last year, the 'No' responses from the pendulum turned to 'Yes'. Others in the group who didn't know where I had 'found' her last year, also had positive responses at that spot from pendulums and dowsing rods.[3]

In her late twenties, Pamela, typically for a woman artist of her time, received little pay or credit for her tarot commission. Her name was not included in the original title, but she consistently managed to include her distinctive signature on each card except The Fool, who begins the tarot journey. Each tarot card bears her mark, a monogram resembling a caduceus with snake-entwined staff formed by letter 'P' overlaid with a 'C' and 'S', a signature she retained.

Her deck is not without its critics. While some see it as an intuitive deck, others find it old-fashioned, even patriarchal. Writer, surrealist artist, and occultist Ithell Colquhoun (1906–1988) who herself illustrated a taro (her preferred spelling) deck saw Pamela's (Waite's) as corrupt, especially in introducing a gender imbalance into the court cards by substituting knaves for princesses, and for introducing pentacles.[4] Curiously, though born later than Pamela, she also moved to West Cornwall where she died in Lamorna, also of heart failure; however, unlike Pamela, whose interest was relatively short-lived, Colquhoun remained an occultist, retaining an interest in organisations like the Hermetic Order of the Golden Dawn. It is Pamela's deck, however, that remains a world bestseller, as tarot is now very much more interpretive, interactive, and empathetic than ever before. Pamela's artwork, if viewed intuitively, as she suggested, allows for this.

Her deck has been very cleverly marketed in recent years. As a woman, Pamela earned little from her labour, but others have since benefited from her work. Tarot for the masses rather than simply occultists was a paradigm shift occurring in the late 1950s after her death, a shift to which Pamela had (unwittingly) contributed. In 1959, the Waite-Smith deck was reproduced for popular sale, along with Waite's book. Then, actress Eden Gray published her book that convinced people anyone could learn to read the tarot; it needed no special gift. Card reading is now more accessible and less mystical, bridging the gap between rationality and belief. Tarot developed a market.

Today, she would be rich on the fruits of her talents, so her global followers are on a mission to restore Pamela to her rightful place in the world of tarot. However, as important as the tarot is, she achieved much more in her life than this inspired artwork of seventy-two divining cards. Having flirted with mysticism for around ten years, tarot played only a small part, having little lasting personal impact, though it is thought on The Lizard that she read the tarot in the attic of Parc Garland, her Cornish home, traditionally the servants' quarters. The paint splatters on the floor there also indicate her continued love of painting. However, the cards in 1909 were a much-needed job for a freelance illustrator. She had more than a passing interest in astrology and the occult, but the evidence insists she was far more devoted to her later Catholic faith.

Her childhood was peripatetic; her early adulthood was, if not bohemian, shared with those notables who were. Her work was prolific but inconsistent. It was her later life that developed most curiously as she progressed from celebrity to obscurity via her chosen religious path. Pamela's Cornwall years (over thirty in all) did not lead her to greatness but her pious years form a vital and until now, ignored, part of her life and history.

2

Childhood: A Bird of Passage

The only surviving child born to a relatively elderly mother, Pamela was artistic and well-travelled from an early age, likely the precocious only child of middle-class American parents. Some writers mention family links to Jamaica, which may explain why Pamela's mother seemed keen to spend time there, but no one has so far verified who this family was. This perpetuates the popular belief that Pamela was a 'woman of colour'.

After the birth/death of her brother Charles (1873), Pamela's birth was proudly announced in *The Standard*. With no siblings to monopolise her parents' time and attention, she did not have the intense childhood friendships, sibling rivalry, and emotional closeness brothers and sisters naturally bring in their wake, though she had cousins with whom she enjoyed amicable relations. Despite a good deal of adult company, in some ways she remained childlike, which was one of the regular comments made of her by contemporaries; she also, no doubt, partly lived in her own fantasy world. Being a communicator, especially remaining in touch with wider family until and during adulthood, was important to her. There is a collection of seventeen letters from Pamela to her cousin, Mary B. Reed, held at Bryn Mawr Library, Pennsylvania.[1] The letters, spanning 1896–1900, were sent from Jamaica, New York, and London, while a young Pamela pursued her fledgling illustrative career.

Those letters report on her various activities of writing and staging amateur plays, designing theatrical sets and costumes, and constructing advertising posters for family and friends, all highly creative; her letters were very self-focused. One dated 25 July 1896 from St Andrew, Jamaica, includes four pages addressed to 'Bobby' (Mary Reed). Pamela describes, like any other young woman, social engagements with friends and books she was reading. She discusses the American presidential race between Bryan and McKinley (the Republican won) while mentioning a parade of soldiers passing her gate. Most of her letters were accompanied by drawings and sketches, adding to their authentic, informative, and engaging nature. She was a prolific producer of creative artwork, also enjoying a busy, socially and politically aware life as a keen learner and commentator, her letters conveying excitement and drama. She noted the way others dressed, their characters, and their speech; indeed, she was an acute and astute observer of people, befitting an artist whose work regularly focused on human form.

An Aquarian, born in Pimlico, London, on 16 February 1878, Pamela was raised in Manchester, England, for the first ten years of her childhood, taking her first long sea voyage while very young; later, by contrast, she lived in St Andrew, Jamaica. Her early socialisation was largely, as was the accepted middle-class norm, by servants. We understandably hear little of Pamela's mother's imprint on her childhood, as servants performed childcare, which was considered an onerous duty for middle-class mothers. Pamela's first address (27 Belgrave Road in SW1) is not unattractive.[2] An elegant road, number 27 is now valued at just under £1 million, indicating her family was affluent, bearing in mind that is just for a share of the freehold building, comprising one bedroom, a bathroom, and one reception room—less than the Colman Smiths presumably rented.

Children born in the late Victorian era to traditional families were expected to be absorbed into their parents' lives and concerns, while often developing primary attachments to the nursemaids who nurtured them. Eileen Janes Yeo noted how in Britain and France, where marriage and motherhood were idealised, the worst fate possible was to be an 'old maid', yet the reality was that most middle-class mothers were not fully immersed in the lives of their children at all.[3] For fathers, this had, of course, long been the case. The myth of motherhood prevailed, but the reality was that few mothers who had other options undertook the tedious full daily care of their children.

Meanwhile, servants were important people to have around; their impact should not be underestimated. Around one in seven employed people by 1900 was a servant, many of whom were women (1.25 million by 1881, although this reduced as other options became available and girls were educated for longer).[4] Many middle-class women only had to concern themselves about organising the servants, not actually doing the housework or actively engaging in childcare. Many were, resultingly, emotionally detached from their children. They loved them, of course, upholding expectations of them, but simply enjoyed or endured more limited interaction than is currently usual, Corinne Colman included. Ellen Jordan explains how women were educated towards marriage and motherhood as expressions of their femininity.[5] Corinne Colman was, like other women, subject to this dominant ideology of her time. Understandably then, when Pamela's parents died, not many years apart, we hear of no massive outpouring of her grief, which is not to say she did not feel any. However, she seemed to pick herself up and move efficiently forward in a very capable, sensible, mature manner, making useful contacts along the way, networking her way through life.

The male was of paramount importance in the household when Pamela was young. Carol Dyhouse explains how households were very much organised around male needs as breadwinners.[6] The male public world was largely inaccessible to women, be they wives or daughters, ably demonstrated by the sisters in the Yeats family, contemporaries and friends of Pamela, whose skills and needs were utterly secondary to those of the men, their brothers and father, yet whose income generation was absolutely vital to sustaining the family.

Women were not expected to have any occupation that stood in the way of the needs of others, be they husbands, brothers, children, or servants. For an intelligent woman, this must have been a major source of frustration. Corinne Colman, Pamela's mother, was considered a very bright, sociable woman, who could memorise huge amounts of text and perform it to an audience within the secure confines of people's homes; therefore, following her husband's work was unlikely to have truly satisfied her. The damp drizzle of Manchester was nothing like the drawing rooms of her home territory of Brooklyn, New York, where she could enjoy performing within a socially acceptable safe environment, nor did it have the warm climate of Jamaica. She provided a role model for the young Pamela, surely sharing tales of her own childhood. Both mother and daughter were performers, liked an appreciative audience, understood the value of a good story, and, most importantly, could captivate others.

Frances Cogan suggested a volatile national climate of boom-bust growth meant men's—and therefore their families'—lives in late nineteenth-century America could turn very quickly.[7] One year, a family would have servants and build a new house, but by the next year, they could easily be bankrupt. Families travelled to be where the work was, as Pamela's father regularly did—hence, the peripatetic nature of her upbringing.

Women like Corinne Colman, however, were growing increasingly aware they also had to learn certain skills to get them through life in times of crisis, to support their male partners, and, at times, themselves. The days of an ornamental, leisured existence had long since gone, yet real opportunities for women were still frustratingly very few during this time of transition. Economic reality urged young women to prepare to engage in the workplace, yet contradictorily, the American womanly ideal was still of a creature of unchallenged leisure; life was a difficult mismatch for these women. As Cogan explained, ideas of fragility clashed with notions of competence. It was during these controversial times of immense social and economic change, especially for women, that Pamela was born. The couple adopted the increasingly popular form of a double-barrelled surname for Pamela's name, without the hyphen, as was the fashion.

Unsurprisingly, Pamela's father travelled widely with his work, with Corinne Colman dutifully following at his side. Her life in England may well have felt comparatively dull after her 'diseuse' days in Brooklyn, where she, a lover of English theatre, would recite dramatic monologues, but she would have had little choice other than to accompany him. In England, it is likely the Colman Smiths were a very autonomous, self-contained unit, far more socially isolated than they would have been among family in America, which made Pamela capable, from an early age, of coping with great change, as well as of entertaining herself. Travel and upheaval to her were both normal, though at times she noted it was difficult to settle.

Little is known of Pamela's relationship with her mother, implying either a certain detached coolness or simply a lack of evidential material, but we do know that following her mother's premature death (about which there seems little detail), she travelled to England with her father. Corinne Colman was born on 4 July 1834 and died in 1896, though there is confusion even about this as she allegedly lied about her age (stating it as thirty on the 1881 census). Susan Wands (2021) has written that Corinne's leg appears to have been amputated prior to her death, implying gangrene. While Corinne was buried in Jamaica, her leg was shipped to Brooklyn's Greenwood Cemetery, where it was buried some months later. This is borne out by cemetery and newspaper references in the public domain. Her husband, Pamela's father, Charles (Chas) Smith, was born in 1846 and died in 1899. Corinne, unusually twelve years older than her husband, was thus in her mid-forties when Pamela arrived, explaining why no more babies followed, and why she often understated her age. In Didsbury, Manchester, the family had two servants listed on the census, one of whom was Pamela's nurse. We know more of Pamela's interactions with her father than we do of her with her mother, despite Susan Wands trying to fill the gap in her fascinating work of fantasy fiction, indicating Corinne Colman knew Pamela was 'special' (as in visionary) from an early age.[8]

3

A Woman of Colour?

Like many Americans, Pamela was originally of immigrant stock, suggests the Tripod website, which includes references to extensive genealogical researches undertaken by others.[1] Her inheritance included movers and shakers, people travelling to succeed, and proactive emigrants. She, too, moved around depending on opportunity, the concept being very familiar to her. Pamela had a distinguished background of economically successful ancestors, so enjoyed a relatively comfortable upbringing and ready source of funds, leading to later accusations of living on unearned income by her one-time friend, Lily Yeats, sister of the poet, who expressed an understandable element of jealousy and resentment as Lily's life was far from financially comfortable, and at times, extremely straitened. No luxury of inheritance came to Lily, alas.

Despite her American parentage and citizenship, Pamela played to her audience, often creating the impression she disliked America (or at least, New York), yet she wanted to remain American, despite her complaints about the people. Regardless of living most of her life in England, perhaps it was, ultimately, home, her identity, her lineage, and a more progressive place where her art was appreciated during her Stieglitz exhibition years. She finally requested her American passport in 1916 when she was living in England, providing a birth certificate and three letters vouching for her American nationality, including one from the actress Dame Ellen Terry. America only seemed to require passports during wartime (including the Civil War). Pretty much anything went in terms of the photograph required, but distinguishing features were listed.

At the age of thirty-eight, we see Pamela described herself as an artist and illustrator, 5 feet and 4 inches in height, with a medium forehead, brown eyes, broad nose, medium mouth, dark brown hair, medium complexion, and a round face.[2] She signed the United States Oath of Allegiance and was personally identified by a Dorothy Walker, who had known Pamela since she was fifteen, a Major Burnet, and Thos. P. George of the Colman Traders' Association.

Her ancestors were the Smiths and the Hookers (paternal), along with the Colmans and the Chandlers (maternal), with her ancestral family hailing from

New England. All these families settled in Massachusetts having originally arrived from England, and all seemed to make their mark on their new land, as one might expect from the kind of enterprising, ahead of the game people who chose to emigrate. Her paternal grandfather, Cyrus Porter Smith, was a wealthy lawyer, merchant, and politician (mayor) in Brooklyn, New York. However, he was also a man of deep social conscience, a Whig. Cyrus was the first mayor (known by many as 'Uncle Cyrus') to be elected by the popular vote in 1839. This founder of Brooklyn Hospital also helped to introduce schools. From poor farming stock, he determined to attend college and did so with honour, paying his way through his studies to become a lawyer. Pamela also developed a social conscience as we see in her work for the Suffrage Atelier and wartime fundraising for the Red Cross.

Cyrus was originally descended from Samuel Smith who arrived at Connecticut, settling in Hartford.[3] A fascinating earlier Smith was Philip (1632–1684/5), who left England as a baby and was later killed by 'witchcraft'. The woman who allegedly led to his demise was Mary Webster, the infamous 'Witch of Hadley'. Sent to Boston and tried for witchcraft, she survived, dying only in 1696. Pamela would surely have loved hearing this story of a woman surviving against the odds. It went rather like this: after Philip Smith died, his corpse had swelling in one breast, bruises on his back, and holes made with awls. He died of delirium and fits one Saturday morning, but by Sunday, his body was still warm despite the eerie chill outside. By Monday, his face was discoloured, with blood running down his cheek. Strange noises were heard in the room where his corpse lay. To achieve 'justice' for his death, some lads dragged poor Mary from her house, hanged her until she was nearly dead, then rolled her in snow before burying her in it. They were either inept or she was very strong, or both. Canadian novelist and poet Margaret Atwood believes she is descended from Mary, so in 1995 wrote a poem, *Half-Hanged Mary*, about her ancestor. Her novel *The Handmaid's Tale* is also dedicated to her.

The Tripod website is so packed with ancestral information, there is no need to reinvent it here, except to mention Thomas Hooker who also moved to Hartford, enjoying the role of preacher.[4] He founded the colony of Connecticut, where a statue of him remains. Thomas Hooker was a prominent Puritan, well-educated in divinity at Cambridge. An eloquent preacher, his son, Samuel, became a merchant, so Pamela's beginnings certainly have a Puritan edge, perhaps at odds with her later conversion to Catholicism, but certainly in line with her (Protestant) work ethic of constant endeavour and her later devotion.

Among her other esteemed ancestors, Thomas Colman was one of the men who purchased Nantucket Island from the Native American Indians in 1660, while Edmund Chandler (1585–1602) became constable and CEO of the Duxbury Colony, Plymouth, in 1637. Again, we see white English ancestry as the Colmans were stock raisers originating from Wiltshire in England. The Chandlers moved to Massachusetts where there are more links with the

Plymouth Colony; they seemed to settle in New England. Sadly, though any Jamaican links may have made Pamela appear more exotic, they are hard to find, so they were probably self-created for enchanting effect.

Later, Samuel Colman (not to be confused with Samuel Coleman) was born on 4 March 1832, dying in 1920, a well-known landscape painter influenced by the Hudson River School. He was a fine arts engraver in both Boston and New York. His eldest daughter, Pamela Atkins Colman, and his wife, Pamela Lewis Chandler Colman, were both successful children's authors. Pamela was a traditional family name, though 'our' Pamela sometimes preferred to use Corinne or even Corine depending on her mood. Certainly, her heritage contained a high degree of creativity, both artistic and literary.

Due to Pamela's exotically engineered appearance, it is often suggested her mother was West Indian. There is a drawing of her mother, Corinne, in Mrs Colman's (Pamela's maternal grandmother) book *The Mother's Present*, which portrays her as decidedly white, plus a photograph of Corinne's older brother, the artist, Samuel, who was likewise white.[5] In *Stories for Corinne*, written by Mrs Colman, published by her husband (as was the way) in Boston, the said Corinne is described as 'pretty and fair'.[6] This does not imply dark-skinned. She was also considered 'a beautiful little girl, who always obeyed her parents, and who loved her brothers and sisters', which tells us nothing of her ethnicity but much about how children were expected to behave.

Many online photographs of Pamela's wider family also suggest white lineage. It would have been highly unlikely Corinne Colman married interracially, and there are no indicators Pamela's father was of mixed race, either. However, the curious books by Mrs Colman provide a taste of what parenting and childhood was like at the time. Children were expected to obey, fit in, be good, and adopt a gender-specific role. 'Seen and not heard' was appropriate for children like Corinne Colman, though precocity was probably acceptable.

An Ancestry search shows Pamela's father as white, with angular features. Pamela seems to favour her mother in appearance, suggesting artist John Yeats's comment on her appearance is unreliable. He wrote in a letter to his son, William:

> Pamela Smith and her father are the funniest-looking people, the most primitive Americans possible, but I like them much ... Miss Smith her father always said even when addressing her ... She does not draw well, but has the right feeling for line and experience and colour. Her dressing is not a decorative success. The bluest of blue dresses, you feel disposed to call it scarlet, blue seems in this connection such a mild word ... the hat is straw, with great black cork feathers sticking out of it. She looks exactly like a Japanese. Nannie says this Japanese appearance comes from constantly drinking iced water...I don't think there is anything great or profound in her, or very emotional or practical. She has the simplicity and naïveté of an old dry as dust savant ...[7]

Pamela's alleged response to this, rather than taking verbal umbrage, was to draw herself wearing a kimono sipping iced water.

The only living person in Bude, Cornwall, who knew Miss Smith was Tony Edwards, her errand boy during the 1940s.[8] Tony described her as 'exotic looking, more Romany than West Indian, or possibly even Japanese'. In 2017, he one day pointed out an unsuspecting lady crossing Nanny Moore's Bridge in Bude, the town where Pamela died, and explained the Miss Smith he knew was of similar height (shortish), stature (solid or plump, but not obese), and complexion (tanned Caucasian). He did say she often looked pale and wan, in need of good Cornish sunshine, indicating how, in her later years, she rarely left her home due to her poor health. Although she was older by this time, there is no indication of West Indian colouring, and earlier photos of Pamela at Smallhythe in Kent again suggest pallor, though a darkness of hair and eyes, as borne out by her passport details.

Pamela's mother, Corinne Colman, married Charles Edward Smith late in life, on 28 September 1870, in New York, leaving an eight-year gap before Pamela was born, indicating conception or pregnancy was not easy. The son of Cyrus Smith and Lydia Lewis (again, no suggestion of West Indian heritage), Charles was born 27 May 1846, in Brooklyn, dying on 1 December 1899, also in Brooklyn. His later funeral service was held at his brother-in-law's residence, Willis L. Ogden of 73 Pierrepont St., Brooklyn, very quickly on 3 December. Living much of the time in London, Charles at one time represented in New York an English firm of decorators and was later an auditor for the West Indian Improvement Company, which involved him in a good deal of travel between St Andrew, Jamaica, and New York, but he retained his strong links with Brooklyn. This is the Jamaican link. It related to work not lineage, despite the persistent rumour Pamela was at least half Jamaican. There is so far also no evidence to support her sometimes alleged adoption either. Her Jamaican traits developed from her acute observations of her nanny who seemed to have entire charge of her.

For brevity's sake, this family history is not thorough but confirms Pamela was born into a fascinating, high-achieving family, with artistic links and some curious history; there was prominence even as far back as Philip Smith. She was a white American, closely linked with England by her history (which may be why she chose to live here) with ancestors who were migrants, the dynamic 'doers' of this world, discovering the new and creating fresh lives, while we see no actual evidence of the mixed-race ethnicity so many assume she has, and which is often used to perpetuate the myth. It seems, in many ways, Pamela simply followed on in the family tradition of storytelling and drawing, using her unusual talents as best she could in a changing world. The fact this storytelling evolved from using Jamaican folklore led to a mythology of its own.

4

Her Letters to Bigelow Paine

What a wonderful treat to read people's letters, as they tell us a far more authentic tale than any author's narrative. Pamela's correspondence with American author and biographer, Albert Bigelow Paine, provides a fascinating insight into her thinking and activities, how much she travelled, her productivity, but also her developing character at a time of deep transition.[1] Her letters were sent as a young woman not only from New York in 1898–99 but also later from England.

Was she aware of Paine's 'secret life'? Max McCoy suggests Albert abandoned his first wife, Minnie, for a woman called Dora.[2] His unresolved divorce case possibly made him a bigamist. He was known to stutter, the origin of 'Tutter', as he was affectionately known, though this was said to be cured in a day during 1921. McCoy, who is no fan of the man, writes: 'Albert Bigelow Paine was a wildly unreliable narrator of his own life story. He was a liar, a cad, a poser'. Well, whatever he was, he was also interesting enough to enjoy an honest exchange of letters with Pamela.

Born in Massachusetts in 1861, Paine was a handsome author and editor, esteemed biographer (three volumes) of Mark Twain, and children's editor of the *New York Sunday Herald*, making him a useful contact for someone in Pamela's field of work, so she cultivated him as was her wont. She learned very early that who you know is important. On 7 August 1898, Pamela was obviously travelling in Somerset with her father, writing to Paine from the compact but beautiful cathedral city of Wells.

She joked to him about her messy scrawl. Ever the mimic, she liberally sprinkled in a few Yankee words, like 'Howdee' and 'Thankee', complaining it was 'bloomin' hot in London' where they had spent four weeks. She described London as 'blingy'. She wrote evocatively of characters met, some 'disgruntled and squeaky-voiced'. Describing the illustrative work she was completing, she also name-dropped Bram Stoker, saying they met:

> … but did not get on very well! He is the original O'Dwyer! In Trelawny! … just as we were getting on all right and he had given us seats to Robespierre,

he went and got sick with pneumonia as usual! They always get that! It's so bloomin' popular.[3]

Her slapstick sense of humour and poor spelling is apparent in her letter dated 7 August.

We saw an adaption of the Tale of Two Cities...and he (actor) just sits on Irving an' squashes him flatttttt! Ha! Best thing we have seen here at all in the play line.... Ireland was blingy, so green. We were twelve days coming over... and so glad to get ashore. Went to Bath for a day—awful hot there and came here to Wells.[4]

There, she was impressed, describing it as 'bully', especially enjoying its clock with jousting knights on horseback rushing around upon every quarter-hour strike. They were then planning to move on to Exeter, followed by a visit to see Devon-born vicar and author Sabine Baring-Gould, a keen teller of folk tales and ballads, who described Widdicombe as marvellous, and whose songs 'Widdicombe Fair' and 'The Golden Vanity' she illustrated. Everywhere she travelled, she had an eye to making contacts and finding work, but the West Country was no stranger to her. When she later moved to Cornwall, she would have remembered happy times in the south-west.

Tomorrow we are going to Glastonbury Abbey and Cheddar where the cheeses come from...we are comin' home dead broke so will give St Nick some old bargains cheap! Ha! Yeats is staying with a Lady Gregory and she has invited me to stay for a day or two with her![5]

She signs off as Pam.

Pamela's father's postscript is also amusing, both very American and of its time—almost a line from an old movie:

Say Tutter, me daughter can't write for a cent but she can pen for a sentiment ... Do I long for my 'appy 'ome? Not often. But at times the artist's assistant thinks she should have fresh water in her color pan and (he) flies to get it. He does not fly back, but saunters. Got it? Yes, indeed.[6]

We see here a charming, easy relationship between 'Miss Smith' and her father, both well-blessed with humour.

By 23 August, they are in Tintagel, Cornwall, at King Arthur's Castle Hotel. We again see her irreverence, this time when talking about Henry Irving:

I wonder if he can manage all the mixy up parts! (of a play) ... was quite merry and puffed and puffed at a Jamaican cigar and wanted to know if I ever designed costumes for a play (may get a job!!) ... we are off to Tavistock tomorrow.[7]

By January 1900, following her father's death, she is signing herself Pixie Pam, and by December, she is in Leeds at The Queen's Hotel, touring with the Lyceum crowd. She is described in an article as scarcely on the boards at all with the Lyceum, but somehow, she remained there. Nonetheless, Pamela enjoyed it.

> So much to do. How is the publishing trade? It's just as bad here. I hear from you sometimes through Dow… I am on tour with E.T. as probably you have heard from some of the Gang!—it is such fun! ... we end next week at Brighton—Scotland was just ripping! Edinburgh—oh my! Glasgow most encouraging! and Manchester very nice—went all over the house I lived in until I was 10—such fun! And walks in the fields and saw the house I used to say Robinson Cruso's mother lived in! Liverpool a very American place and of course I didn't like it! What kind of books are selling now?[8]

Her writing hurtles from topic to topic, a sign of her ever-active mind. Her next letter is dated 16 January 1901, from Winchelsea, where we find she has no permanent home.

> I have not any settled place to be In ... Pixie poetry book—a collection of 60 fairy poems—still being considered by Richards! who is as conventional as the rest of the tribe of publishers! pigs all ... I am here with Edy and Chris for a week or so—such a delightful place, backgrounds galore, all to be used for 'Little Charles'. A huge gray stone church with ivy on it and red tile roof—splendid. The largest village church in England. Rye in the distance on top of a little hill, red-roofed ... with the gray sea beyond and little ships in the harbour.[9]

By 17 March 1901, she is writing in green ink from Whitstable, though there are more apologies for having no time for writing. Outspoken in her condemnation, by now, she is peeved by the publisher's response to *Little Charles* 'is finished and gone to Grant Richards! pig! Last thing he said was "it's too artistic". What ROT!' She writes emphatically and emotionally, her letters crammed with exclamation marks of surprise, annoyance, and excitement.

More positively, she attended a studio tea with W. B. Yeats. She also describes Mrs Beatrice Erskine, co-editor and the hostess, as a 'pig' for making silly remarks and interrupting the great poet.

> Ha! It was fun! Held by Mrs Erskine, editoress (we know 'em) of a new magazine called The Kensington and for which I am doing a lot of drawings. 4 sketches

> and a full- page drawing! The Studio tea was held in 2 studios in a mews! Stables all about! When it got too crowded in one! little bands of company crossed the stable yard—through flocks of chickens and hens and straw![10]

A friend, Christabel Marshall, also attended the event. Pamela mentions many people in passing in her letters but we note that rarely, if friends, does she tell us much about them. Her descriptions are mainly reserved for acquaintances. Her speech, like many of her drawings, is sheer caricature, exaggerated, and grotesquely comic at times. She was not only a keen observer of people but also noticed changes in the natural world, something less obvious in her later correspondences, when money troubles seem to overtake everything else. She mentions Peter the Great, a Shetland pony exercised in a little cart, and various caged birds.

> Primroses in the Canterbury woods, where I went t'other day with some nice farm people who live 3 miles across squashy fields and stiles and streams—larks in fields 'a singing', cold wind, showers and cocks a crowin'. It's so nice![11]

Despite this reverie, work was in London, so she planned to return to see if she was needed for rehearsals. At a more practical level, she also discussed her (art) fixative doing strange things, which needed attending to. Her letters would flit from the sublime to the dull, making them engaging but largely self-obsessed.

By 28 May 1901, she was back in the theatre.

> Been very busy! Dress rehearsals and new plays. Helping Edy and getting my office and theatre in order. We call it the Henrietta Theatre ...
>
> E.T. is very well! Better than she has been for months and months! ... Thanks for papers you sent. I should say magazines. Chris dipped into them freely for 'Far & Near' which she writes for 'The Lady' every week ... I told Teddy Craig some weeks ago to write you and send some drawings—he is so very cracky! ... you might get an idea for a sort of mad person for a book!—from his letters!
>
> I have been to Chislehurst ... a nice place ... lovely woods ... clouds of bluebells ...[12]

There was the occasional descriptive gem among the ordinary.

By August 1901, she has a much more regular hand, with vastly improved writing. Maybe this is because she is commiserating with Albert.

> Poor Old Tutter. I'm so sorry. Such sad things do happen. There isn't any more to say, so I won't...
>
> I am getting into some colour prints ... and starting A Broad Sheet with Jack Yeats. He is brother to Willy the 'oatmeal meal chest' and draws such bully things! I have been staying in Devonshire for more than a week. Mrs Yeats draws

> awfully nice (damned with faint praise?) things too and they have a lovely house in the deepest valley in Devon and a studio in an apple orchard! Please do you know any rich publishers who might subscribe to A Broad Sheet? The Yeatses are going to try to persuade Willy (the mildewed one as E.T. calls him) to write something we could use. I would have liked to have come over and first peeked in on you all but it does cost a lot and my books don't sell well enough! [1]
>
> I got a royalty on The Golden Vanity for six months (1 dollar!) It must have been hard for Doubleday to part with it!
>
> Will you sometime go and call on cousin Ella Howard? I know she would be awful glad to see you and she'd cheer you up a lot! She is living with her mother, Mrs Lewis, 125 Hicks Street, Brooklyn (almost next to the corner of Clark Street)—it's on the Heights and not far. Do go and tell her I told you to be cheered up![13]

She adds:

> I had a splendid summer in Devon. 3 weeks at a farm with the Davises, and then at the Yeatses - I went to Widdicombe! ... it's a big church and almshouse built in 1600 and 3 or 4 cottages, that's all! A lovely valley in the middle of the moor, and clover. I never saw so many clover plants anywhere—awful windy on the moor! I got beastly neuralgia with the wind—I think that's what the old gray mare had! The Devon people talk so strangely—they say 'is fay' when they mean 'yes, faith'. At Dartmouth, they fish for mackerel and when they see the fish playing they call out 'these 'um play!'
>
> Uncle Teddy is coming to see me in October.[14]

Pixie Pamela, again making practical suggestions, exhorts him to keep his spirits up and not to get down.

December 1901 provides more information about Pamela and the Yeats family. This is when Pamela seems to have decided to stay in England, organising delivery of her belongings from America.

> I have got my things over the deep water and here they are again—just as they used to be—a little more battered, a little more friendly, and more than ever welcome! I've been working hard ever since I decided not to go over to N.Y. and heaps more to do!
>
> I went over to Dublin in October ... and had just a bully time with Lolly and Lilly and Jack Yeats and Willie! He is a treat! The poet—so like an owl! Kind of chants in his talk—and looks through his glasses sort of kockeyed [*sic.*]! Ha! Forced!
>
> The Broad Sheet isn't out yet! Do get us a few subscribers! ... I go to the Irish Literary on Fridays to a Galic [*sic.*] class—don't learn much, but it's so funny![15]

By 1904, she is writing *The Green Sheaf*, which she is reducing in output as there are so many other things to do. She is also storytelling, her big success.

> I am telling *Annancy Stories* very often now. I hope in time to make some money by it. *Green Sheaf* does not pay yet—it is most discouraging to go on working at it. I have a good scheam [*sic.*]—a hand press! ... a lot of work but anyway no printers' bills if you print yourself!
>
> Lately, I've not seen many visions, but some dreams many and wonderful. Do you see things? Do you know anything of astrology? It seems to me more practical than most other things—don't you think so?[16]

Do we see here the beginnings of some interest in astrology as she is by now involved in the Hermetic Order of the Golden Dawn?

> The *Annancy Stories* amuse me but are very small and outside but it is amusing to watch the people.
>
> I saw a book in a dream the other day with a picture of 'angels at the well getting water'—very nice! Also, two angels with fans of happiness! Like Honey Pots! There is a wonderful exhibition of Blake drawings and paintings on view now here—I never knew his colour was so rich! ... The River of Life is a beautiful one. [2]
>
> What is happening in New York? Have they all stuck where they all were 4 years ago? What people from America I've seen seem to be very much stick in the mud hampered—weighted down dull - narrow without feeling sort of people! And those that have feeling all so dull! So empty! They seem to suck in all you give 'em and give nothing back! Why can't people be simple? They are all so affected and empty dull dull dull!!! Stupid. Well, I think I've blown off enough to you and now can go on working![17]

During 1906, she visited New York again and was very excited visitors from Jamaica were going to arrive for a few days on their way to England. She signed herself as 'Pam' regularly mentioning she is always in mad haste. By 1907, she is back in London. Her writing becomes scrappy, note-like, makes little sense, and her communications are far fewer. She seems hasty, always busy, rushed but, of course, still short of money.

On 29 October, in purple ink, she writes:

> This is a queer world the more I see of it! I doubt I will get to America! This winter! I think things look bad - bad over there for money things! And I want to sell drawings and tell stories if I come! I should like to for many reasons! 2 or 3 months! Not more![18]

5

Mixing with the Great and Good

As her letters tell us, by 1899, following her mother's death, Pamela and her father were both back in England and Ireland to meet the well-known artistic and literary Yeats family. Sometimes, it seemed like Pamela spent much of her life on ships; she was a frequent seasoned traveller, voyaging the Atlantic from an early age. Additionally, her father seemed ambitious for her or maybe simply knew what a tough time ahead an outspoken, unmarried, and motherless female artist might have.

By this time, Pamela was already busily writing; she had published her *Annancy Stories* of Jamaican folk tales but was additionally working hard as an illustrator. She was undeniably prolific in output, creative and imaginative, brimful of potential, with noticeable talent, combined with her propensity for hard work when she enjoyed the tasks involved. We can assume her father planned a future in England for them both, but this was sadly not to be, for he died suddenly and unexpectedly when back in America in 1899. Pamela thus had to make her own way forward. It was a tough struggle for a young single female, parentless, as she transitioned into early womanhood.

When her father died, she was touring with the Lyceum Theatre Company in America, acting 'bit' parts. A thespian, she enjoyed being a small but involved part of the travelling theatrical community, sanctuary following her life-changing bereavements. It helped her to earn some money. The Lyceum, for around thirty years between 1871 and 1902, was the acting home of the indomitable Sir Henry Irving and the captivating Dame Ellen Terry, excelling and complementing each other in their productions of Shakespeare's plays. Despite an erratic education, we know Pamela enjoyed Shakespeare, for one of her many book ideas that never succeeded involved illustrations of Shakespeare's heroines.

Today, it is hard to imagine how unbelievably popular these plays were, the actors being the major superstar celebrities of their day. To give a taste, Irving's production of *Hamlet* ran for 200 nights. *The Merchant of Venice* remained for 250, though in total was performed on 1,000 occasions. By 1901, Irving was sixty-three years old and a Sir. It was much later, in 1925, three years before her death, that Ellen Terry was made a Dame. Their reputations were immense and unmatched; combined, they were an even greater whole. Pamela was incredibly fortunate to work with both; they would become her so-called 'surrogate parents', another of the myths surrounding her.

In addition to Irving and Terry, Dubliner Bram (Abraham) Stoker, the author of *Dracula* (a character thought to have been based on Irving), also worked for twenty years between 1878 and 1905 as the theatre's business manager. Here, we see where Pamela's circle interrelated as she knew them all. Irishman Bram shared an interest with the Yeats sisters in their mother's home town of Sligo, becoming friends with the poet, their brother, William Butler Yeats. Stoker's role as manager included travelling with the Lyceum Company, but also involved writing, by hand, up to fifty letters a day for his idol, Henry Irving. Included in this book is a lovely photograph from 1902 of a rather older and portly Ellen Terry, with (it is thought) Lindsay Jardine, described as a close friend of Edith Craig, writer and activist Christabel Marshall, and Pamela, who by then was aged twenty-four. Pamela, hatless, wearing conventional attire, is sitting with her left hand on Ellen's skirt. Here, Pamela displays none of the frivolity and extraversion of the self-created images of her as Gelukiezanger or Gypsy, the storyteller.

We can only imagine the celebrity of this Irving–Terry acting duo who enjoyed immense admiration, applause, and respect for their art. They were rewarded with numerous invitations to events, where they were feted, lauded, and fed sumptuous dinners. To be taken under their wing was an amazing stroke of luck. Pamela was mixing with the great and good of English theatre at its best, while learning performance skills from incredible talents. Extremely hard working, Henry and Ellen were leading lights at the Lyceum in London but they also engaged on lengthy backbreaking provincial tours, both at home and abroad, where Pamela first encountered them. Lest we think the partnership was equal, Ellen Terry's son, Gordon Craig, in 1932, reminds us of the reality, it was still very much a man's world, something of which Pamela would have been only too aware:

> We hear of the partnership of Irving and Ellen Terry, as meaning that both had the same power—it was no such thing. There was only one head of the house, and it was Irving. This house was the Lyceum Theatre, which was head of the English theatrical world.[1]

It seems from humble origins, these renowned and internationally famous actors, superstars of their day, were not without compassion, for they sheltered the lone adult Pamela as temporary mentors or 'substitute parents'. Arguably, despite her personal losses, she landed on her feet, for they provided work and numerous contacts. It was a good place to be in many ways, for Pamela was a natural performer, knowing how to take advantage of opportunities. It led to a steady flow of interesting work, though not always well paid.

Pamela, for example, completed the illustrations for a pamphlet commissioned and written by Bram Stoker when Irving performed Robespierre. From this, we discover Sir Henry Irving was extremely hard-working and exacting but would spurn a prompter when delivering his lines. His 'artistic exactness' among other things contributed to his theatrical genius. Meanwhile, she captured the expressions of the leading lights in her many illustrations, especially her colour ones held at Smallhythe.[2] She and Bram became good friends. To her, he was Uncle Bramy, whom she teased mercilessly, calling the red-headed Irishman 'Bramy Joker' in one of her drawings.

She also enjoyed performing with the toy theatre she had since her childhood. Her education was irregular due to travel, but one of her favourite childhood pastimes was making theatres, managing puppets, and writing plays. This was not unusual as toy theatres were very popular; it probably helped prepare her for real life as by 1901, she was deeply involved in stage design theatrical work with the key personnel of the Lyceum. Unfortunately, she had also suffered a few publishing 'rejection' slips for books she had written. Pamela, it seemed, was at the stage of her life where she tried every which way to make her creative mark. Some of her gambles paid off, while others did not.

6

The Flavour of Rejection

Like many, Pamela did not take rejection from publishers with good grace, a commonly recurring theme during her life. Any would-be author can imagine her disappointment. No one likes to be told their work is not publishable. To be fair, reasons given for her rejection were not really within her control, as we saw in her letters to Paine, so revising her work and starting again was not an option.[1] Notably, reasons given were the economic impact of the costly, drawn-out Boer War and, alternatively, that her work was 'too artistic'. How could it be otherwise?

Maybe the publishers wanted more words and fewer pictures, but illustration, not writing, was Pamela's forte, though she worked hard at both. If her writing was like her letters, then it would have required considerable editing. She wrote as she spoke, with her letters liberally and erratically punctuated with superfluous exclamation marks and underlining, some of which seemed to be the fashion of the time, as Ellen Terry's letters were similar, though slightly better organised (edited by Christabel Marshall). Yet, time and again, she was drawn to writing to accompany illustrating. Changeable, she enjoyed variety and wanted it all. Her urge to write was understandable given her undeniable storytelling skills and her literary family history.

It became apparent that book writing and publishing, as for so many even now, was not going to be the sensible way forward to earn a living income; it is here that her intense, longstanding dislike of publishers undoubtedly kicked in. She complained loudly and often about them to anyone who would listen. Her writing was not particularly special; her art was certainly more noteworthy and lucrative. However, Pamela was nothing if not flexible. A prolific producer not easily deterred, by 1902, she instead grew increasingly involved with the Celtic Revival of lore and legend using the Yeats Irish influence her father had cultivated, this having a massive impact on Pamela's work and life. Often, she worked with her friend, Ellen Terry's daughter, Edy Craig. The two made a productive, seemingly harmonious pair, Edy the older of the two, but also the key source of questions relating to Pamela's sexuality that refused to wane.

In 1901, Pamela fatefully joined the ritualistic, hierarchical occult group, the Hermetic Order of the Golden Dawn, under the guidance of the poet W. B. Yeats (who previously flirted with Buddhism and other esoteric belief systems). There, she later came to design the very tarot deck that gave her a place in posterity. Coldwell explains she had, 'always been inclined to the occult, having second sight herself and being absorbed in imaginary visions ... this step marked the point at which her art work began to be dominated by mysticism', but how accurate is this?[2]

Yeats later resigned from the Order after political infighting and a schism within the group, following the expulsion of its founder, MacGregor Mathers, and the interloper, Aleister Crowley, alleged by the Order to have been a member of the British Secret Service sent to scupper the organisation. Much has already been written about this in other books. Mary Greer noted the secretive Order, founded in 1888, was 'the first time men and women worked together as equals in magical ceremonies whose purpose was to test, purify and exalt the individual's spiritual nature'.[3] However, while the women may have been at the heart of the organisation, as usual, the men received the credit, the fame and indeed, the notoriety.

There is little convincing evidence Pamela was ever fully engaged in the Order to the levels its more ardent followers were, though she did enjoy a deep fondness for ritual and attended for some years. By November 1903, she was one of twenty-eight members who joined Arthur Waite in his Independent and Rectified Order, focused more on mysticism than ceremonial 'magick'. She stayed on at least through to 1909—a fair time. This connection brought her the job for which she is most well-known—the artistry of the tarot deck. Waite believed her to be 'a most imaginative and most abnormally psychic artist' so was keen to have her on his side.[4] When she left the Golden Dawn, it was probably to pursue her attraction to Catholicism, for she converted in 1911; the two organisations were incompatible. Many aesthetes were drawn to the imagery, ritual, and art of the Catholic Church (likewise, occult groups), converting around this time. Pamela, more than most, seemed to wholeheartedly embrace not just the iconography but the belief system of the Church. Meanwhile, she still had to work to live.

Professionally, it is hard to keep an enthusiastic writer down so, a determined woman, Pamela diversified, another of her characteristics, changing to magazine production. Her confidence belied a deep-seated self-belief but also an understandable refusal to put sustained time and effort into anything unrewarding. In an ambitious project, she created hand-coloured illustrated magazines with fellow illustrator, Jack Yeats, younger brother of William. Elkin Matthews, the publisher of Oscar Wilde, prominent in London literary life, agreed to publish the project. This magazine did not last, perhaps because the target audience was uncertain, but also because of the sheer effort involved in such time-consuming work for little recompense.

Hand-colouring was as it sounds, manually adding colour to photographs and illustrations using watercolours, oils, pastels, paints, and dyes in the days before colour photography. The technique was refined and popular in Japan since the 1860s. Pamela had learned Japanese techniques at her art college, Pratt, which she had obviously enjoyed. Unfortunately, it was a laborious process, as Pamela (not the most patient of individuals) found, and may have been worth it if the pecuniary reward had matched the effort. There are some accusations from Lily Yeats that Pamela was lazy, but like most of us, her enthusiasm and effort seemed to depend on how committed she felt to any one project, and the novelty of making a huge effort for little return naturally soon wore off.

7

Ellen Terry, Surrogate Mother?

It was her much-lauded 'mother–daughter' relationship with actress Ellen Terry that opened so many doors for Pamela in the first instance but how close were they? Ellen Terry was a dynamic, magnetic, charismatic, and well-loved character, someone Pamela needed in her life. Pre-Raphaelite in appearance, Ellen was strikingly beautiful with the most arresting pale blue eyes and large expressive hands. Her red hair and intense energy (in performance, writing, and life) paralleled her playfulness—extremely attractive traits making her almost goddess material. An immensely talented actress, she knew exactly how to capture and imprison any audience in her thrall. However, she did, said her son, have some shortcomings as a mother; additionally, she picked up waifs and strays along the way, of which Pamela was probably one.

Curiously, in Ellen's own copious memoirs, we find another mystery, for Pamela is rarely mentioned, which seems strange if Ellen was Pamela's 'substitute mother'. They knew each other very well, with Pamela making numerous visits to see Ellen and her daughter, Edy. Ellen wrote huge amounts about her children, but Pamela barely features, despite her 'adopted daughter' status. There is scant mention in her biographies, too.

Ellen's son, Edward Gordon Craig, suggested there were two sides to Ellen Terry, one being the actress he calls E. T., the other Nelly, his mother.[1] Nelly was a good mother, thought her son, but E. T. got in the way, not allowing her inner domesticated creature to rest. This could probably be said by the children of most successful professional women. Craig was a man of his time, prizing the domestic above all in women. He wanted a mother more than a famous actress.

However, in their highly literate and articulate family, even his memoirs do not mention Pamela much, and her friend, his sister Edy, also pays her scant attention in her writings. Again, this seems highly unusual for such prolific wordsmiths regarding someone thought to be almost family. Was Pamela the kind of person who inveigled herself into company where she was not wanted? Did she lack the social empathy to know or did she simply not make enough impact for anyone to record it? Perhaps, they were simply kind. It is hard to believe the great Ellen Terry would have bothered spending time with someone too dull to mention, but this 'mother–daughter' relationship may well be one of many over-exaggerated Pamela myths that have developed over time. Ellen and her family certainly assisted Pamela and invited her to visit, but was she any more than a visitor?

People obsessed over Ellen Terry. Gordon Craig's book was a defence of Ellen in her dealings with George Bernard Shaw (as obsessed with her as everyone else, desiring her to perform his modern plays rather than Irving's Shakespearean productions).[2] Shaw and Terry communicated by letter for decades, though meeting only once or twice. It was a curious fan relationship, one that did not impress her son.

Craig reckoned his mother took pains to remember people but 'unless they impressed her very powerfully, they just vanished from her memory'. He mentioned the words of artist Graham Robertson, who worshipped her:

> One thing strikes me in reading her letters and looking back—that people had less influence in her life than might be imagined. Things, thoughts, dreams, memories seemed to affect her more. She would write often and lovingly of her friends with that playful affection that was specially her own, but the note of deep feeling is absent with which she would write or speak of things that really moved her.[3]

These included her family, lover Edward Godwin, daughter Edy, and Ted. If this is so, to be mentioned at all was no small achievement.

Pamela enjoyed visiting the cosy enclave of Smallhythe, Ellen's enchanting family home in the Kent countryside. In Ellen's letters, she mentioned Pamela's productivity and grasp of marketing, traits she felt may benefit her own son, Gordon (Ted), as she was always looking out for her children's welfare while encouraging their economic activity, aware she was constantly paying out for them. She was eager to have a better and closer relationship with her son.

Ellen Terry led an unconventional life. She was perhaps a role model for Pamela but whether this was a good thing is moot, certainly romantically. It is interesting to read of Ellen's marriages in the somewhat romanticised account of *The Red Shoes* ballerina, Moira Shearer, which suggests at least one of her marriages was unconsummated (her first marriage to artist G. F. Watts, when she was an ingenue of just sixteen and he was forty-six, in a peculiar short-lasting affair reminiscent of John Ruskin and Effie Gray).[4] Ellen craved the attention of many far more than she needed the attention of one:

> If this is true, it suggests that after Edward Godwin [number two man and the father of her children]—the one unforgettable, unforgotten love in her life—she craved male attention but preferred love to come to her through

> excessive and ardent correspondence with many men … she would not have been the first fascinating, adored woman who, after a great love, found sex an unnecessary part of life.[5]

Pamela, similarly to Terry, corresponded with a great many people; she too seemed to enjoy being courted, feted, and admired. Her salon society lifestyle fed her love of attention given by a group of interesting individuals, both male and female. She did not have Terry's beauty, dominance, irrepressible energy, and charisma, but she did attract curiosity, attention, and had self-cultivated presence. Ellen was described as Pamela never was: 'Ellen Terry is an enigma. Her eyes are pale, her nose rather long … her hair rather like tow. Yet somehow she is beautiful'.[6]

By comparison, Pamela was characterful, not beautiful. She did not attract romantic partners, nor is there any sign she herself found any men or women particularly sexually attractive. Indeed, there is little evidence of a romantic relationship with any one person, male or female. Perhaps Ellen Terry deterred her from the idea of men, as she did Edy. Alternatively, arguably, the feminist non-conformist within was not comfortable with the idea of a husband. Maybe men were simply thin on the ground, if we assume heterosexuality. Perhaps she simply was not interested in the opposite sex, or possibly even her own—all part of the childlike persona often attributed to her.

From her biographies and her own words, Ellen was a devoted mother, who constantly bailed out her children financially, but she also struggled with motherhood in many respects. It is hard to imagine she would have taken on yet more unnecessary responsibility. From biographies and her own memoirs, Ellen found motherhood very challenging, but perhaps parentless Pamela was hard to resist. It is hard to imagine why, with Gordon and Edy Craig to contend with, she would want any more stray young adults in her nest, especially one as unmalleable as Pam.

Indeed, if we look more closely at the life of this 'mother figure' of Pamela's, it seems she had quite matter-of-factly discussed 'giving away' her illegitimate son to his father when they separated. It appeared neither parent wanted the challenge of him, though Ellen was keen to keep her equally illegitimate daughter. It is little wonder her son was a controversial character and as a partner, struggled with commitment. He had five children with his wife, Helen Gibson, followed by three with his lover, Elena Meo. Then came a daughter with Isadora Duncan (their daughter sadly died of drowning at the age of seven) and a son by his lover, Dorothy Lees. His sister, Edy, by contrast, had none. Ellen had, during her life, courted backlash with her unpredictable and controversial actions in affairs of the heart; she seemed intent on her own daughter avoiding her mother's mistakes, but her son was a loose cannon she failed to similarly contain.

Gordon Craig noted his mother, Nelly, had few 'theories', but Ellen Terry (E. T.) had many:

> Before long my mother, Nelly, gave to E. T. the bringing up of my sister—and then it was that E. T. came out with all her 'theories'. She told my mother that she'd soon show her what a grand result could be achieved with the daughter, and left her to deal with the son.[7]

He also mentioned his mother had a great respect for the institution of marriage but no love of it; after all, she had tried it three times. It appears to be something she wanted her daughter to avoid. He added:

> While she did one thing, she preached another. She would do as she wished ... but to every younger person she preached 'forbearance'—they were to be 'slow and sure': 'orderliness' and 'caution' were to be their watchwords: she wished them all the attributes of a 'lovable personality.' She, who lived life, did all she could to prevent girls living their lives—her counsel to them was negative and led to nothing—her own actions positive and led to everything. It wasn't that she did not want them to suffer through experience—it was, strangely enough, that, rightly or wrongly, she really thought that suffering would be not a scrap of use to their small or unbalanced natures.[8]

Nina Auerbach, influenced by Craig's writings, intelligently suggests Terry felt the only love she could give out was 'artistic love', in the way of a fine actress, a fascinating insight. She writes:

> It was in large part Ellen Terry's work to make people love her by pretending she loved them: the artist survived by performing the loving woman while barricading herself against the grasping need for engulfing intimacy she aroused in others.[9]

It is quite the celebrity's response. Undoubtedly, the celebrity and the woman at times overlapped.

Ellen Terry, it seemed, loved people on her own terms. Her feelings for others, apart from those very closest to her, lacked authenticity, but then she was a very fine actress. She wanted to be loved but was not keen on any of the neediness associated with it; essentially, such distancing was part of self-preservation for someone in her position. Auerbach indicates Terry slid into others' visions of her life without them ever slipping into hers. This may explain why Terry's own memoirs and biographies contain scant information about Pamela. For a time, at least, Pamela simply slipped into Ellen's life and just as easily faded out of it.

As for Pamela, she learned from the best. Motherhood was probably the hardest role Ellen ever had to play, and it went on for years. Whirlwind Ellen would undoubtedly have been very attracted by Pamela's productivity; as she worked so incredibly hard herself, a positive work ethic was a trait she deeply admired. People in her company felt they had encountered a tornado when they met Ellen. She had the work ethic of someone who never felt quite 'good enough', never resting on her laurels, of someone who had known what it was like to be poor. Pamela just tried everything she could to make money (a living) through her art, despite not knowing poverty during her youth. The two had some congruence in this respect. Gordon Craig advised his mother would sometimes need time out from social life, but being in the public eye, had to make excuses to do so:

> [She] was ever prone, from her youth, to take refuge in the Victorian excuse, 'not very well'. As she grew in years—indeed, as early as 1900—this habit of hers increased alarmingly ... She preferred this excuse to another, because she knew it absolved her from hurting other people's feelings.[10]

In Pamela's letters to Bigelow Paine, she mentions E. T. being 'better than she had been for months'.[11] However, Ellen seemed to have an empathy Pamela lacked. When Ellen later died (in 1928), it is noticeable that Pamela, in a very non-daughterly fashion, did not attend her funeral and was trying to sell her drawings of Ellen rather than give them to the family, creating afresh a sense of a more distant and professional relationship than a close familial one, unless geographical remoteness and Ellen's advancing years and senility had severely cooled things between them. Had her desperation for money forced her into the embarrassing situation of having to sell pictures of the woman who had once allegedly treated her like a daughter, or was this an example of her interludes of social ineptitude, the self-focused approach that so often irritated others, and which regularly made its presence felt in a variety of circumstances?

It was through the Lyceum that Pamela and Ellen grew to know each other in the first place. In 1893, the theatre company set sail from England to New York on their fourth American tour. However, it was in the summer of 1899 that Pamela and her father made a trip to England to investigate employment opportunities and promote Pamela's book of folk tales written in Jamaican patois, her *Annancy Stories*. On the trip, they called upon Bram Stoker, business manager of the London Lyceum. He was impressed by Pamela's artwork, engaging her to illustrate an eighteen-page souvenir brochure which was very exciting and high-profile for her at the time. She gelled very well with the troupe, especially Ellen, who was there for her when her father unexpectedly and suddenly died, so accidentally or otherwise, Pamela found her way into Terry's inner circle.

The suggestion Pamela had a romantic relationship with Ellen's daughter, Edy Craig, is a mystery that persists; there may be something in it, but we lack hard evidence. Certainly, we know Pamela was good friends with Edy as she visited Edy along with her family and friends, but whether she viewed Edy as a love interest is seriously questionable. There are various clues that suggest that while Edy enjoyed the company of both men and women, she was not a physical person. One comes from her mother: 'she loathes emotional people, yet adores me. I scarcely ever dare kiss her, and I'm always dying to, but she hates it from anyone'.[12] Partner Christopher St John in 1949 added that while they lived together, they also had separate interests: 'as we all had another life, apart, in our work, we did not really see much of one another. The fine point of our pleasure in being together was not blunted by excess of it'.[13]

When Ellen Terry and Edy Craig sailed with the Lyceum on the mail steamer, the *New York,* young Edy was contemplating a relationship with Birmingham-born Sydney Valentine, a married man, with whom she appeared madly besotted. People are rarely besotted with more than one person at a time; it tends to be exclusive. It is thus very unlikely she was simultaneously romantically inclined towards Pamela, indicating friendship not sexual attraction. Whether Pamela was attracted to women we do not know. However, if she was, there seems no real evidence she ever acted upon it; maybe she chose celibacy, was asexual, or simply kept her private affairs just that.

There are various interpretations of Edy's attentions towards men. One suggests she was merely toying with the idea of heterosexuality, going through the motions, doing what was expected; the other suggests she did feel a real physical attraction towards men although she seemed to have a penchant for those sporting some physical disability. Although her 'love life' is well-documented, the latter idea is tempting, not least because of a complaining comment made by her female partner, Christopher St John, about the non-physicality of their relationship. Perhaps bearing her own relationship difficulties in mind, Ellen Terry had no patience for her daughter's potentially ruinous relationship with a married man and swiftly ended the affair, thereby pushing her towards the society of women. On the ship, Edy cemented her friendships with two American women, one of whom was Pamela, the other Satty (Sarah) Fairchild, a longstanding friend of Ellen and Edy, hailing from Boston. Ellen, an amusingly honest diarist, wrote in her memoirs how Satty had listened to *Arms and the Man*, recited by George Bernard Shaw.

> My daughter Edy was present at the reading, and appeared so much absorbed in some embroidery, and paid the reader so few compliments about his play, that he expressed the opinion that she behaved as if she had been married to him for twenty years.[14]

Pamela completed some fabulous, colourful artwork on this trip; much of it still held at Smallhythe, including caricatures capturing the tensions of the characters within the Company during their off-stage, off-duty moments. She was an acute observer of character and appearance, absorbing the subtle interactions between individuals, which she then painted with great humour. The sense of vibrant and vivid colour in her painting demonstrates her colourist abilities, despite her spending so much time illustrating books with black-and-white line India ink drawings. The actors were doubtless enamoured by such care and attention bestowed upon them, capturing their quirkiest traits within their portraits and representations.

Earlier, when Pamela's mother died, she and her father lived in New York where she earned money selling hand-coloured books, prints, and illustrations in a gallery on Fifth Avenue. She also wrote plays and designed miniature theatre settings. Her father worked hard at touting around Pamela's work, probably already very aware of tough times ahead. It was at the Pratt Institute of Art in New York where Coldwell believes she met the Lyceum Theatre company on their American tour, as her illustrations appear in Bram Stoker's souvenir publication at that time. When her father died in 1899, she returned to England joining Sir Henry Irving and Ellen Terry at the Lyceum Company, helping with set and costume design and playing minor parts. Pamela appeared talented and confident. It seemed an ideal world for her to join and feel a part of, for she was a natural performer. Her relationship with Edy Craig was undoubtedly friendly yet professional, for Edy was a useful colleague. There is no indication of sexual intrigue.

Previously a hard to contain, free-spirited student at Pratt, Pamela sold prints of Shakespearean scenes and illustrated books of fairy tales and ballads, developing an eclectic set of skills and interests, some of which overlapped with Edy's. Pamela's early career consisted of illustrating children's books and collections of folk tales, ballads and verse. Her published works include *Widdicombe Fair* (1899), *Annancy Stories* (1899), *The Golden Vanity and the Green Bed* (1899), and *Chim-Chim: Folk Stories from Jamaica* (1905). She also illustrated works by other authors such as *Christmas Carol* by the Lancashire dialect poet, Edwin Waugh (1898), and *In Chimney Corners: Merry Tales of Irish Folk-lore* by Seamus MacManus (1899). She was hard-working, lively, and spirited, with a keen interest in folktales and lore.

The collection of her letters at Bryn Mawr library informs us of her immense productivity around this time. The plays she worked on included *Henry Morgan, Herne the Hunter*, and *The Magic Carbuncle*. The library collection also contains additional materials, including newspaper clippings, sketches, with an advertisement for a shop she opened in London to sell her prints and services as an illustrator of cards, bookplates, and sign boards.

In one of her letters to Mary (Bobby) Reed, Pamela discussed the actors Sir Henry Irving, Harry Irving, and Dorothea Baird. Regarding social engagements, she asked about Bobby's studies at the Pratt Institute and mentioned she was anxious to know the results of the presidential election. On the back of the last page is a note: 'We've just heard McKinley's elected! Ha Ha!'[15] In a letter sent in 1897, Pamela mentioned dresses she had made for the daughters of family friends, expressing her irritation that the dresses were found to be 'not nice enough'. She also attended the rehearsal of a local play, acted out by schoolboys. By January 1898, she mentioned she had sold three works: *Bill Hart* for $50, *Wind* for $50, and *Fruits and Flowers* for $100. Her letters were invariably accompanied by sketches.

In one, she described a visit to the Drexel Institute, where she met the popular American illustrator and storyteller, Howard Pyle. She observed his class, and Mr Pyle looked at her portfolio. She reported he found her illustrations 'very ingenious and interesting'.[16] Her ambitious father inquired about the possibility of her enrolling in the school. Mr Pyle said she probably could, but in the event the summer school was full, so she did not attend. However, by March 1998, she was back in St Andrew, Jamaica, complaining there they were behind a month on American newspapers and only saw the latest telegrams about the Spanish–American War (1898) mainly focused on Cuban independence.

Delightfully, she worked on a Shakespearean alphabet for children. The characters were listed as Ariel, Banquo, Caliban, and so on. By June, a publisher, Mr Russell, had taken the alphabet to London. He also asked her to take examples of her illustrations and scenery to show Maude Adams, an American actress who later achieved great success playing *Peter Pan*. She did not see Maude but left her card and expected a visit from the actress. Then she heard Mr Macbeth wanted to put on an exhibition of her artwork in his gallery. By this time, Pamela was giddy with interest and attention. Her star was on the ascendant.

By September 1998, she excitedly mentioned to her cousin writing and illustrating *Annancy Stories*, plus the alphabet was to be published as an *Edition de Luxe* in London, Paris, Berlin, and New York. By late 1899, she planned to travel to Philadelphia to visit Ellen Terry, to whom she had become quite close. Her letter was signed Pixie Pamela, a nickname she said Ellen Terry gave her. By 1900, she was excited over her pending return to England. She described socialising with Sir Henry Irving, Ellen Terry, and other actors, as well as performing in crowd scenes in *Robespierre* and *The Merchant of Venice*. She discussed her part in a production of *Robespierre*, in which she played a prisoner, and mentioned a brief trip to Edinburgh. Her sheer exuberance, energy, and imagination overflowed at this highly productive time of her life. Her future was surely looking bright; it was certainly never dull. Her constant endeavour continued back in England.

Pamela collaborated with Edy Craig, on *Ellen Peg's Book of Merry Joys*, created in watercolour, graphite, ink, and gouache, the characters being Pixie and Puck, known as 'two little devils' based on Pamela and Edy. Pamela's artwork, at this time, was humorous but was in some ways also childlike. She mischievously represented Gordon (Edward) Craig as 'Tedpecker', for example. The two acted like naughty schoolgirls. Pamela, it seems, did not take men as seriously as they did themselves. She enjoyed teasing them, though generally, they seemed to get along well with her, perhaps because she was not seeking to impress, or to find a husband. Despite the failure of many of her money-making schemes, Pamela often remained on friendly terms with those she worked with. In 1901, she created a portrait of W. B. Yeats, with his characteristic lock of hair on his forehead and his rimless spectacles, describing him as 'owlish' but also 'demonic'.

Edy and Pamela together also designed scenery for a play by Yeats called *Where There Is Nothing*, working collaboratively on many designs. There was a mutual sense of communal usefulness between Yeats, Edy, and Pamela. Pamela worked well with the Yeats family. She remained on good terms with Jack Yeats, who visited New York in 1904, and probably recommended her agent to him. Gordon and Edy, meanwhile, had the usual kind of brother–sister love–hate relationship. Pamela and Edy together amusingly used some of Gordon Craig's production techniques (so-called 'stage dodges'), which annoyed him, such was the rivalry between Edy and her brother, and such was Edy's delight in tormenting him. Pamela was her partner in crime, so creative sisterly banter was rife. Yeats valued the creativity of the two friends whose ideas bounced off each other, perhaps the whole being far greater than the sum of its parts.

In the Masquers theatrical group created by Edy and Pamela, Cockin tells us Pamela was 'inexplicably designated librarian rather than artist or costumier'.[17] This does seem inexplicable, indeed, for who less like a librarian was there? Pamela was frenetic but she never gave the impression of being especially organised. Several members of the Masquers published work in Pamela's magazine, the hand-coloured *The Green Sheaf*, Edy's partner, Christopher St John (Christabel Marshall) being one of them. Cockin seems to have hit the nail on the head when she writes that the magazine seemed to lack a clear manifesto. It is difficult to know who would have bought it, or why. It is reminiscent of schoolgirl magazine humour, though reading material was very different then. However, Ellen Terry was also sceptical: 'Pixie is starting another paper—an affected dilettante sort of affair, but as her Irish God "Mr Willie" has blessed it, she thinks it will be the most original journal ever produced'.[18] 'Dilettante' is an interesting word; indeed, the whole phrasing of Ellen Terry is curious. There is almost an air of boredom, a feeling of 'here we go again', that Pamela is writing (in a non-committed kind of way) affected, non-populist material, so probably doomed to failure. She associated such editorial self-importance with the poet, Yeats.

Curiously, Pamela does not merit even the slightest mention in Holroyd's immense book on the dramatic lives of Ellen Terry, Henry Irving (the stage name of one Johnnie Brodribb from Somerset), and their remarkable families, but we do learn a little about these key people with whom Pamela socialised.[19] By 1899, the Lyceum was falling on hard times. Past her heyday, the shining light that was Ellen Terry was greying and struggling with poor eyesight and rheumatism. She was feeling distinctly middle-aged. Like many ageing actresses (she was born in 1847 so was in her early fifties), she was finding a dearth of decent parts available on the stage, possibly partly also because of Henry Irving's reduced personal interest in her as his eyes fell on his new romantic partner. Meanwhile, Ellen explained in her memoirs: 'My hair is getting nicely grey ... I feel I can't look young'.[20] The Irving Society mentions Henry Irving had endured a difficult year in 1898, not least affected by the cult of personality that floundered when he became ill and could not perform:

> In February fire destroyed £30,000 worth of scenery stored in a railway arch. In the ferocity of the flames HI lost almost his entire stock-in-trade—the only sets left were those in the Lyceum at the time. That he had recently reduced his insurance from £10,000 to £6,000, against Bram's advice, did little to soften the blow. Worse was to come. In October while on tour HI was struck down with pleurisy and pneumonia; without the actor-knight topping the bill takings plunged. The onset of emphysema further depleted his energies.[21]

Irving had, by this time, indeed taken up with a Jewish journalist and gossip columnist, Eliza Davis Aria (1866–1931), who praised his unusually sympathetic treatment of Shylock, normally portrayed as a villain. She had taken him, following his illness, to convalesce on holiday at King Arthur Castle Hotel, in Tintagel, Cornwall, mentioned at the start of this book, a Gothic building, windswept, isolated and positioned on a rocky promontory overlooking the castle ruins. It is a place that, from her letters, Pamela also visited, though the hotel has no record of her stay, despite the existence of a letter written on headed hotel paper. Henry Irving mentioned he intended to retire to Cornwall to write his memoirs, but this never happened. A young Henry had been sent to Cornwall at the age of four to live with relations in a mining town. He would see his poverty-stricken parents once a year when he travelled by packet steamer from St Ives to Bristol. Known as a loner, he was a difficult man to know, but Cornwall presumably retained a magical draw for him.

Ellen, meanwhile, had fallen in love with the dilapidated building at Smallhythe in Kent, which she decided to buy, encouraged by her daughter, Edy. She wanted somewhere to relax and recuperate from the hard life of a touring actress as, during the Lyceum American tour, they visited thirty American and Canadian cities in six months. The workload was phenomenal and the travel extensive. Fortunately, the Lyceum was still supported there rather more than at home where it was by now making a loss. Pamela thus joined the company at a time when costs were high, while profits were low, Henry and Ellen, despite their combined charisma, were on the wane in their glittering careers, and Pixie Pamela was probably a useful and cheap option to have around, with her clever design skills.

Once she moved to England, Pamela wanted and needed to forge a more lucrative career for herself. The stage designs she offered Irving and Stoker did not come off but instead, she developed a close relationship with the Lyceum, touring the provinces, and publishing scenes from the tour in *The Kensington Magazine* (April–May 1901). This is where we find informal sketches of the actress, Ellen Terry, with whom she remained friends, creating illustrations for Terry's book, *The Russian Ballet*, in 1913. Michael Holroyd wrote:

> Ellen still dreamed of finding some dramatic enterprise to bring her son (Gordon Craig) back into her life… The Russian Ballet … celebrated a country which has no nationality and no barriers, the kingdom of dreams … formed by the coming together of Diaghilev, Nijinsky, Pavlova and others. Christopher St John helped to draft the 5000-word narrative which accompanied some rather crude illustrations from Pamela Colman Smith from Les Sylphides, Le Carnaval and Spectre de la Rose. 'Pixie' Smith was a young, elderly-looking American artist and folklorist, long associated with Edy's theatre productions and well known for her chanting performances of Yeats's poetry ... Ellen liked to recommend her to Gordon Craig as an example of how he might successfully manage his career.[22]

Did Pamela look elderly? Photographs suggest so, perhaps because of her unfashionable form of dress, for she did not dress to be attractive. Her industry was less in question than her dress sense. If an item sold, Pamela would make it. This reinforces questions about Ellen's and Pamela's relationship. Ellen was taken with Pamela's industriousness. A newspaper source mentioned her ballet drawings were clever but would have been better in colour, as befitted the Ballet Russes. Ellen often called her a 'funny little creature', which sounds a more pitying description of someone socially odd; that said, she also used similar terms to describe her daughter, Edy.

Katharine Cockin mentions the informal adoption of Pamela by Ellen, writing: 'Edith Craig acquired another sibling of sorts when in 1899 her mother informally adopted the adult Pamela Colman Smith'.[23] Pamela was, by then, twenty and a storyteller. Her Gelukiezanger Jamaican folk tales were called 'an absolute novelty' in New York; they also went down well in London. Cockin reports Ellen Terry as saying: 'since hearing your stories I have told no others'. Pamela was certainly unusual, novel, and a fresh talent. However, Ellen also described Pamela as 'The Japanese Toy'. Was this positioning her in terms of her questioned ethnicity and her unusual values, orientalising and infantilising her, or merely colluding with Pamela's own self-created image?

Meanwhile, various other plaudits appeared from the well-known. Cockin tells of Arthur Symons' description of her storytelling performance, written beautifully and evocatively: 'What you do seems to me exquisitely right, like an instinct; out your croon comes into silence like a bird's chuckle among the leaves outside the window'.

His rich description indicates instinctive storytelling skills with an extremely effective vocal range. Pamela was an author, performer, and visual artist, something of a minstrel, a heady combination of skills that entwined well together yet still failed to make her wealthy or even financially comfortable. It was this same year Edith Craig met Christopher St John. Did Pamela see Chris as another welcome 'sister' or was there something else? Did she feel herself usurped in Edy's affections by Chris? Was this part of the reason she later left London for Cornwall? Possibly, but doubtful, for the time gap is surely too wide.

Ellen Terry's letters reveal a few other thoughts about Pamela. She had obviously heard about her ongoing tussles with publishers, her continuous complaints about overdue payment for her completed work, and her constant workflow. Ellen was impressed by such productivity. However, it is possible to see how Pamela, at one stage a spectacularly successful exhibitor, somehow diluted or tarnished and devalued her own output by painting cards, wooden boxes, souvenirs and other low-value bric-a-brac. Ellen's description of her peddling her wares, fast selling, but with a small income, suggests she found her odd, but she did listen to and heed Pamela's grumbling. Possibly, she did not quite know where to socially situate her. It is potentially a sign of her financial desperation and desire for independence that Pamela was making and selling virtually anything she could, even low-value items. Ellen wrote of 'this girl':

> The girl of 20 Pamela Smith I told you about, has an order from a New York publisher to do 30 drawings of Henry and me in our characters. I'm finding out today how much is paid to her … Pamela Smith suffers horribly from the Publishers. She says they are nearly all like that and that the best thing to do is to try and get one publisher for all one's work and then keep him in good temper. She writes me: last week I received a royalty on The Golden Vanity and Widdicombe Fair. Give a guess how much it was! 432 dollars and 50 for 4 bookmarks which they never used …
>
> This girl Pamela has quite wonderful business instincts and she is a real good sort. Her address is 142, East Street 18th St, NYC. I think she goes to England in the spring—was there last year at Tintagel Castle, Cornwall. She is the sharpest little creature I ever met.
>
> Will you make a bookplate for Pamela, if she makes one for you? The souvenirs are selling very well but she gets just 5 cents apiece on each copy sold and no lump sum down. She is extraordinarily industrious and is everlastingly making (and selling as fast as she makes) lampshades, candle shades, paints

> wee wooden boxes, cards, etc. She gets 25 cents I think for the boxes and she does a dozen a day. 50 cents a pair for candle shades and she can't do them fast enough for the supply. She just trots them around. A funny little creature.[24]

The Forbes website states bookplates enjoyed a golden age from the 1890s to 1920, as individual and unique works of art, not the mass-produced items we buy today.[25] Books and bookplates were objects worthy of display, things of beauty, indicative of the holder's personality. Like a pedlar, however, Pamela was creating and selling whatever and wherever she could for whatever she could get, almost the equivalent of a modern-day craft fair exhibitor. Ellen obviously wanted to help her, having heard the ongoing saga of Pamela and her publishers, but it seems she did not quite know how, perhaps because there was no real answer.

Ellen also writes of her relationship with Edy, known by the family as 'The Frump' in contrast to her beautiful, flamboyant mother and more ostentatious brother. It is a strange combination of motherly affection and criticism. Joy Melville's book reflects upon this dual attitude, explaining how Ellen regularly turned to Edy for emotional support but also often complained publicly about her.[26] In turn, Edy relied on Ellen's money but also emotionally; they were co-dependent. It seems everyone who was not too closely attached to her (and had limited emotional expectations) loved Ellen. Yet Ellen had a seriously soft spot for effort. She made time for people who strived and struggled. In this respect, her own children, financially dependent, sometimes seemed to disappoint. This was the parent who resented all the giving she had to do for her offspring. For example, Ellen wrote of Edy's confirmation:

> Edith confirmed today (January 11, 1887) by the Bishop of Exeter (Dr. Bickersteth). A private single ceremony by the Bishop for Edith. Strange! Over thirty years ago Father and Mother (with Kate and me) walked (necessity!) from Bristol to Exeter, and now today my child is given half-an-hour's private talk with the Bishop before her confirmation.[27]

Despite her American heritage, Pamela enjoyed the English character, so Ellen Terry's passion felt authentic especially compared to the empty vacuous nature Pamela perceived in some Americans.

8

Earning Some Pennies

Like many women of her time, Pamela had many strings to her bow, possibly too many to be taken seriously at any one of them. The diversification of her talent diluted it. She enjoyed writing, drawing, and painting, but also enjoyed performing, though more in reciting poetry and folk tales rather than in stage acting.

We imagine performers as extremely self-confident lovers of people, though that is not always so. Gordon Craig said, after his mother's death, how not only did Ellen feign illness to avoid socialising, she also preferred the company of men as women, she declared, always wanted something from her.[1] It is possible Pamela also had two aspects to her character, the popular performer, Gelukiezanger, and the authentic woman who later discovered a deep and sincere faith in God. Given her interest in the Golden Dawn, she was obviously seeking and striving for belief and structure for a long period. Many an introvert can psych themselves up to perform but has no real connection with people. Pamela enjoyed storytelling, and her unique take, her strangeness, was part of her attraction in this role—her unique selling point. She also enjoyed entertaining children, as seen in the utter delight on her face in the company of youngsters in some Smallhythe photographs. She seemed to find children easy—undemanding yet exuberant companions.

Possibly, Pamela's fondness for folk tales and children's literature stemmed from her own childlike imagination, but also her long-lasting love of toy theatre and storytelling, for children are surely the best audience for this. Toy theatre was introduced in Britain around 1810, so it was well established by the time Pamela arrived on the scene. The aim was to faithfully reproduce popular plays but in miniature, so it was a very creative and imaginative activity. Therefore, reproductions of actors and actresses, costumes, and sets would be faithful. Stages were built of wood or cardboard; printed figures and scenery were pasted on to stiff backing and manipulated on stage via tin slides. Colour and drama were the desired outcome. The Victoria & Albert website explains their appeal:

Toy theatres (or 'juvenile drama') were hugely popular in the 19th Century, and were collected by adults and children. Every successful production staged in London's West End theatres would be reproduced in miniature.[2]

Generally more popular with boys who liked controlling the theatrical activity, toy theatres were souvenirs that were popular toys until their decline at the end of the nineteenth century; they lasted longer in America. Miniature stages, characters, scenery, and props were printed on paper from copper plates and sold by publishers and stationers as individual sheets. A 'Penny Plain' could be coloured or a 'Tuppence Coloured' came ready done, so this was a pastime for the middle classes. Children would spend hours setting up their theatre, colouring the characters, and learning lines to put on performances. Pamela likely encountered them during her childhood in Manchester. Actor Peter Baldwin wrote of the fascination of a Pollocks' toy theatre: 'You push the characters on and off, change the scenery, take the curtain up and down, change the lighting. You're totally in charge, it's an actor's dream'.[3]

For a storyteller and illustrator like Pamela, we can clearly see the attraction. She built her own stage and created her own gaudily painted figures from pasteboard, to illustrate her storytelling, well before 1899. The style of theatrical sheets informs some of her early painting. Pamela hand-coloured and stencilled her theatre items, writing in 1908, in *The Craftsman* where she advised:

> Go and see all the plays you can. Next time you go to the play look at the clothes ... an actor should be able to show the period and manner of the time in the way he puts on his clothes, as well as the way he uses his hands, head, legs ... the stage has taught me almost all I know of clothes, of action and of pictorial gestures.[4]

Gordon Craig mentioned how Ellen Terry's timing, her sense of dramatic movement, and especially her use of her hands captivated most audiences. Pamela reiterates these ploys and techniques here.

It was certainly a useful introduction to artistic accuracy and theatrical props. Additionally, Pamela's time in Jamaica had a massive impact on her life. She was a natural mimic but also spent a good deal of time with her Jamaican nanny who told her folk stories such as 'Annancy the Spider', 'Recundabundabrumunday the Witch', or 'Gingy Fly' (the bluebottle), tales of terror to Jamaican children. Losing her mother meant Pamela fell back even more strongly on her relationship with older women, receiving loving care from her Jamaican nanny. She readily picked up the dialect, a keen listener to the oral tradition, a re-teller of the folk stories she encountered. She enjoyed relating them to a wider audience, and for a good while, audiences loved them.

Whether she simply felt exceedingly comfortable retelling these tales, merely enjoyed the attention they brought, found they were a valuable source of income, or all three, she developed her role as an avid and fashionable storyteller to whom people in London flocked. She was a refreshing novelty. The American press exclaimed 'as a whimsical tale teller she has all fashionable London at her feet'.[5] For most bohemians, Jamaica was a place they would not have known or have visited; therefore, Pamela, who grew up unconventionally and strangely, seemed exotic, a part of the spirited lifestyle they wished so much to embrace. The tales, the language, her form of dress, and performance were all new and exciting to them. Her eccentricity, difference, and oddness made for interesting amusement and entertainment. It was novelty Pamela relied upon as she wanted to make an impression. Bohemians were happy to spend what limited money they had on entertainment and scintillation, more so than food and home comforts.

9

Bad Bohemians

Between the end of the Victorian age and the start of the First World War, it was close to impossible for a London artist to avoid the unconventional culture of bohemianism, not that they would have wanted to, for the freedom it offered from traditional societal norms and values formed the exhilarating backbone of fresh approaches to art and life. Bohemians wanted new and different things; they desired art, travel, exotica, and erotica. Understandably, they were intrigued by Pamela's storytelling as, while many travelled to Europe, notably Paris and Perugia, few if any would have encountered the West Indies, creating a demand for her tales in the oral tradition.

Even Ellen Terry was embroiled to the extent of taking a lively interest in the new creative trends of the time. Her book *The Russian Ballet* (illustrated by Pamela) was written because the Ballet Russes, formed by impresario Diaghilev, set her contemporary world on scandalous fire, performing stunning, sensual boundary-pushing ballets like Rimsky-Korsakov's *Scheherazade* and Stravinsky's *Firebird,* accentuated by Bakst's opulent costume design. The Victoria & Albert website describes Diaghilev as 'dictator, devil, charlatan, sorcerer, charmer'.[1] Diaghilev epitomised bohemianism; he had no money but plenty of charm, promoting dazzling performance on a shoestring budget. Notoriously, he borrowed money from others, never paying it back, yet somehow brought together artists and creatives in balletic works of the highest order. Male dancers and choreographers (such as Diaghilev's one-time lover, the technically astonishing Nijinsky) were now elevated in this high art form, while remarkable principal dancers (like classical English dancer, Alicia Markova, and the Russian prima ballerina, Anna Pavlova, the latter probably most known for her performance of the Dying Swan in Saint-Saen's *Carnival of the Animals*) were still the stuff of dreams for young girls well into the 1960s.

The 1948 film, *The Red Shoes,* starring Moira Shearer, is loosely based on this period. As the illustrator of *The Russian Ballet*, Pamela was well-acquainted with this folklore character-based dancing, a cultural phenomenon associated with the upper classes, exoticism, and decadence. She tapped into the fashions of the time to produce income through her own storytelling and illustration. It was not at all harmful to her career as an illustrator to be involved with such an illustrious character as Ellen Terry, although Pixie's drawings were not universally popular.

Virginia Nicholson wrote of Ballet Russes-inspired home furnishings.[2] There, we begin to see why Pamela's soirees felt so welcoming and attractive to this self-absorbed group of people. Ostentation, even gaudiness, colourful, Moorish, oriental, and Asiatic influences were all on the ascendancy. Vibrancy, incense, alcohol, and difference were the order of the day. Her environment could not have more at odds to her line drawings with poorly constructed hands and feet. This was a very different persona. Nicholson mentions Pamela, though not by name, in Arthur Ransome's description of an evening with her:

> A bohemian Chelsea hostess known as 'Gypsy' (no one ever calls her anything else). Her backdrop was a mad room out of a fairy tale. This was clutter with a vengeance, but not fusty, dusty, musty ... kind. The room in which Gypsy entertained her circle of artist friends was reminiscent of a curiosity shop, but with elements of exoticism that recalled Gypsy's obscure West Indian origins. The walls were dark green, and every available space on them was hung with brightly-coloured sketches, paintings and a gigantic double-edge sword hanging from a hook. Besides bottles of painting ink, strange paperweights, books and portfolios, the room was stuffed with loose sheet music, heaps of crimson silk, and lit with a multitude of candles. Incense burnt in an urn suspended from the ceiling. Oriental ceramics and Hindu deities crowded the shelves along with miscellaneous gimcracks of every kind. On top of a pile of folders a woolly monkey perched grinning at the company.[3]

Her studio was described by writer and artist, Gardner Teall, at the turn of the century as quivering with bottles of ink, pigments and chemicals, so much of it that she had quite an emporium. There are various tales of Pamela's storytelling evenings or salons from Ransome.

> She simply puts on one of her gorgeous robes, wraps her hair in a queer oriental scarf, hangs a few strings of coral and amber beads around her neck, and sits cross-legged on the floor with five candles twinkling before her. Her marvellous hands and her slanting eyes fascinate you, as she tells stories that the old mammies in Jamaica tell ...
>
> They call her Pixie in England and it exactly fits her. [4]

Indeed, it did as she celebrated deeply ingrained cultural prejudices through her Pixie persona. She made the press through her storytelling of Jamaican tales, even as late as 1917. She is described by Ransome thus:

> ... a little round woman, scarcely more than a girl ... looked as if she had been the same age all her life. She was dressed in an orange-coloured coat that hung loose over a green skirt with black tassels sewn all over the orange silk ... She welcomed us with the most uncanny little shriek, half laugh, half exclamation ... She was very dark ... with a smile that was peculiarly infectious and the eyes of a joyous, excited child meeting the guests of a birthday party.[5]

It was quite a setting. A room full of eclectic junk for the telling of strange tales was Pamela's contribution to bohemian London. Yet, as Nicholson says, poverty among these unworldly creatives was widespread, so meetings like this were pure escapism; it is doubtful she was paid a huge amount for her time and hospitality. However, the company was interesting and seemed more lucrative than illustration for a while. 'Gypsy' receives another mention in the Nicholson book, taken from another Ransome visit:

> The guests are picture dealers and artists, models and actors. They clamour for Gypsy to sing them a song but (she is thirsty) first she offers them drinks ... She offered opal hush ... and squirted lemonade from a syphon into a glass of red claret, so that a beautiful amethystine foam rose shimmering to the brim. The Irish poets in Dublin called it so ... It was very good, and as I drank I thought of those Irish poets, whose verses had meant so much to me, and sipped the stuff with reverence as if it had been nectar from Olympus.[6]

She would then sing the 'googoo bird' and perhaps chant a Yeats poem in monotone:

> Enthroned in a chair covered with gold and purple embroidery, Gypsy tells Caribbean folk tales in the old Jamaican dialect which she had learnt at her nurse's knee. She sings, and recites Yeats's poetry. Then a beautiful Scottish girl performs sea shanties while incense rises over the piano and perfumes the room. Ransome feels he has returned to the days of the troubadours. This was 'my first evening of friendliness in Chelsea'; there were to be many more.

There are yet more description of her salons:

> Gypsy had spent some of her life in the Indies, and knew a number of the old folk tales. She told them in old dialect, in a manner of her own. Fastening a strip of ruddy tow about her head, so that it mingled with her own black hair, she flopped down on the floor behind a couple of lighted candles, and after a little introductory song that she had learned from a Jamaican nurse, told story after story, illustrating them with the help of wooden toys that she had made herself. She told them with such precision of phrasing that those who came

> often to listen soon knew them by heart and would interrupt her, like children when, in a single word, she went astray.
>
> For a long time, I never let a week pass without going to that strange room to listen to the songs and tales, and to see the odd parties of poets and painters, actors and actresses, and nondescript irregulars who were there almost as regularly as I. Sometimes there would be half a dozen of us, sometimes twenty. Always we were merry. The evening was never wasted. There, too, we used to bring our work when we were busy upon some new thing, a painting or a book, and work on it with fresh ardour after cheers or criticism.
>
> We waved our goodnights to her as we saw her disappear into the house next door where she lodged.[7]

Nicholson explains how such structured evenings added coherence to the *laissez-faire* bohemian lifestyle but for Pamela, it would have been exhausting. However, her evenings were of short duration, ephemeral as she says, the kind of evening fully enjoyed at the time but which leaves a sense of emptiness and pointlessness behind, slightly souring the aftertaste. A 2015 BBC Four series by Victoria Coren Mitchell tried to pin down what made someone bohemian as did Arthur Ransome, but as the adage goes if you must ask you will never know. There is no formula.

Boyd Parsons, who was fortunately able to interview Edward Craig in 1974, says Pamela's storytelling was well loved at Smallhythe, too:

> Here around 1912–14, Pixie would entertain us and other children - she sat us around her in a circle and, with the aid of little figures that she had made out of wood and paper, she would tell us wonderful stories about a' Nancy. She generally wound a scarf around her head ... the special background to the stories. She was ... rather plump and very soft and lovable—we all adored her. She taught us West Indian songs and games.[8]

Smallhythe was a rural enclave. For some bohemians, the rural idyll appealed as an escape from the rat race, just as it does today, but outside London, it was even harder to earn a living by following a creative star. Survival was difficult for bohemians living alternative lifestyles unless there was a very wealthy family pumping through funds. Although Pamela did not describe herself as a bohemian, she often felt out of step or time with others, namely those buying her art. She complained the British public was not ready for the work she wished to unleash upon them, such was the conservative, unimaginative British attitude towards the arts. Of course, it has long been a common cry among the unsuccessful that the public are not yet ready for their greatness. Shortage of money and artistic popularity, combined with the desire to escape to something more authentic may well have contributed to Pamela's decision move to Cornwall. She was used to moving around, so another move was not difficult. There was no great emotional attachment to London, for she had no family or early memories of the city. Giving away her visitor book on 7 April 1914 indicated her loss of desire to keep up the act, a pretence that often became the way of life of performers simply to survive. A room with a view in Cornwall, safely held within the bosom of the mighty Catholic Church, was perhaps meant to make everything better, but even there she was plagued by money worries and unreliable people.

At the turn of the century, as Nicholson points out, Britain was relatively isolated from the ferment happening on the continent but this was set to change and not in a sympathetic way towards Pamela's undoubted skills.[8] The rise of modernism was quite terrifying to many, especially the aristocracy and middle classes, who viewed it as an attack on English values. Modernism and the avant-garde embraced massive change, both societally and artistically. Tradition was *passé*. Pamela's work was oddly challenging in some ways, but not in others; however, it was not challenging enough in the face of social and artistic turmoil.

It is difficult to know quite what Pamela's identity was, what persona she adopted, as she experimented with her performance. She sang songs from Jamaica and Devon, recited poems, and emulated the techniques of Yeats's close friend, Florence Farr, whose recitation the poet described as 'exquisite'. No wonder people were confused by Pamela, for it seemed she could turn her hand to anything, a natural mimic but with multiple identities. If people wanted it, somehow Pamela could supply. She should have been wealthy.

10
The Yeats Connection

The fascinating Yeats family were a creative yet dysfunctional group with whom Pamela became firm friends for a while. She would work with Jack, recite poetry by William, and develop a friendship with Lily, with whom she shared artistic interests. Lily Yeats was interested in Buddhism for its affinities with Sligo folklore while her unfortunate poorly treated sister, Lolly Yeats, published texts advocating Japanese brushwork for children—what curious pastimes for these young Irish women, yet both pertinent to Pamela for she adored folklore and had also studied Japanese art. Both sisters worked closely with Pam, whose studies influenced their aesthetic, though she seemed personally closer to Lily. The Japanese connection is a little-explored facet of Lily's and Lolly's craft work. A press release for the embassy of Ireland in Japan stated:

> Yeats was already well-acquainted with Japanese art through his collaboration on set design with Edward Gordon Craig and Pamela Colman Smith. Fenollosa had been one of Smith's teachers and she shared his esthetic with Jack B. Yeats and with Lily and Lolly Yeats, who were 'sisters at war'.[1]

Lily and Lolly certainly struggled to happily co-exist as sisters. Indeed, none of Lolly's family appreciated her contribution to their wellbeing and often treated her quite appallingly, especially in later life.

An article by Marianne MacDonald in *The Independent* suggested the girls supported an arrogant W. B. Yeats financially.[2] They personally published the first editions of his poetry. Their father, John, trained as a barrister but instead of practising law to provide for his family, he followed his bohemian heart, taking up painting, forcing his wife and children to endure constant financial struggle and, at times, abject poverty. It was only four years into his marriage that he decided to pursue art instead of law. His unfortunate wife, Susan Pollexfen, and their children were miserably, unhappily poor, living in grim circumstances in both Ireland and London. Yeats's biographer, Roy Foster, wrote of Susan:

> Sligo remained her emotional base; reticent and occasionally caustic in the Pollexfen mode, she hated what she construed as the pretensions and social frivolity of 'artistic' life. Nor did she share the Yeats fascination with ... people.[3]

Poverty was no joke. Poor Susan never recovered from the disillusioning, harsh reality of her marriage; marrying was probably one of the worst decisions of her life, but she certainly mothered some exceptional children. Whether she took any comfort from this is hard to tell given she spent much of her time depressed and socially isolated. Like many bohemians, her husband never quite made a living from his work, despite his talent. He was not averse to borrowing money (usually with no intention of paying it back) from his family, friends, and children. His own interests were paramount, which might have been fine if Susan had been like-minded or acquiescent. Situations like this were all too common; it is no wonder Pamela, a friend of the family who would have seen all this first-hand, did not embrace marriage.

The Yeats girls were oppositional, different personalities. Lolly (Elizabeth) was energetic and nervous, to some irritatingly so, while Lily, ten years older than Pamela, was more sanguine (like her mother) but also more deferential to men, making her more acceptable to them and therefore the more conventional of the two. The girls had no choice but to work given their economic situation, Lily as an embroiderer for William Morris and Lolly as a nursery teacher, maintaining a family of six on their income for years while the males followed their ambitious, creative stars. Despite their mother's fate, the girls still seemed oddly keen to find husbands, for the single life was non-stop work.

It is easy to see why Lily, while friends with Pamela, resented her unearned income from her uncle Theodore. Helpful as she was, Pamela in Lily's view could probably afford to experiment creatively and indulge herself rather than seriously need to earn a living; she had a safety net. Lily, whose mother was from strict Protestant stock, also disliked Pamela's later Catholic lifestyle, claiming it tedious and dull. Lolly was also judged. Later in life, her family claimed she was mad, so her evenings were spent in bed, shut away like some 'madwoman in the attic'. Pamela certainly met some amazing people in her day, all of whom would have had a huge impact on her life and choices. The Yeats sisters were two of them. T. S. Eliot reckoned: 'Yeats's relationship with his two sisters was a curious one. I have two sisters, he told Sturge Moore. One is an angel (Lily), the other a demon (Lolly)'.[4] His interpretation deduced Lolly had a mind of her own, which men did not like. Given the men she met during her life, it is easy to see why Pamela may have been put off.

Pamela spent a good deal of her early time back in England, working with the curious yet prolific Yeats family, suggests Joan Coldwell.[5] She created stage designs for W. B. Yeats and collaborated on magazines with Jack Yeats, but she also contributed designs to the Dun Emer Industries in Dublin through the Yeats sisters.

She was twenty-one when she met the family and worked hard (some may say hard-headedly) to establish herself with them. Coldwell suggests the use of Yeats's first play in her miniature theatre productions 'is an indication of her up-to-date reading, her experimentalism and her ready response to Yeats's poetry'.[6] Although Yeats was considered a great twentieth-century poet, which was no mean feat, Pamela gave no impression of being overawed by him, indeed poking fun at his solemn social circle of sycophantic female admirers who were awestruck by his poetry and growing reputation.

Yeats was popular with the ladies, embarking on many affairs with young women, even as his virility waned. His fame and celebrity seemed to have little impact upon Pamela, however; she was more impressed by his folk stories than his social standing or his appearance. She wrote, astutely and scathingly of his adoring followers, cutting through the nonsense:

> W.B.Y. was there and he is a rummy critter! Seemed most stupid and had on a tea party air and posed about and looked bored ... And when all the ladies with ermine collars had gone, who all told him how very much they liked his bloomin' poetry, which probably they had never read or heard of ... then W.B. began to talk! ... folklore, songs, plays, Irish language, and lots more—reciting a sort of folksong which was splendid, and not stopping for silly interruptions by Mrs E. pig ... who made silly remarks; it was fun and we all liked it very much![7,8]

Pamela, ever scathing of assumed social airs and pretensions, liked the real character behind the façade, while Yeats seemed to find her refreshing, too. She would surely never have settled in Brooklyn where the *Daily Eagle* (1904) described her:

> Far removed from ordinary girls' point of view. She even dressed strangely, with a love for bizarre and barbaric colours ... she was a bird of passage ... before and after her father's death. In the ordinary fashionable households, she could not be happy ... Pamela found no charm in even the life of art ... Her *métier* was to lie in bed until midday, to do all her painting and designing under artificial light. It was not until she came across Ellen Terry that she found real solace ... her drawing has been called bad, but it is not only odd, unusual, with a touch of the grotesque, the wandering of figures quite untrained. It is one of the most interesting things in *Brooklyn Life* that such a personality should have come out of the heart of the Heights.
>
> Miss Smith's instant success here is a bit unusual. I think it is largely due to her absence of all pose; queer, unexpected, absolutely original as Miss Smith is, one realizes her unmistakable genuineness as well as appreciates her talents.

> She is a gentlewoman, presenting an odd type of thoroughly unconventional femininity—therein lies her greatest charm.[9]

She mentioned giggling in her hanky during a reading of *The Shadowy Waters*. Her comments about others were often very personal and rude, though we must remember these were made privately as comments to her friends. She often described people judgementally as 'pigs', joking about squeaky voices, as well as incongruous couplings and situations. She later described Yeats as Willie, which suggests an informal, friendly relationship developed.

She seemed to get along well with the more private, subdued younger brother, Jack Yeats, at least as a friend, if not professionally. He had a miniature circus, so there was common ground. They worked together on their *Broad Sheet* which, patterned on nineteenth-century ballad sheets, measured 18.5 × 15 inches, containing hand-coloured pictures by them both. Coldwell mentions the publication reflected the varying interests of both parties. There are many claims it was Jack Yeats who started the publication, despite the world at large thinking it an equal collaboration, but was anything then involving a male–female partnership ever equal? In a letter to John Quinn in 1902, Jack wrote:

> Pamela Smith did not start the *Broad Sheet*. I did. In fact, I had a weird thing called the Broad Sheet two years ago, just stencils that I used to print myself ... Between you and me and the wall ... Miss Pamela Smith (though I think a fine imaginative illustrator with a fine eye for colour, and just the artist for illuminating verse) is a little bit erratic, and she being a woman I can't take a very high hand with things, so there is often a lot of bother about the numbers, and I don't like being responsible for anything that I have not got absolute control of.[10]

Lily also recalled difficulties with the restless, highly-strung Pamela whom she found clever and charming but lazy.

> When Jack brought out the Broadsheet, I used to go to her studio once a month and colour Jack's picture while she did hers, only a hundred. Yet she often lay on the sofa and cried because, she said, I was bullying her and making her work when she did not feel like work.[11]

We could, of course, ask why Pamela had to colour her own and Jack's sister did his. This flies in the face of Pamela's previously noted work ethic, but she seemed to work hard when she felt it was worth the reward. We also must bear in mind the Yeats brothers did not seem to have particularly high opinions of the work of women, which probably impacted upon Lily's opinions. Hilary Pyle, in her biography of Jack Yeats, writes:

> [Pamela] had been caught up in the tail end of the decorative wave ... greatly under the influence of Walter Crane. She left Jamaica in 1899, and came to London, where she called on the Yeats family in Bedford Park. The following year, in the summer of 1900, she stayed with Jack and Cottie at Snails Castle, and enjoyed their performances of the miniature theatre, just as they must have approved of her telling Jamaican folk stories for children. She had illustrated several art printings of nursery tales. Her style is distinctive, though rather conventional. She was impressionable, and gradually adopted several of Jack Yeats's ideas.[12]

Her view then reiterates Jack was the creative talent, with Pamela merely adopting and adapting his ideas (the same later happened with Pamela and Arthur Waite) though he eventually rid himself of Pamela without hurting her feelings, giving colouring work to his sister, Lolly, instead. Pyle later describes the *Broad Sheet* as: 'romantic linear style, curvilinear with frills and strong outlines [Pamela] and rugged or rectilinear with strong shade contrasts [Jack]'. The September 1902 edition included a poem by a Mrs Barbauld. While an adept self-publicist, Pamela had compiled a book of illustrations to accompany her poems but failed to find a publisher. These days, she would probably have self-published or blogged, but then her options were limited. Her illustration in this case was of chubby infants on a fairy-tale hill, 'in the style she favoured for children's books'. By January 1903, Pamela had tired of the *Broad Sheet*. She and Jack remained friends but she, like Jack, wanted sole responsibility for a periodical, which is how *The Green Sheaf* (published and edited solely by her) began. W. B. Yeats helpfully thought *Hour Glass* a better title, as he saw it as a vehicle for idealised, beautiful work, with his poet's disregard for income. Pamela probably had more of an eye to sales and survival, choosing more saleable ballads, tales of love, war, pirates and the sea, with which to fill it.

Pamela also used the publication to advertise her work. The John Burns Library Blog advises:

> In addition to advertising hand-colored prints, Colman Smith offered custom orders for books, programs and advertising cards as part of the 'Green Sheaf School of Hand Coloring'. The seventh issue includes an advertisement for 'BOOKPLATES and PRIVATE CHRISTMAS CARDS Designed, Printed, and Hand-coloured to order' as well as a hand-colored print of '"Cathleen Ni Hoolihan" an illustration of the play by W.B. Yeats'. By the 12th issue, published in 1904, the Green Sheaf School of Hand-Colouring had opened a shop in Knightsbridge, London.[13]

Given she found hand-colouring onerous, it is a strange route she followed, but perhaps the attraction was controlling her work, rather than collaborating with someone like Jack Yeats, who also wanted control and, as a man, was more likely to get it. Notably, *The Green Sheaf* did not include any Colman Smith retellings of Jamaican folk tales (probably better spoken than read) although, beginning with the sixth issue, the magazine did contain advertisements for readers to hire Gelukiezanger (Pamela's stage name/pseudonym for her performance) to tell stories at parties.

The Green Sheaf was very catholic in its content, printing a wide variety of fairy and folktales from several different countries. Its content was written in Standard English, so it may be the fear of losing subscribers that caused Pamela to avoid publishing any of her patois retellings in the pages of her magazine. Despite persistent problems with money throughout her adult life, Pamela's letters reveal she was very attuned to financial concerns and quite savvy in at least some of her financial decisions, though later she seemed to struggle very much with money, more through low levels of earned income rather than profligacy.

Sizewise, her publication was smaller than the *Broad Sheet*, measuring nine by eleven inches, containing fifteen pages and sometimes loose-leaf supplements. A yearly subscription was thirteen shillings but offered thirteen issues for the price. There appeared to be plans to later produce it quarterly, but this never seemed to happen. O'Connor says:

> The Green Sheaf also published the work of a host of seemingly unknown women writers as well as anonymous contributions which increased as the numbers progressed. Some of these women's names appear to be pseudonyms, possibly even for Colman Smith herself.[14]

Anonymous writing was not uncommon, nor was publishing. The first issue of *The Green Sheaf* contained an illustration of a portly gentleman, poking fun at patriarchal culture but also of bookish learning rather than real activity. The publication also contained some bleak pieces, such as a short poem or ditty called 'The Town': 'O deary me how idle is/is great and weary town./For people talk and never do/As they go up and down', which is more of an attack on complacency and human emptiness than any specific sense of isolation within Pamela. It is not a brilliant rhyme. Pamela's attempts at earning a living through writing and publishing were, as for many today, seriously difficult; the inconsistency in her work did not help her to continually fill her magazines with quality content.

She completed twenty-four copies in all from January 1902 to December 1903, including some high-profile work from the Yeats brothers, John Masefield, and Synge, with poetry, art, and illustration among the lesser items. Who bought them, we can only guess. The back cover (as was common) contained various adverts for Pamela's money-making schemes, but she also used it as a networking tool to advertise items for her friends and acquaintances. However, it was also a vehicle to publish items by women, demonstrating an ongoing interest in female literature and creativity, giving women a voice.

Along with her Gelukiezanger tale-telling, she also briefly chanted (rather than recited) Yeats's poetry to small audiences when she joined the theatrical group, the Masquers. She was obviously good at remembering lines, but her contemporaries observed the rhythmic way she sang poems, maybe a skill inherited from her mother. She had found a niche. In 1904, Pamela's shop was advertised in *The Green Sheaf*, based at 3 Park Mansions Arcade, Knightsbridge. At this point, her storytelling was far more lucrative than her other creative works.

11

Fine Artist or Jobbing Illustrator?

To understand more of Pamela's situation, we need to know something of the mid-Victorian artistic and political cultures. Nunn suggests women artists were not taken seriously.[1] They were considered worthier of the craft movement than fine art, which required less talent. Craft was ideal for the 'fairer sex', who, of course, in a patriarchal society, obviously lacked skill. Pamela was born after this period and did not live her entire early life in London, but she could not escape immersion into prevailing attitudes, as a product of the society in which she lived. Women were largely hidden from art history throughout the 1800s. However, this was also the time of the burning issue of 'the woman question' with a serious fight for women's suffrage as well as discussion of legal issues of marriage and property, with more women moving outside the domestic sphere. The lives of men and women were seriously differentiated in a way which is difficult for us to fully understand, with the female role extremely limited by gender. Women artists were not taken seriously, for their lives were meant to be domesticated and home-based.

This is closely linked to ideas prevalent at that time about femininity. Feminine meant a semi-sacred mother figure, incapable of sexual enjoyment, morally and spiritually superior to man, intellectually and in terms of personality, inferior, idolised for her physical charms while normal sexual processes were labelled pathological. Women were assumed weak and frivolous, there to be married, to produce children, to be led by men. The work women artists produced would be different to that of men for ladies were considered unable to paint. Great art was bound up with notions of genius, and women could not be that, either. John Ruskin (art critic)—who appeared to be no lover of women if we look at his treatment of his young wife, Effie Gray—encouraged girls to learn technical skills when drawing, but to accept the limitations of their gender. They were indeed considered more suited to craft than art. In short, women were condemned for their shortage of creativity and inspiration they were told not to aspire to. They were simply not special enough, requiring men to legitimate their existence.

Nunn uses the term 'ghettoisation' to explain the position of women in art in the mid-1800s.[2] Art was a middle-class career, but it was not fully open to middle-class women who were caught up very much in the identity of the privatised domestic sphere. Life was dull for these women, but it was even harder (financially and socially) for women who did not fulfil their destiny of marriage and motherhood—a double bind. Women paid for and maintained by their husbands would not earn a living through art; therefore, they were consigned as amateurs (their work thus unsaleable). To be taken seriously as a woman artist probably required eschewing men and marriage. Yet, family connection was also vitally important in the art world. Pamela had no such kin immediately available but she could eschew marriage.

Not only was art discouraged among women, it was considered a threat to the *status quo* if they painted. Nunn suggests that women taking non-domestic activities amounted to a serious threat on the continuance of marriage and family.[3] Pamela was very much a working artist, seeking commissions to earn a living. It is difficult for us now to realise quite how seriously a woman's role within the home and family was taken. Certainly, earning a living from art was also very hit and miss for a woman, so Pamela did very well for many years, exploited mainly because she was a woman who could not quite command the respect of a male artist.

What is particularly interesting when considering Pamela's life is Nunn's mention of deliberate 'singleness', which she suspects to be the case of women who enjoyed long and successful careers as painters.[4] This is an enticing idea, one which probably applied to many women who enjoyed same-sex companions, maybe with or perhaps without the sex, but certainly with affection. She cites Emily Mary Osborn, unmarried, who was artistically active for over fifty years, and the Mutrie sisters, who exhibited for twenty-five to thirty years but never married. Marriage was severely deleterious to artistic careers as wifely time would then be devoted to domesticity and childcare, and enforced domesticity, where art became merely an amateur hobby. The tide had begun to turn against women as middle-class ornaments, and by the 1860s, women were acknowledged as participants in the British art scene; however, the barriers to women were still immensely, persistently significant, with the process of change stubbornly slow. Women whose families encouraged them, and whose art was taken seriously by them, flourished most.

Art and feminism were linked. When we see Pamela's incredible drive and energy, we see the remnants of attitudes that endured, requiring that women had to work incredibly hard to stand their artistic ground, in order not to be condemned for a 'feminine' lack of industry or application. In 1871, women still could not put the coveted letters of RA (Royal Academy) next to their names, something Pamela later achieved, and of which she was presumably proud. Pamela was born at a very interesting time, one that began to allow women to follow artistic careers though not without a struggle (which persisted throughout her life, despite her prodigious work rate).

In an article, Pamela turns tutor, advising artists and illustrators on studying people.[5] She advises them to go and see all the plays they can, to study emotions, faces and bodily positioning. She sees art as storytelling, at first a simple story but later elaborated with detail, a belt, a sword, a dagger, and a swagger. Here, we see links to her dramatic side. It gives a glimpse into Pamela's world. She not only had to draw, paint, and illustrate, but she also had to tell stories and effectively 'teach', too. Pamela would have probably fared well in modern-day Cornwall where artists can thrive but are often involved in a multitude of related work to earn an appropriate income. She also suggests as an exercise that students draw a composition of fear or sadness, in just a few lines, to tell a story, then show it to friends and ask them to explain what it is meant to portray. We can see from her urge to tell stories through illustration where her illumination for the tarot worked. Pamela learned a great deal from her many and varied life experiences, so wanted to communicate that to others.

In 1897, at the tender age of nineteen, Pamela held her first art exhibition at William Macbeth's gallery in New York, where she sold four of her watercolours. Four may not sound many but for a new artist beginning her career, it was very encouraging. Macbeth's gallery founded in 1892, was created to deal entirely with American art, surviving until 1953, after Pamela's death. By the end of 1897, Pamela's Christmas cards, illustrations, and prints were sold regularly through the gallery; whether this extended or diluted her appeal is moot, but she was surely thrilled to have such a high-profile spot to show her work.

She also attracted critical praise from her exhibition. Some found her work untainted by convention, while others found it crude and unformed, such is the qualitative and subjective nature of art criticism. However, it was also easy for critics to overlook her work, the sad lot of many women artists during Pamela's lifetime. She had to have more strings to her bow yet did she overdo it? Artist Hannah Rose Shaw, who compiled an exhibition on Pamela for the National Trust, wrote on her blog: 'She dabbled in many areas, which is maybe why she was never distinguished in any field'.[6] This dilution and dissipation of talent was perhaps her undoing but was largely down to economic circumstances at the time. In trying to be a Jack of all trades, she literally became master of none. Her eccentricity exacerbated this: 'She has always been strange. There is not a page of her life, not an incident, that is not overflowing with romance', asserted *The Brooklyn Daily Eagle* of 1 November 1904.[7]

> In London drawing rooms the enthusiasm and the fashion of the hour is Pamela Colman Smith, who, in a brilliant frock of orange with a red turban, sits on a board with two lighted candles in front of her and tells before crowds of delighted people weird and strange folklore tales of Jamaica.

It also noted she was 'highly unconventional and full of mystery in her art, as well as in her life, a wonderful colorist ... a most "ungirlish" individuality, yet full of curious attraction.' The words tell us a great deal. 'The fashion of the hour' indicates how quickly trends could turn and change during this great social upheaval. C. K. Stead said at the 2004 Hay Festival, 'they [bohemians, people who would visit Pamela to hear her stories] had the insecurity of the rich who are poor, not of the poor who are poor'.[8] The problem with those middle-classes who wanted freedom and an openness to transcend social norms and mores was they were also extremely keen on change and novelty. Pamela had to make the most of her storytelling while it was popular. Audiences were fickle and could turn on a sixpence.

Similar happened with the modernist turn in the art world, which was ultimately to Pamela's detriment. In 1907, aged nearly thirty, a triumphant Pamela had her first exhibition in the Photo-Secession Gallery in New York, followed by another in 1909. The Photo-Secession focused on the potential of photographs to 'approach the aesthetic quality of a painting', including the comparison of paintings and photographs to judge the limitations and possibilities of photography as a medium.[9] Alfred Stieglitz was keen to present amateur photographs as works of art, 'discovering' Gertrude Käsebier (who created the most fetching photograph seen of Pamela) and Clarence White. The works were promoted at 291–293 Fifth Avenue. It was thought to be Käsebier who introduced Pamela to Stieglitz.

Pamela briefly began to hit the big time when she moved on from telling stories to Stieglitz's exhibition. Stieglitz, states *Mary Greer's Tarot Blog*, purchased quite a few of Pamela's paintings but soon after he died, these were allegedly sold off (separately) by his wife, Georgia O'Keeffe, due to, as Greer intimates, decades worth of jealousy.[10] David Coale felt Pamela was close to Stieglitz in the early 1900s, even sending him a copy of her tarot designs before they were publicly released, but lamenting the likely poor printing quality.[11] For Pamela, this was an ambitious way to keep her at the forefront of his professional mind, to keep him intrigued. As he developed professional (and personal in O'Keeffe's case) relationships with other creatives; after Pamela returned to England, their mutually beneficial artistic partnership quickly faded. There is no indication Stieglitz was sexually attracted to Pamela, so it is hard to know what Georgia O'Keeffe's issue was, but presumably not professional jealousy.

In Nancy Hopkins Reily's book on Georgia O'Keeffe, Manchester is described as 'a hotbed of women voicing their political views disguised as spiritualism'.[12] Did this descriptor apply to Pamela's drawings? Pamela and Georgia O'Keeffe exhibited work together in New York under the wings of Stieglitz, whom Miss O'Keeffe later married. Unlike Pamela's (whose work is mainly confined to tarot circles), the work of Georgia O'Keeffe is still celebrated in the art world. In 2017, an exhibition was held in Brooklyn, comparing her minimalist monochrome portrayal of herself, through black and white photography, with her immensely colourful magnified flower images.

O'Keeffe's androgyny was often cause for comment. Her appearance the opposite of Pamela, she wore clothes coded as male, rather than dresses and jewellery. In the article, her persona is considered 'self-crafted', as seemed to be the case for all artists. She seemed, appropriately, as a feminist, very much in control of her own image and her fate, living to be ninety-eight years. Like Pamela, she too turned her back on fame, leaving behind her career in the city of New York for solitude in New Mexico where she lived close to the land, gardening and cooking. Yet, despite being a loner after Stieglitz's death, she remained a celebrity, unlike Pamela who would pretty much be a nonentity without her famous tarot art, though Pamela chose her new path much earlier in life.

How closely Pamela gelled with Stieglitz is difficult to assess but her letters intimate a certain 'buttering up' of the said gentleman to achieve her exhibition and sell paintings, saying what she thought he wanted to hear. She tried the same tactic later with the Bishop of Plymouth when in need of money for her mission, but was unsuccessful. Her relationship with Stieglitz was professional, not personal, and there appeared to be no chemistry between them; she was no Georgia O'Keeffe. How did they meet? The idea may have come from Robert H. Russell, publisher of some of Stieglitz's photographs, or as earlier suggested, from mutual friends, Gertrude Käsebier or photographer, Alice Broughton, who for a while lived in a studio apartment with Pamela. Stieglitz described it, thus:

> One day a young woman appeared ... She asked me to look at her work, drawings in black and white ... with a view to exhibiting them ... The artist called (one) picture *Death in the House*. Since it illustrated exactly what I was feeling at the time and what was in danger of happening to the Photo-Secession I decided then and there to present her work. I wanted also to destroy the idea that the Secession was dedicated solely to photography.[13]

It is hard to imagine the impact of one picture led to an exhibition offer for Pamela. A review of her work in the *New York Sun* was positive:

> Pamela Colman Smith is a young woman with that quality rare in either sex—imagination ... Miss Smith is in every design, many of them mere memoranda of a spiritual exaltation, of the soul under the influence of music, or haunted by some sinister imagining. 'Death in the House' is absolutely nerve-shuddering ... Munch (he of the expressionist painting, *The Scream*) himself a master magician of the terrible, could not have succeeded better in arousing a profound disquiet.[14]

This mirrors Whelan. He says Pamela appeared unannounced at No. 291 one day in early December, when Stieglitz was not in the best of moods. When she asked whether Mr Stieglitz was in, he replied rather testily, 'No, I'm not'. Whelan goes on to say he was intrigued by the twenty-eight-year-old 'eccentric-seeming' American woman, who had lived in London and explained to him dealers were afraid to show her work. Her fortunes had dropped since her two-person show with Robert Henri at the Macbeth Gallery in 1897 when Pamela was only nineteen. Whelan writes:

> One reviewer had then praised the 'remarkable decorative quality' of her work, though the titles of two of the drawings—*Our Pets* and *Hark! The Dogs Do Bark*—suggest that he was being over-generous.[15]

There was already a strong element of impression management in Pamela's outward appearance and persona at her first exhibition, in *Brooklyn Life*'s description.

> The well-bred crowd at the Macbeth Gallery was too polite to stare at Miss Smith as she made her rounds, but when she left the room one heard many inquiries as to who that remarkably picturesque little woman could be. Her gown and coat were long and floppy and of a sort of pussy-willow gray. On top of her curly coal black hair she wore a high-crowned gray hat, which in place of a brim, had a box pleating of bottle-green ribbon. When she entered the room, you felt as if a little Kat Greenaway girl had suddenly been endowed with life and walked right out from the covers of a book.[16]

By 1906, Pamela had matured; name-dropped into the conversation, mentioning her friends Yeats, Ellen Terry, and Arthur Symons; and showed him portfolios of her work, which were said to be largely inspired by the French symbolist, Odilon Redon, by Shakespeare and theatre, and by Schumann's music, *Carnaval*. It is said Stieglitz was particularly taken with her small blue and yellow wash drawing of an Icelandic folk tale 'Death in the House', which contained a skeleton as part of the Icelandic story she was representing.

Much is made of the fact that Pamela was the only non-photographer to exhibit at the photo secession; however, Whelan suggests Stieglitz had planned all along to also exhibit non-photographic works, so if we accept this, Pamela was not quite as special as is sometimes assumed. Stieglitz was keen for people to understand he was not simply their publicist, so to some extent, exhibiting Pamela's work was a rebuke to the photographers. That was not, to him, what the Secession was about. It seems for the first ten days or so of Pamela's exhibition, the gallery was mainly empty, but a complimentary review brought in the crowds, and her work sold out, leaving Stieglitz in the happy position of selling books of photographs he had taken of her work. The reviewer, James Gibbons, also loved 'Death in the House', her *pièce de résistance*. A sold-out exhibition did not make Pamela any more popular with many of the Photo-Secessionists, as they rightly felt there were numerous galleries for non-photographic artists to exhibit.

Her artwork was incredibly popular in its day, accentuated by Pamela's decision to immerse herself in the naïve fantasy world of children, wearing her gypsy attire, chanting her Jamaican folk tales, and reciting ballads by W. B. Yeats. Whatever one's views of Pamela, her exhibition opening must have been an incredible event. It was said by Benjamin de Casseres that her paintings at the Photo Secession (1909) were curious and fascinating.[17] He was obviously transfixed by Pamela's work, which seemed of inconsistent quality, at times completed in a hurry, lyrically stating:

> She is a blender of visions, a mystic, a symbolist, one who transfigures the world she lives in by the overwhelming simplicity of her imagination. To me, these wonderful little drawings are not merely art; they are poems, ideas, life-values and cosmic values that have long gestated within the subconscious world of their creator.
>
> The minds of the greatest visionaries are infantile—and here Miss Smith approaches Blake and Beardsley. Only dullards believe in the commonplace; only mediocrity feels life to be stale ...
>
> I have spoken of the overwhelming simplicity of her work. They are so simple that fat practical brains will either see in them nothing or lunacy ... a poet, such as Pamela Colman Smith, who speaks directly of things as they are perceived by the mind not yet overlaid by the painted illusions of sight and not affected by the deadly automatism of routine, is believed to have a touch of insanity. All absolute simplicity startles, is eccentric and bears about it the mark of other-worldness...
>
> Also, is Pamela Colman Smith the *évocatrice* of Wonder. Her world is a world of romance—a world seen with the divining and transforming spiritual power of a child.
>
> Pamela Colman Smith has seen by closing the eyes.[18]

Could he have been her greatest admirer? He refers to her childlike manner, her naïve way of representing the world, her untainted thinking, and her simplicity that makes her somehow innocent and unworldly, which specifically appealed to some people, but not all. In some ways, Pamela was very worldly, but her art could be manipulated to suggest otherwise. Stieglitz liked Pamela's imagination and sympathised with her about the alleged British apathy towards her work. Her January 2007 exhibition was so successful it was extended for eight days. Despite poor weather, the crowds thronged, including critics and other artists, educators, collectors, and students. Sales were vibrant. Stieglitz maintained Pamela's work fitted the spirit of the Photo-Secession, which was not the product of, or in servitude to, any one medium.

Pamela exhibited successfully again in 1909, but her one-person show of drawings in monochrome and colour evoked by music, sketched during concert or opera, while popular, was to be her last exhibition there before Stieglitz moved emphatically towards modernism. At the private opening on the evening of 16 March, her Secessionist friends were enthralled by her recital of West Indian nursery rhymes and Yeats's poetry, a combination of her talents.

Alas, Pamela did not feel comfortable with most of the Americans she met in New York, aside from Stieglitz and a few others whom she regarded as kindred spirits, though she also played to her audience. She was anxious to return to what she felt was the more congenial environment in London, despite the alleged apathy of its people. Brooklyn was depopulating around this time, so while not exactly suburban, it was developing more offices and commercial buildings in an area too expensive for housing; Brooklyn was changing. Maybe she found it unsettling.

In the early 1900s, newspapers mentioned the *Annancy Stories*, claiming Pamela's childhood and youth were spent in Jamaica, thereby enabling her to tell tales in the style of Uncle Remus, her recital skills like old bards and troubadours, but that she was also an artist of childlike simplicity, naïve yet colourful, though generally accepted to lack artistic technique. Pamela was an all-round performer, using her considerably varied skills to promote herself and her work. American newspapers were impressed by her list of personal friends who were famous painters, musicians, actors and the literati. In 1907, for example, newspapers mentioned her:

> Unique program of entertainment which seemed to consist of singing old English ballads and songs in a s'teenth century costume, also by 'lilting' such modern Irish poems as W. B. Yeats 'Dream of the Wandering Angus' in the manner of ye ancient bards and troubadours.[19]

Seen as an unusual entertainment, she was feted for her recital skills.

Like any artist, Pamela's self-doubt focused on her own deficiencies, but even she realised she was something special as a storyteller. When telling tales to children she illustrated them with hand-made wooden dolls, focusing on language, facial expression, gesture, and intonation. This would work for all groups, be it children on the east side of New York, or adults in sophisticated salons. Her humour shone through her performances. Mary Greer's blog contains many extracts pertaining to her storytelling skills.[20]

The rationale for Pamela's storytelling was described in article for *The Columbus Journal* from 1904:

> A woman who has struck upon an unusual way to bring in the pennies is Miss Pamela Colman Smith, who is entertaining London audiences with West Indian folklore stories. Clad in a flame coloured robe, she sits in Eastern fashion on the floor, on which she manipulates the toys which represent the dramatis personae of her stories. In front of the board are two candles for footlights, while in the background a grate fire sheds a warm, red glow over the weird picture. Every story begins with the formula: 'In a long-before time, before Queen Victoria came to reign over we' instead of our 'once upon a time …'[21]

Bringing in the pennies is precisely what Pamela was doing, and why not? She enjoyed performing; she was fascinated by folklore and was an exceedingly accomplished storyteller. Does this diminish her as an artist? Perhaps not, but her artistic career was relatively short-lived as fashions changed and as she turned to other pursuits to survive. The penniless bohemian lifestyle was not for her if she could possibly avoid it.

12

A Diluted Talent

Even today, there is a distinct snobbery and difference between the art world and the craft world. Crafting is still perceived as the inferior cousin of fine art, illustration straddling the great divide. It is Pamela's illustrative career that makes her difficult to place in the art world. The Illustration Art Blog explains that quality reproduction attracts many viewers for marginal payments.[1] Illustration is therefore more mass market than fine art, which often provides higher payment for fewer views. Largely, it depends on the exclusivity of the audience.

Pamela was prolific, though she was spending more of her time as an illustrator drawing quality pictures to earn a crust than as a top-notch artist painting what she (maybe) really wanted. For example, she wanted to draw Shakespearean heroines but there was no market, so it did not happen. She had to be market-led. Pamela's output as a jobbing artist was intensely industrious and sadly badly paid, but hers were probably not the kind of paintings many wanted on their walls. Most books suggest she stopped painting in later life. This appears to be incorrect. Discussions with Tony Edwards, her errand boy, suggest she was still painting in Bude during her sixties as she generally offered to pay him in pictures unless these were old ones she was trying to offload. He later, of course, wished he had accepted them. She is also believed to have painted while living on The Lizard.

There are many resources, some included on the wonderful Mary Greer tarot blog, discussing Pamela's eclectic artwork.[2] Her pictures have been described variably as 'interesting, colourful and accomplished'. She learned to draw as soon as she could hold a pencil but her work soared when she attended Pratt. 'Original, wonderful, almost garish' have also been used to describe her. She was also described as too versatile to confine herself to one form of work. Her recitals were mentioned but also work at children's parties 'as all youngsters plainly adore her'.

One such resource mentioned:

> Under the auspices of the Pratt Art Club, Miss Pamela Colman Smith gave an extremely interesting recital at the Institute last Saturday evening. While

telling her Jamaica folk stories, Miss Smith sat upon a low platform with her feet tucked under her, and a row of half-dozen big fat candles before her to serve as footlights. The room was darkened and the young narrator presented a very picturesque figure gowned in a loose robe of flame colored silk, with an arrangement of tulle and beads bound about her head like a kerchief. Her capital West Indian dialect rendered the stories all the more piquant. In a charming recital of old English ballads, this clever artist dressed the part in soft gray and white with a quaint cap; while in her tragical odd lilting of a group of poems by William B. Yeats, Miss Smith again showed her rare knowledge of dramatic values by wearing a long dark green cloak with hood drawn close about her face, and only one nervous hand visible.[3]

Additionally, on Saturday, 9 February 1907, it was noted:

Possibly the best number on the program—certainly the greatest novelty—was furnished by Miss Pamela Colman Smith, who gave Jamaica folk stories. Having passed many years on that island, Miss Smith is conversant with the correct Jamaican costume and has acquired a capital West Indian dialect. Gowned in old rose cashmere, with deep black fringe, and wearing beads about her neck and chiffon twined about her bead to represent a kerchief, Miss Smith sat flat upon a small round table with her feet tucked beneath her gown and a row of half a dozen short fat candles at her knees to represent footlights. An artist of quite exceptional brilliancy and absolute originality, Miss Smith knows the value of every gesture, every smile and every inflection. The Entertainment Club, nearing its majority, can surely be congratulated upon its twentieth celebration.[4]

However, 16 February claims:

Miss Smith's instant success here is a bit unusual. I think it is largely due to her absence of all pose; queer, unexpected, absolutely original as Miss Smith is, one realizes her unmistakable genuineness as well as appreciates her talents. She is a gentlewoman, presenting an odd type of thoroughly unconventional femininity—therein lies her greatest charm.[5]

Also in 1907, 'An alligator brought by Miss Smith from Jamaica was an attractive exhibit' (presumably this was stuffed). This account, also listed on Greer's blog, describes Mark Twain's glee at her skill:

Miss Pamela Colman Smith, who made such a success in London a year or two ago as a storyteller, is now enchanting America with her quaint art. She recently entertained Mark Twain, and he was so delighted that he laughed like a child the whole time. In the weird dialect of the Jamaican negroes—a sort

> of cockney English with Spanish colouring, a rhythmic rising inflection at the end of each sentence, and barbaric words and idioms sprinkled through it that must have come directly from the voodoo worshippers of the African jungle—she tells fairy folk-tales of 'de long ago before time, when Queen Victoria didn't yet rule over we'.[6]

She is listed as an alumna of the Pratt Institute of New York, a Pratt icon, despite Pratt being unable to curb or train her. The Institute still has campuses in the creative hubs of Brooklyn and Manhattan. Founded in 1887 by industrialist Charles Pratt, its objective was and still is to provide affordable education for working women and men. Even in 1887, it welcomed all through its doors regardless of class, colour, or gender. When Pamela attended, it was already a forward-thinking institution, ideal for her unusual style. While there, she lived in an old glossy-floored, polished 'French' apartment house in Manhattan.

Like most young people, she pursued her course vocationally, to make art or illustration her career. Fortunately, life drawing was heavily emphasised at the Institute, which in turn informed the figure drawing which brought her so much work. It was in her fourth year she joined the life, composition and design course taught by key art educator, Arthur Wesley Dow, where a photograph of one of his classes around 1899 shows it to be dominated by women. He focused more on abstract composition rather than imitative drawing, so she learned a great deal from him and made good use of her lessons.

Pamela's obvious talent shone through from a young age, as she was merely fifteen when she started her art studies at Pratt. Her approach was visionary, further exploited through real, alleged (or adopted) synaesthesia, a mystery condition then and still not terribly well understood; she was generally presented as a mystic, an exotic persona she seemed to enjoy. Her love of miniature theatre and her nickname, Pixie, further added to her self-created image of a woman of childlike simplicity and naïveté with magical qualities. Usefully, this childlike persona freed her from the constraints of domesticity applied to the work of most women, allowing her some success in New York, so it was worth cultivating.

As ever, she sold herself well. She was not above saying what people like Stieglitz wanted to hear to sell her work, if it was to her own advantage, but her appeal, which was initially useful to Stieglitz, had by 1909–10, begun to wear off. The novelty of the so-called 'woman-child' had dulled, as the more explicit innovation and experimentation of modernism took a hold on the art world. It is curious yet ironic how the concept of the 'feminine' within Stieglitz's modernism ultimately appeared to be defined or controlled by a man.

Understandably, as with any new wave movement, when modernism developed, Pamela's more symbolist artistic work was sidelined within artistic circles to create space for a new way of thinking, a trend where male artists once again took centre-stage (Rodin, Matisse, Picasso, and others) while female artists who were versatile enough developed new forms of painting or photography. The uncertainties of industrial change and the horrors of the First World War had led to a whole new forward-looking dynamic into which Pamela's charming quirkiness did not fit. It is easy to see how, in times of great turmoil, her work seemed less relevant to the modern age.

Frankly, she did not 'fit' with the modernist turn in many ways. She was not a creator of big statement pieces, nor did she embrace the female nude rapidly becoming popular as a symbol of women's emancipation. By 1909, Stieglitz had Anne Brigman on board, a photographer from the far west of America whose photographic nudes were far removed from the genderless, often comedic qualities of Pamela's figures. Her naïveté quickly fell 'off trend'.

Additionally, modernism was increasingly shaping itself around sexuality, as the influence of the work of Sigmund Freud, Havelock Ellis, and other early sexologists took effect. Ellis presented the first objective study of homosexuality, which was a massive shift in thinking. From the 'childlike' of Pamela's work to the unconscious darkness of sexual desire marked a huge change in thought, a gap, once open, too wide to breach, which was beloved of the bohemians who embraced freethinking and free love, among other contentious thinking and behaviours.

Elizabeth Foley O'Connor claims Pamela was multi-talented, attempting to blaze her own trail, achieving some success before being defeated by the expected subjects and behaviour of women, constraints with which she constantly battled and notedly rejected.[7] It is this that many believe led to her retreat from public life, so a theme of disillusionment with women's lot, and her particular lot, persists. Certainly, to receive little remuneration for her talents cannot have made life easy; it was disillusioning and disenchanting.

Nonetheless, we should not underestimate Pamela's contribution to the art world, although most of it now lies forgotten. She was commercially active from 1890 into the 1920s, which gave her thirty decent working years, longer than many. Her work was exhibited in Europe and America, while she also illustrated over twenty books—no mean feat. She was nothing if not prolific, yet her view of publishing and publishers remained negative; this attitude probably did not help her and was a misguided or ill-judged response, childlike rather than rational and adult. It is often said that had she not illustrated the tarot deck, Pamela Colman Smith would have slid into total obscurity, which is probably true.

In 1897, she left Pratt (reputedly without graduating) taking up residence with her father in New York. Soon, an energetic and innovative artist, she was selling various items while also seeking commissions for illustrations. It was through this work that she met Mark Twain's biographer, Albert Bigelow Paine. Professionally, he was a useful man to know within children's book illustrating but they also seemed to get along well. In her early letter to him dated 29 December 1898, writing from 142 East Eighteenth Street, New York, Pamela wrote to Mr Paine, thanking him for his package of inscribed books (presumably sent for Christmas) mentioning, 'Daddy joins me in expressing thanks to you for your kind gift'.[8]

Pamela was experimental by nature, enjoying playing in the world of her imagination. She liked building elaborate props, stages, and wooden characters, theatre in miniature, which is partly what drew her to the attention of the Lyceum theatre crowd. She was additionally praised for her imaginative book illustrations and her colourist abilities. Already a chameleon unbound by convention, in 1899, she and her father returned to England where her work encouraged a response, good or bad. It was rare for someone to have no opinion of it or her. People were also not shy about expressing their opinions.

Artistically, her upbringing was unorthodox. Most people view her as part of the symbolist movement occurring towards the end of the nineteenth century, given her focus on the introspective symbolic world, rather than the accuracy of naturalism. Pamela's paintings were never meant to be faithful reproductions of real life. This, understandably, made her individualistic in her expression. The *Annancy Stories* illustrations are a good example of her work in this respect, imaginative and creative.

Katz and Goodwin state when it came to her best-known work, the tarot deck, Waite hired Pamela as 'a very skilful and original artist' who also had some knowledge of tarot values and was 'deeply versed in the subject'.[9] It is often suggested Pamela was no intellectual but was intuitive and immersive in her art where it was needed. Images suggest Pamela created a black and white pen and ink version of the tarot cards first; she seemed to have a real talent for pen portraits and compositions. The whole tarot project is said to have taken about five and a half months to complete and seems to have been her one and only real link to the cards. Spirituality had to give way to pragmatism, for she knew she needed to earn a living.

Despite Waite, who had a reputation for dullness, describing her as an 'abnormally psychic artist', her cards were not particularly well-received in her time, only growing in popularity after her death. She seems to have had little knowledge and deep understanding of the subject *per se*, though some would disagree. Waite reckoned he worked hard to stop Pamela casually picking up 'floating images' (a reference to her alleged synaesthesia though that was likely another artistic device and a fabulously effective way for a woman to control her own work rather than accede to the demands of others, especially men), feeding her the designs of some of the Major Arcana. It is widely believed Pamela treated the tarot as a symbolist would, seeing the cards as without fixed meaning but subject to individual interpretation. Inspiration for them apparently came from a stay at Smallhythe Place around 1903, where she visited her actress friend, Ellen Terry.

Like many, Miss Smith struggled with drawing feet and hands, despite the detail of her drawings. It is often suggested that Pamela ghost-wrote *The Russian*

Ballet, but it seems unlikely. Pamela's letters were haphazard, non-sequential, and brimful of errors. Her capacity and focus to write a book not based on copied dialogue from stories was surely limited, unless she was simply slapdash with her correspondence. Ellen herself was not concise with language; there is more of a case for Christopher St John, who was an adept writer and editor.

Pamela, however, had a problem. Having created her 'stage' persona, real life was quite different. Nowhere, it seems, did Pamela feel quite at home and comfortable, to fit in, but her perceptions of her fellow Americans as affected, dull and vacuous gives us some indication she sought meaning in her interactions; game playing was not enough; social niceties were not enough. She sought a sense of belonging, of community, of being.

There are many digitised letters from Pamela to Stieglitz held at the Yale University Library, Beinecke Rare Book and Manuscript Library, Alfred Stieglitz/Georgia O'Keeffe archive, some written in America, some London, and even one on SS *Minnehaha* dated 23 March 1907.[7] The letters are crammed and chaotic, not always spelled correctly, and using many variants of her name such as Pamela Smith, Colman Smith, and Pamela Coleman Smith.

By 27 April 1907, Pamela was writing from 84 York Mansions, Battersea Park. Her letters were always very precise about money in the way of someone for whom money is an issue. Her letter is about her art sales, but she mentions: 'London is delightful—but spring is late and it is still very cold'.[10] By 26 October, she has her customary initials signature 'PCS' as her letterhead in green. Writing in turquoise ink, she explained:

> My Uncle was over here and seemed to think it would be unwise if I went to New York this winter—so I put it off until January—and now things look so dark (financially) that I fear I shall not go after all. Anyway—I am getting a show ready for you—I will send you over 30 or 40 drawings—about the last week in December.—if that is all right for your arrangements.[11]

She discussed her musically inspired works thus:

> I am having an exhibition here—beginning on Nov 22—of 22 drawings (all music). But I expect wild rage from the British Public!
>
> I hope you will think my things have improved ... There are several that I dare not show here - they are too much...
>
> I have never been able to draw much to Liszt. but strangely enough I have 3! Liszt drawings in my show! & 1 Strauss—5 Beethoven. & 3 Bach. I have 4 sketchbooks of music drawings done at concerts with ink and a brush—and they are certainly bolder and more definite than those of a year ago.
>
> I make hardly any money here—and so it entirely depends on how things look in New York later on—if I come. Of course I should like to see my show

at the Photo Secession and rail at the foolish Bromides! [here, she was playing to her audience].

The show here is nothing like so well done as yours. I will send you notices that may amuse you! Good luck to the 'garret'.[12]

Pamela was relying more on American art sales than British ones, as well as flattering Stieglitz. She was not in vogue in England. If we look at some of the exhibiting painters in Europe around this time, we see Pamela was somewhat out of tune. Compare her to Sickert (avant-garde, urban) and the American John Singer Sargent (Edwardian portraits) who featured. By 27 December 1907, she explained:

> I am getting another show here ready for a new show all of January. So am very busy! Had a show in Edinburgh—for 2 weeks in December—3rd to the 15th—and I sold 2 drawings & exchanged 1 (James Paterson—ARSA) great swell—does ripping things of Scotland![13]

She sent Stieglitz more drawings—all 'music pictures'—and was sending a word about them (effectively her own press release) in the hope 'some paper would publish it'. 'The London notices are good as things go here—but they have all got hold of the wrong end of the stick'; she goes on to hope he can make head or tail of her scrawl.

> I have had a letter from Henry Wood the conductor of the Queen's Hall Orchestra here: allow me to say quite frankly, how your imagination, fancy, form and colour delighted me, I too see musical things from a colour point of view, but the impression and mood you portray … are to me of deep psychological importance, & are so fresh and new—and your lines on Fear are splendid! So you see, from a musician's point of view this is something! (triple underlined).
>
> This Observer notice seems to me good. People were especially sympathetic in Edinburgh which I think is like Boston compared to N.Y. to Edinburgh London! Maurice Hewlett woke up enough to buy two drawings from the London Show. 1 other I sold here so I hope I'll do better in N.Y.[14]

Her exhibitions were not a resounding success north of the border and possibly cost her more money in travel and accommodation costs than she made. She constantly self-publicised, exhaustingly so, given no one else would do it for her.

In a letter sent December 1907, she talked about another show and sending more pictures, saying:

> I think some of them are a step ahead! I met a Chinese man in Edinburgh who said that my things were the only pictures he had seen in western countries that he could understand! So I am glad!

> Enclosed you will find a few words on how I do and see the music pictures. Perhaps you can get some enterprising paper to use it!!
>
> The bells are ringing in a new Year! & I hope it will be successful to the Photo Secession and you! - and to all workers in the true way! Everyone always thinks theirs is the true way! But if we did not believe, we should never do![15]

By January 1, 1908, she is talking pricing and asking Stieglitz to critique her work. She is sending more pictures come February 1908.

> There is an 1812 which I think would sell if anything will! ... some of them have been taken by The Strand magazine for an article - though the pigs won't pay anything! It may help the sales for they have a very large circulation ...
>
> Do you think there is any likelihood of having a show—or of getting any drawings in a magazine or such in Munich? This spring I shall have lots of new and I think better paintings.
>
> The publishers and public are just as bad here—won't buy anything—& if they do, don't pay!!! Fuller Maitland (musical critic of *The Times*) is very keen on them and has played me a lot of Bach which I did drawings for. I find the more I do the more I see. The last week I have done 94 drawings, almost all useable ones! (this is a colossal workload by anyone's standard).
>
> I cannot do drawings of New York in London! People sometimes think I have no sensibilities. I have been sticking to the music drawings only for I cannot tell how long they will go on! It seems as if they were going to lead on to some other work. I can't tell what![16]

The fear the music drawings will cease suggest whatever visions Pamela had, they were not synaesthetic. She also indicates that to draw a place she needed to be there; she was so more observation-led than psychic.

> I find that the picture and art public are the wrong people—altogether! Those interested from a psychological standpoint and a music one see a view of the drawings quite invisible to the arty point of view. These are the people to go for. I hope you will be able to sell some for me. BUT I know you will do your best and talk to them in a way I cannot, and convince people![17]

This is interesting as it indicates she needs to sell to people more interested in subliminal messages than artistic form.

> There is much talk of conviction here just now in all things—stage & music & books—that is one of the things one feels lacking in the art of the day, lack of belief in anything!

> All art, pictures and illustrations, with the exception of a very few things is a hollow sham, and the more students put off it the better. I feel a … revolutionist that would make the hair of any self-respecting art instructor rise! The false cant of the arty makes me ill! So sorry about the Camera Club turning you out. Pigs![18]

Pamela herself saw problems with her work. People liked their artistic quality, their musical quality or their psychological quality, but rarely all three combined, so they were not prepared to pay much for them. Again, she railed against the whole art establishment. She certainly seemed to feel underappreciated and misunderstood. By March 1908, she was prepared to accept any money rather than none, as she fought a growing disenchanted mood, she was painting for nothing. In March 1908, she was beginning to feel seriously depressed, writing:

> I would rather sell at a small price to the people you would be glad to have the things than not at all. I do want some money very badly as I have not been able to get paid for the pictures sold here last December—yet! I am looking forward to every post to bring more news …
>
> It is very cold here and I am very depressed, swearing at everybody! I have 5 more fat sketchbooks like the ones I sent over just sitting here. If only there were something in view to work for. The publishers are as dull here as elsewhere! except for the usual harmless dull insipid stuff by feeble females! I know plenty of 'em who are living well by their inanities! We disgruntled devils don't please anybody![19]

She asked him to choose a picture for himself with her good wishes and to send one to someone who she promised a wedding present long ago. By 9 May, she is signing herself Pamela Smith; by 19 November 1909, she needs money again from Stieglitz:

> I want some money for Christmas … I have 8 or 9 new things. I am sending one next week. You will like them, I think. Perhaps a few people may like 1 or 2. They are carefree and nice colour and larger …
>
> I've just finished a big job for very little cash! A set of designs for a pack of tarot cards. 80 designs. I shall send some over of the original drawings as some people may like them. I will send you a pack (printed in colour by lithography) (probably very badly!) as soon as they are ready by Dec 1 I think.[20]

By now, she is Pamela Coleman Smith. We see her money problems growing. The tarot cards were by now completed.

Melinda Boyd Parsons, who completed a masters' thesis on Pamela in the 1970s, was a big part of Pamela's rediscovery; to Parsons, Pamela was as follows:

> An exceptionally imaginative painter and illustrator who was prominent in Britain from 1900 to 1915. During that period, she produced paintings and drawings which embodied her subconscious fantasy world and foreshadowed surrealist art.[21]

In her day, she was compared with, as Boyd Parsons says, Munch, Redon, Ensor, Beardsley, and Blake.

Pamela, described as a 'visionary' with her deepening friendships with members of occult groups, increased her interest in both mysticism and synaesthesia, when she experimented with the idea of incorporating musical interpretations into paintings. Whether she was an actual synaesthete or whether she merely tapped into the idea and developed it, as she did with so many things, is moot. The popular belief is her work was not conscious but spontaneous, suggesting that whatever prompted musical composition in the first place also prompted Pam's paintings. This may explain why her style was so very varied, if it depended upon music, but she was not above trying any commercial wheeze to raise funds.

After 1920, Pamela dropped off the artistic radar, no longer exhibiting, her post-war state of mind no longer quite the same as artistic fashions changed.

13

Synaesthesia or Simply Technique?

Pamela is considered by some to have been blessed with synaesthesia, a crossover of the senses where, for example, music may be perceived as colours. Most writers avoid calling her a synaesthete and for very good reason, though she certainly used music in her paintings.

Synaesthesia is little understood, affects only a small percentage of people, and, importantly, is present from birth; therefore, it was a useful concept to use in the anti-rational mysticism prevalent at the time in England and Ireland. To be noticed, claiming to be special was a useful ploy. Many painters who are not synaesthetes employ 'synaesthetic techniques', which Pamela learned at Pratt. There is a difference between the condition and the technique. To think of her as a synaesthete is more romantic, certainly. Some researchers speculate that the conditions leading to synaesthesia may be a window into how abstract thought developed from disparate senses.

A medical condition, synaesthesia is where a sensation in one of the senses, like hearing, triggers a sensation in another. Evidence suggests it can be distracting or, conversely, gives slight learning advantages, especially in terms of visual learning. It is more common in people with autistic spectrum conditions, sitting at 17–19 per cent for those with autism. However, most people with autism do not have synaesthesia and *vice versa*. There is no evidence Pamela was autistic, though her feelings of being an outsider may indicate a sense of difference. The Synaesthesia Association says it is a truly fascinating condition, a union of the senses usually experienced separately, as they become involuntarily and automatically joined together—a difficult concept for most of us to understand.[1]

As most synaesthetic artists paint abstract works, this makes sense. The mystical qualities of Pamela's paintings attracted attention, so assuming this was due to a special 'psychic' characteristic was a popular idea. The mystical was valued way above rationalism in many creative circles; in others, there was a harking back to intuitive working. In a contemporary source, M. Irwin. MacDonald wrote of the 'fairy faith' espoused by W. B. Yeats in a fight against scepticism, indicating people accepted the reality of the subjective world in the days before materialism and rationalism.[2]

Pamela was a potential bridge between academic cynicism and everyday leanings towards folklore, life and humanity. She not only asserted she saw fairies and other beings but also painted and drew them. Of course, anyone could say this, but her super-ordinary vision differentiated Pamela's paintings and illustrations. Irwin noticed her drawings drew the crowds in New York, despite them being 'not especially remarkable for technique. There were hundreds of as good or better pictures shown in other galleries at the same time'.[3] It was the simplicity and sincerity that appealed, accentuated by the use of pencil or India ink. The fantastical world Pamela captured fired the imagination.

Irwin adds Miss Smith is described as follows:

> Not a musician nor an aficionado of it, but the changing rhythms and hormones stir her consciousness so she draws exactly what she sees. She sees music rather than listens to it, and she expresses - as perfectly as she can and with the literal directness of a child—exactly what she sees.[4]

It sounds like synaesthesia but is it? Importantly, Irwin suggests we all have this power for if we have the mind of a child (open, perceptive, honest), then we can make pictures, regardless of such fabrications as technique. There is a difference between having the mind of a child and synaesthesia. If his assertion is correct, then synaesthesia it was not; it was imagination.

Hugo Heyrman suggests there are two types of naturally occurring synaesthesia, but also created forms in art, asserting many artists around Pamela's time actively tried to demonstrate the complementary nature of the senses and correspondences.[5] Paul Klee reiterated this approach: 'Art does not reproduce the visible; rather it makes visible'.[6] He explains from 1900–1950, the crossing of borders in art was part of the technique of the *fin-de-siècle* avant-garde, a component of the origins of modernism, starting with expressionism, a term Pamela used to describe her own work. He describes Munch's *The Scream* as an expression of the synaesthetic experience, 'a hallucinatory level, a pictorial metaphor of primal fear: you scream and scream but no one can hear you'. The crossing over of forms, therefore, was not necessarily true synaesthesia but a legitimate artistic approach.

Pamela was affected differently by various composers, something with which modern-day synaesthete artist, Jane Mackay, would agree.[7] Grieg to Pamela was pleasant, while Wagner, profoundly sensuous to many, created only a violent blur for her. Schumann created within her emotional paintings. Rather than interpret the music, the 'vision' was the emotion inspired by the sound. It was Debussy whose work revealed the most vivid pictures in Pamela's collection.

Affected by so many influences, Pamela was believed by her contemporaries to have the gift of second sight, yet, she never perceived this as clairvoyance but as something everyone has within them. Pamela nurtured the natural, childlike, naïve persona, the artist who knew little academically of psychological or philosophical theories.

She certainly played to her audience. Her interest in folklore appeared in Jamaica during her youth, where she expressed the oral tradition in writing. In England, she employed a Lucy Atwell tendency towards the quaint and whimsical, which appealed to her sense of humour, and probably to English audiences. She drew lots of pictures of children, following the fashion of Walter Crane, to incorporate decoration and colour. Humour oversaw much of her work, but she was especially keen on illustrations for children's tales.

During the Celtic Revival of the late nineteenth–early twentieth centuries, she encountered Maeterlinck and Debussy, among others, who allegedly saw other beings, especially in Ireland; they were the Sidhe, the children of the Dana, who, in Celtic lore, were driven out. Pamela had a vivid imagination, or maybe visions from her 'second sight'. Conversely, she was simply fascinated by and open to folklore (as in Jamaica) able to tap into belief in supernatural beings. Fascinated and inspired by such beliefs, she used them in her work. Pamela probably saw a market; she was willing and able to use her observational skills in a way focusing on the bizarre vagaries of some weird underworld which made her different to the rest and was at least briefly, successful in her quest.

Depending on what we read, around 1–4 per cent of the population are synaesthetes, a trait far from universal. For someone who is not, it is a complex concept to truly grasp because most people's brains work quite differently. At an objective, academic level, it is understandable, but at an experiential level, it is almost impossible. Much of the work written about Pamela questionably takes it for granted; 'because she was described as working in a synaesthetic way', she was a synaesthete. Pamela's contemporary, the Russian artist Kandinsky (1866–1944) adopted a synaesthetic approach to his art, which was much more abstract than Pamela's. It seems any synaesthetic art would be likely to be abstract. Given his affinity for the composer Schoenberg, however, it is easy to see why Kandinsky might have developed such a non-objective form.

Pamela's work was never truly like this. It was creative and eclectic, but we might argue, observation-led, as we see in so much of her figure work. Boyd Parsons suggests the reason her work has been generally forgotten was due to 'her pictorial dependence on the quickly outmoded visual vocabulary of *fin-de-siècle* art'.[8] She remained a competent illustrator but was no Romantic, enthralled by nature. This was clear in her later life when her errand boy, Tony Edwards, had no recollection of her ever going near the tremendously energising, powerful sea in Bude, despite living only ten minutes' walk away from it. On The Lizard, she posted letters from immensely beautiful places like Kynance

Cove, but for someone with keen observation skills, she made no mention of her incredibly scenic surroundings. Maybe she was more concerned with her created world than the real one, or had little sense of place. Her interest seemed to be in people rather than nature, landscapes, or seascapes. This makes her move to The Lizard even more intriguing.

As an artist, she would apply various styles to see what worked best for her in specific contexts. Her landscapes invariably have some folklore connection or human form involved. Pamela, as we know, was a consummate performer, so impression management formed a key element of this. It is unlikely anyone truly knows her authentic views on most things except from her letters, when she was annoyed, and from her actions. We are told she was spontaneous and well she might have been. At times, such spontaneity may also have led to quality inconsistency, a slapdash approach, which may also have affected her artistic impact.

We also cannot assume that because Pamela related to both music and art she connected the two in a synaesthetic way but she certainly used music to inform her art. Boyd Parsons mentions how Dow discussed 'creation of rhythm and harmony independent of meaning as the goal of painting'.[9] He used musical terms to describe the act of painting, so tones were, for example, notes. Of course, as she developed her sense of spirituality through her involvement with the Golden Dawn and other of Yeats' mystical concerns, art could be perceived as representing other related ideas, akin to synaesthesia. Synaesthetes, however, experience this naturally, rather than as an artistic style. While her music paintings in America between 1907 and 1912 were enthusiastically received, we must question of whether she did them consciously or not.

Boyd Parsons suggested Pamela enjoyed 'hermetic visions', which may be synaesthesia. Some of her descriptions of drawing to music suggest it, yet was she like this from birth? Musical painting appeared to become an element of her work from around 1900, which would not have been the case for a true synaesthete. Was she simply an incredibly good storyteller and marketeer, not above creating the persona she felt would sell her artwork and make her money? Probably. It is an attractive thought, that music not only inspired her to paint but directed her artwork; however, when visiting Pamela's life, one may take nothing for granted. She did her utmost to appear exotic, unusual, and mysterious, to attract an audience in an ever-changing bohemian setting, so why would she not use synaesthesia to the same end? If so, she was certainly open to feelings and trends, not as naïve as we might think. Over and again, we hear drama was constantly on her agenda.

Certainly, Pamela had her own style and way of doing things placing her on the fringes. Two things usually happen when an artist is on the fringe. She either falls off the edge and disappears without a trace or becomes incorporated into the avant-garde, then eventually the mainstream. It is a risky business being different but with potentially high stakes and rewards. Unfortunately for Pamela, after a period of popularity, she fell off the edge. It is easy to see why she may have felt like an outsider, at least partly a consequence of perpetuating an illusion of mystery and intrigue, living an almost double existence. Parsons wrote in her abstract:

> Smith told him [Stieglitz] she painted 'automatically'—that is, without conscious control—claiming simply to record passively the hermetic visions that came to her unbidden when she listened to music (a crossing of aural and optical sensation called synaesthesia). Both this 'automatism' and Smith's Symbolist subjects—strange goddesses, zodiacal symbols, star-crossed lovers, ancient heroes and folkloric nature-spirits—were remarkably progressive in New York at a time when Naturalism and Impressionism were the new plus ultra of avant-garde endeavor.[10]

Obviously, this was enticing. Art is innovative, constantly requiring new ways of thinking and doing things; it is difficult to be noticed. Stieglitz was also breaking new ground, so he needed new ideas, types of creativity, and the unusual. What better way to make yourself attractive to a person with power to than to incorporate an air of mystery to your life, actions, and work? However, most things that seem mysterious do not retain it for very long. The extraordinary becomes ordinary.

By December 1900, she had begun to draw what she called 'visions'. She explained them:

> They are not pictures of the music themes—pictures of the flying notes—not conscious illustrations of the name given to a piece of music, but just what I see when I hear music—thoughts loosened and set free by the spell of sound.[11]

In 1927, Mrs Forbes-Sempill wrote how Pamela told her she created her first music picture on the afternoon of Christmas Day 1900, at Ellen Terry's house while Gordon Craig played Bach on the piano.[12] She said suddenly, in front of her eyes, a shutter clicked, leaving a hole containing a very vivid and clear picture. The point made about Pamela was she was unmusical, often not having a clue about the titles of pieces of music no matter how many times she heard them. Given Pamela was born in 1878, however, she would not have waited until she was twenty-two to have her first synaesthetic experience.

Pamela suggested during her interview that if she tried to alter the first detail of her drawing, the picture would break up and disappear instantly. She also explained she felt detached about her drawings as if she had no recognition of them. She would begin her drawings at the lower left-hand corner of the paper, working upwards with big sweeping strokes and no sense of hesitation. She seemed to respond better to some composers rather than others such as Bach, Beethoven, or Debussy, more than Chopin, Mendelssohn, or Brahms. Wagner, however, would drive her mad with anger and fury:

> Scratchy little brown fir trees rising through a brown fog; my scalp tingles and my hair pricks; I feel so full of rage that I want to crack the heads of people together like nuts. When it is played in a room, thick curtains of brown spiders' webs appear, sticky and evil-smelling. I have come into a room after Wagner music had been played and found that sickly, sweet evil smell clinging to everything. I have had to leave a concert when Wagner was being played ...
>
> The music of Debussy seems to her more natural than that of any other composer, to have more in common with the sounds in nature—not the ordinary singing or chirruping of birds, but sounds like bells in the wind, and a curious pulsing under-rhythm, beating and throbbing—like the breathing of living things and the sap running in the trees.[13]

Neuroscience was not advanced even by the time Pamela died in 1951, so the only way to investigate the synaesthesia claim further is through Pamela's own words and in conversation with a living synaesthete, sound-colour London artist, Jane Mackay.[14]

Jane Mackay feels if Pamela was a synaesthete, then she would have been one from birth, so ideally, we need to know more about her early childhood to understand more. When she attended Pratt at the age of fifteen, she was thought to be something of a prodigy, so she was obviously a talented child. Music would have driven her art from an early age as a synaesthete.

Some of her paintings were certainly inspired by well-known musical pieces. Her 1907 exhibition was visited by 2,200 visitors and she sold thirty-three paintings and drawings, but it was her later exhibition where music became more of a factor. An article in *The Delineator* in November 1912 says her last exhibition in New York created a furore because reporters heralded her drawings of music as a little freakish, but they are described as interpretations of music.[15] Pamela, when asked what kind of artist she was, apparently answered: 'Why, I suppose if I am anything, I am an expressionist. I try to express myself in the best way possible', hence her meeting with Debussy, something of an artistic admirer. Debussy's music sounded to Pamela like the sounds of nature. While the music played, she would, says Professor John Vance, give a brush drawing of what she saw.[16] 'Her hand works feverishly while the music lasts. When it ceases, the brush falls from her hand and she sees no more'. Pamela said: 'Once I begin to focus on the drawing instead of the music, I lose the image'.

Pamela's gift gained press coverage during her life, including a period when it was thought Pamela did little artistic work. *The Illustrated London News* in 1927, for example, included several drawings of Pamela's:

> It is a fascinating question whether music can be interpreted in terms of pictorial art. Many musical works purport to express aspects of nature, and some even have geographical titles, while musical critics frequently talk of 'colour'. Whether there is any definite connection between certain sounds and certain forms is a matter for scientific investigation. Very interesting evidence of such a connection is afforded by the remarkable drawings of Miss Pamela Colman Smith, described by Lewis Hind as 'sign-posts on a bye-path to the art of the future'.[17]

By 1909, she had widened her artistic horizons, so her music paintings were perhaps just another form of self-expression. She worked on the Waite-Smith tarot and joined the London Suffrage Atelier, which worked closely with the Women's Social and Political Union (WSPU) to produce propaganda in the form of postcards, posters, banners, and similar. The Atelier was founded in Shepherd's Bush by Laurence Housman, Clemence Housman (his sister), and Alfred Pearce in February 1909 to encourage artists to promote votes for women. Pamela probably encountered them via her friend, Edith Craig, who produced one of Laurence Housman's plays. Her music paintings were only discussed when she was trying to sell the idea, not for example, when she was illustrating for a cause.

A piece of research by Hartmann and Kunzendorf reviews many studies on boundaries (differentiated as 'thick' and 'thin' boundaries) and the links to synaesthesia, which is interesting when trying to understand Pamela, as it also relates to behaviour.[18] Boundaries relate to parts of the mind which are separate, yet interconnected. They can also be used to measure personality. A person with thick boundaries in all senses has a very sharp sense of focus and concentration on any matter in hand. They can ignore distractions, and are unlikely to experience synaesthesia. These are people who do not let feelings get in the way of rational thought, for example, or people who are totally clear when they are awake or dreaming. The researchers write:

> This person has a clear sense of the separation of past, present, and future ('that was then, this is now'), a very definite sense of space around him/herself ('this is my space, this is yours'), and a clear, delineated sense of sexual identity ('I am a man, you are a woman, *vive la difference*'). The person will have a definite group identity ('this is my group, we do such and such; other groups are totally different') and will tend to see the world in terms of black and white, us versus them, good versus evil.
>
> By contrast, a person with thin boundaries may experience some synaesthesia, letting a good deal of sensory material in, so have difficulty focusing on one element. These are the daydreamers who are acutely aware of thoughts and feelings, so that the real-life boundaries become less clear.[19]

Where Pamela is concerned, this next part of their description is especially pertinent to some contemporary descriptions of her.

> This person may be very aware of the past, and have it blend with the present, for example, 'I am grown-up, but in a lot of ways I'm still a child'). Similarly, this person will accept mixtures in sexual identity (such as 'I am a man, but there's a lot of feminine in me too'). He or she will not feel solidly a member of one group, but may be an individual taking part at times in many different groups, or perhaps a 'citizen of the world'. In judgments or opinions about the world, this person will tend to think in terms of shades of grey, rather than black and white ('it all depends, s/he's good in some ways and bad in others,' 'it's different at different times,' and so on).[20]

These are the extreme ends or dichotomy of a continuum and most people fall somewhere along the line, but dreams and daydreams are linked. Artist Jane Mackay gives us an indication of how Pamela may have felt if she was a synaesthete:

> I can't remember not linking sounds and vision Sound was always linked to vision for me. I can remember specific things from my childhood which, very much later, I realised were synaesthetic manifestations. From quite early on, I remember painting not only music but poetry and words and sounds generally. One of my first memories was the colour of birdsong in my mother's garden, for example.[21]

We never see such expressions in Pamela's writing, apart from the occasional ambiguous note. Jane adds:

> There are different layers of synaesthesia for me and I get it in different ways. I'm very aware of loud noise, like banging a door. I get a sensation very like an electric current or pins and needles, usually around my face, my lips, mouth and in my shoulders or the crook of my back. These are fundamental low-level examples of synaesthesia.
>
> When listening to music it is sometimes like watching a film or like floating in the sea over the top of a coral reef. You have all these wonderful colours, sometimes sensations, with textures, shapes, movement, perspective. They just hit you as the music comes along but I think you are responding to completely different things in the such as the Hallelujah Chorus in Messiah where the words have particular colours. The shape of the phrases is the image. Often, we are responding to change, unexpected things in the music, so I get my greatest visions from things like change of key, change from major to minor or minor to major, very loud crashing astonishing chords like Britten's Gloriana opera.

> When Elizabeth has just signed Essex's death warrant, that was such a strong image, I did an enormous oil painting of that. I might respond to something particular like what the tymps are doing, what the cellos are doing. Live music which really hits you between the eyes.[22]

She also explains artistic techniques and interpretation to make some of the images she creates more workable.

> It's multi-layered. As an artist, you do play with images. Often the synaesthetic images I get aren't going to make good compositions or paintings, so I often take the energy of the original image and then play with it later. Some of my sketches are direct and the colours are often very specific and have to be mixed to get the right colour, but that might not be terribly interesting as a painting. I can remember some images would just have been a colour field slanting across a grey background and I wouldn't want to necessarily spend ages painting that. My music painting is very much played with, experimental, processed but my inspiration comes from the synaesthetic images and sensations that I'm getting.
>
> Synaesthesia is just abnormal connections between parts of the brain. Every baby is a synaesthete as all their pathways are undifferentiated. If you give a sound to a baby and measure its brain wave, its visual area will light up. This happens until approximately 6 months of age in non-synaesthetes. Synaesthesia runs in families. I only put a name to all this when talking to a psychiatrist in the 1980s about painting music. Retrospectively, everything made sense.[23]

Synaesthesia is not a new condition but it was hidden for many years in the realms of neuroscience. Jane explained:

> From the late 1600s onwards, within music, people were quoted as saying trumpet sounds were red and so on. In the Bauhaus movement, it was fashionable to link art and music. Kandinsky called his paintings after musical themes (though I don't think he was a synaesthete). All went quiet until the 1960s/70s when scanning came into being (MRI, etc) and scientists/medics could actually look into the brain. Synaesthesia was not a word in common usage around 1951, when Pamela died.
>
> It is a condition a little like colour blindness. It's not that special really. Artistically it may confer advantage as many artists/creative are synaesthetes. In terms of Pamela Colman Smith, it is probably impossible to know if she was a synaesthete unless we uncover something about her childhood but synaesthesia provides a looseness of association, an openness to seeing life in different ways, opening up opportunities.[24]

If she was a synaesthete, then Jane's wonderful description of how she experiences it may give us some insight into Pamela's world. If not, then we can still see what she was trying to capture. Pamela expressed this in her own words:

> When I take a brush in hand and the music begins, it is like unlocking the door into a beautiful country. There, stretched far away, are plains and mountains and the billowy sea, and as the music forms a net of sound the people who dwell there enter the scene; tall, slow-moving, stately queens, with jewelled crowns and garments gay or sad, who walk on mountain—tops or stand beside the shore, watching the water—people. These water-folk are passionless, and sway or fall with little heed of time; they toss the spray and, bending down, dive headlong through the deep.
>
> There are the dwellers, too, of the great plain, who sit and brood, made of stone and motionless; the trees, which slumber till some elf goes by with magic spear and wakes the green to life; towers, white and tall, standing against the darkening sky—
>
> Those tall white towers that one sees afar,
> Topping the mountain crests like crowns of snow.
> Their silence hangs so heavy in the air
> That thoughts are stifled.
>
> Then huddling crowds, who carry spears, hasten across the changing scene. Sunsets fade from rose to grey, and clouds scud across the sky.
>
> For a long time the land I saw when hearing Beethoven was unpeopled; hills, plains, ruined towers, churches by the sea. After a time I saw far off a little company of spearmen ride away across the plain. But now the clanging sea is strong with the salt of the lashing spray and full of elemental life; the riders of the waves, the Queen of Tides, who carries in her hand the pearl-like moon, and bubbles gleaming on the inky wave.
>
> Often when hearing Bach I hear bells ringing in the sky, rung by whirling cords held in the hands of maidens dressed in brown. There is a rare freshness in the air, like morning on a mountain-top, with opal-coloured mists that chase each other fast across the scene.
>
> Chopin brings night; gardens where mystery and dread lurk under every bush, but joy and passion throb within the air, and the cold moon bewitches all the scene. There is a garden that I often see, with moonlight glistening on the vine-leaves, and drooping roses with pale petals fluttering down, tall, misty trees and purple sky, and lovers wandering there. A drawing of that garden I have shown to several people and asked them if they could play the music that I heard when I drew it. They have all, without any hesitation, played the same. I do not know the name, but—well, I know the music of that place.[25]

What Irwin implies is how all great poets, artists, and musicians are attuned to make people see what is merely in the subconscious; maybe music becomes a form of meditation for some artists. He continues:

> Pamela Colman Smith is so naturally a mystic that she has but little intellectual interest in mysticism. From childhood, she has had the gift of 'second sight' ... she never thinks of this power as clairvoyance, or exploits it as such, but uses it precisely as she does the senses and faculties which are common to all. In temperament and personality, she is as much as an anachronism as William Morris, for like him she belongs to an earlier age, but the only outward evidence of this is a childlike and utterly unconventional sincerity which finds expression with fearless freedom. She does not dabble in psychology, as is the fashion now, and she knows next to nothing of philosophical theories, transcendental or otherwise. Her understanding and knowledge are wholly intuitional. Perhaps this is why she sees so much that is hidden from ordinary sight.[26]

Synaesthetic effects can be like drug-induced ones. For instance, Albert Hoffmann was the first person to note the psychoactive properties of LSD when he accidentally ingested or breathed it. His laboratory notes clearly describe synaesthesia.[27]

In a research article 'Synaesthesia, creativity and art: What is the link?', Jamie Ward *et al* suggest:

> There seems to be a link between synaesthesia and creativity...Synaesthetes may not be more creative but may be biased towards the creative arts. 24% of synaesthetes were in artistic professions compared to 2% of population average ... the tendency to be engaged in arts is related to the particular phenomenological (based on subjectivity of human consciousness, not objectivity) characteristics of the synaesthesia. Individuals experiencing vision from music have particularly rich experiences (movement, textures, colour, shapes) and this may provide a source of motivation.[28]

To say all synaesthetes are more creative is too simplistic and not helpful. Georgia O'Keeffe, too, claimed music affected her painting. Her teachers, like Arthur Wesley Dow, encouraged the visualisation of music and listening to music when drawing. It seems anyone who met Dow was synaesthetic or perhaps, more likely, they were simply encouraged to use music in their painting.

14

Seeking Meaning: Mysticism and Religion

In 1901, Pamela joined the occult group the Hermetic Order of the Golden Dawn, a secret society focused on alchemy, spiritualism and metaphysics; most importantly, it was where she met Arthur Waite. Resulting from this, people have viewed her as a naturally mystical person, but was she? Kaplan suggests the Colman branch of her family's long-term interest the Swedenborgian movement swayed Pamela towards an interest in the occult; maybe, or like others around her, her interest in the occult was a response to scientific rationalism.[1]

Though slightly offbeat, the Swedenborgians is a branch of Christianity, not an occult group. Worshippers follow Christ not Swedenborg. In his writings, Swedenborg predicted God would replace the traditional Christian Church, establishing a 'New Church', to worship God in one person: Jesus Christ, so it is a branch of Christianity related to the second coming. While Swedenborg spoke of a 'new church', he never tried to establish one, and it was not a cult of the individual. However, it was also not remotely related to Catholicism with its reliance on Papal supremacy, which the Swedenborgians would not accept, for dominance of scripture is paramount to them. Her connection opened her up to religious reflection.

We do not know why Pamela joined the Hermetic Order, but her friends and acquaintances were involved, so why not, if it was a part of her social world and she was seeking meaning? She met many members of the occult community in London through professional contacts and friends, W. B. Yeats and Bram Stoker; she enjoyed the social and ritualistic aspects of the Order, and it was part of her social life, much as the Catholic Church later grew to be.

Some may disagree, but Pamela seemed to drift into the Golden Dawn without ever truly embracing it at a deep, philosophical, or academic level. As Arthur Waite wrote, she never pretended to or attempted to understand anything subsurface about the movement, her interest was superficial. However, she loved the sense of ritual and ceremony, which partly explains why she was also later attracted to Catholicism with its similar focus. In an article explaining the benefits of ritual, it seems they help alleviate a sense of loss, reduce anxiety and increase confidence.[2] There is always a reason for them, and why some people, more than others, are attracted to them. Remember, Pamela had lost both of her parents close together, at a young age. In an article for a monthly publication concerned with the supernatural and 'psychological problems', Arthur Waite explained why he specifically chose Pamela to illustrate the cards:

> I have embraced an opportunity which has been somewhat of the unexpected kind and have interested a very skilful and original artist in the proposal to design a set, Miss Pamela Coleman Smith in addition to her obvious gifts, has some knowledge of Tarot values; she has lent a sympathetic ear to my proposal to rectify the symbolism by reference to channels of knowledge, which are not in the open day.[3]

He did not mention cost but it was probably a consideration, too. Likewise, the tarot cards were not, to Pamela, a particularly religious experience, although she described how to use them intuitively, probably the only way she knew. They were a paid commission, and not a very well-paid one, as she bitterly complained to anyone who would listen. Her mentality was bound to be like most freelance creatives; work is work, not to be turned down. She borrowed from her previous work, and from others, to complete the so-called Minor Arcana (pip cards) and certainly, as that would happen for 'very little cash' why not? Reinventing the wheel does not come cheaply, after all. Ronald Decker and Michael Dummett wrote:

> She evidently received from Waite or from the publisher, Rider & Co, a flat sum in recompense for the work she did in 1909 ... If she had insisted upon royalties, this would surely have eased, and perhaps dispelled altogether, the financial difficulties from which she increasingly suffered: for the pack was, and has continued to be a triumphant success. Not only was it the first complete commercially available cartomantic Tarot pack to be produced in Britain, and the first independent of the Etteila (first tarot designed for occult purposes) tradition to be produced anywhere, but, in the face of all the competition put up against it over the years, it has remained the most popular.[4]

Pamela was naïve in not pursuing royalties, or was perhaps cash-strapped enough to prefer the quick fix of a one-off payment, especially as she was used to people evading or delaying paying for her work, or maybe she offered 'mates' rates', but how popular was the deck in her own lifetime? Well, not very, so would it have made her rich? Doubtful. Decker and Dummett continue:

> Waite ... went so far as ... saying that the Tarot de Marseille was no longer extant, but had been 'superseded in all respects' by the pack designed by Miss

> Smith at his instructions. Many of the later occultist packs have borrowed from Pamela Colman Smith's design; it could almost be said to have established a standard pattern for occultist Tarot packs. But the designer never benefited from its success; conventional nomenclature was not even to attach her name to it.[5]

Of course, many people express concern that Pamela's name was omitted. Conventional nomenclature or not, the publisher and Waite certainly included their names, but not hers because she was a woman illustrator in what was a man's world. The tarot was not, in 1909, something the public was terribly excited about. Pamela had no inkling her cards would enter more mainstream culture, maybe why she failed at the time to push for more pecuniary advantage from her work. In 1938, Waite still failed to give Pamela her full due when he wrote *Shadows of Life and Thought*, where he downgrades her from 'artist' to 'draughtswoman' (who needed proper guidance) but by this time, maybe she no longer cared.[6]

She had drifted towards the Golden Dawn, if Waite is right. Pamela worked prolifically but she also needed some fun, to enjoy life, to socialise, to feel a sense of purpose, to be a part of something. The people she knew at the Golden Dawn fulfilled some elements of this role. It was also new and exciting. She liked them. Waite wrote:

> Pamela Coleman Smith ... had drifted into the Golden Dawn and found its ceremonies—as transformed by myself—without pretending or indeed attempting to understand their sub-surface consequence. It seemed to some of us in the circle that there was a draughtswoman among us who, under proper guidance, could produce a tarot with an appeal to the world of art and a suggestion of significance behind the Symbols which would put on them another construction than had ever been dreamed by those who, through many generations, had produced and used them for mere divinatory purposes.[7]

Australian academic Helen Farley agrees the cards were just a job to Pamela, paid by Waite as: 'a flat fee, to bring his designs to fruition', though she too later explains the design of the Minor Arcana or pip cards was left to Pamela.[8] Interestingly, the *Rider Pictorial Key to the Tarot*, by Waite, which was first published in 1910, did not grow to a second edition until 1971, which is quite a timespan. It was then reprinted at regular intervals during the 1970s–80s, having regained popularity, becoming financially viable. Whose designs they truly are is the subject of intense debate, with many people today dismayed how Pamela seems to have been treated by history as Waite's pawn, who never received the accolades—nor indeed the money—she deserved when alive. This is not necessarily the case. As she aged, no one is known to have heard her complain about the rate for that job. She had doubtless moved on, while Waite continued to tell people about his input and control of the production.

When she illustrated the deck, it appears Pamela was well acquainted with the esotericists and intellectuals who were influential within the emerging occult revival, where people were searching for answers, which rationalism was not providing. Pamela had an eye for a trend. If mysticism might help her to sell her work, then she would use it. Mysticism gained popularity at a time of massive cultural shift, where there was comfort to be found in alternative knowledge. The Puritan Board Blog suggests, 'if you reject Christianity and God's straightforward creation, yet yearn for some kind of truth, you naturally will get sucked into the occult'.[9]

In Pamela's case, God readily reeled her back in. There are few other indications Pamela was particularly mystically-minded or psychic. Edy Craig, in her memoirs, noticed Pamela perceived the same spiritual presence in a haunted London house that everyone else did. So, she was sensitive and open to new ideas, but was she any more so than anyone else?

The structure of the Golden Dawn is based upon the Rosicrucians (Master Masons). The Neophyte is a probationary grade. Pamela did not progress very far in the First Order reaching Zelator. Regardless of whether she joined the Order from curiosity, recommendation, or even to tout for work (stranger things have happened), we begin to see her develop her love of ritual and ceremony shared by the Catholic Church, an institution she later wholeheartedly embraced. The Neophyte grade is rudimentary, largely based on astrological symbols (she mentioned astrology in correspondence with Bigelow Paine) but it is in the Zelator grade where she would first have encountered the tarot.

A 1959 book entitled *The Pictorial Key to the Tarot,* originally by Waite, with numerous illustrations originally by Pamela, contains an introduction by Gertrude Moakley.[10] She firmly believed the rectified tarot deck was developed collaboratively by Arthur Waite and Pamela (though the book again mentions Pamela was under instruction) but also how she was not first to illustrate the pip (minor cards) as the Sola Busca had done this before. She believed Pamela had visited the British Museum or the British Library to research the Sola Busca, upon which she heavily drew inspiration. Moakley, a New York librarian, rightly says the tarot work was almost a side issue for Pamela. The work was long and the pay was poor; Pamela never expected to become famous from this piece of work:

> This set of mystical tarot cards ... developed together, seemed at the time a mere trifle to both of them compared to their more ambitious projects. Yet their Tarot is one of the few published works by either of them that has remained almost continuously in print for nearly fifty years.[11]

She calls it something minor, a 'delightful avocation' or effectively a hobby or minor occupation. Moakley adds: 'When a brilliant man and woman like Waite and Pamela Smith work together, his masculinity and her femininity are sometimes flint and steel to produce new brilliance.'

A woman of her time, Moakley did not take Pamela too seriously, damning with faint praise. Mentioning Waite's and Pamela's links to the Golden Dawn, which Waite especially wholeheartedly embraced, Pamela is condescendingly described as an 'American girl who had grown up in Jamaica. There she had amused herself by trying to draw, and by collecting the Ashanti folk tales told by the Negroes of the island'. An article in *The Delineator*, 1912, adds to this sense of naïveté, stating that when she lived in Jamaica, she rode all over the island on her little pony (Jamaica is nearly 11,000 square miles so it is a curious observation) 'with a penny copy-book for the stories the negro mammies told her'. It all sounds a touch fanciful and of its time, but it is easy to see why people felt she may be partly of Jamaican extraction.

To Moakley, Pamela was just what Waite needed to help him express his thinking. Much as the feminist within dislikes the idea of Pamela, the woman, being secondary to Waite's ideas, there may well be something in it, if she was not too seriously interested in the Order or the tarot. To Waite, Pamela, with her 'clairvoyance', her imagination, and her artistic competence, was just the right person to produce, 'under his guidance', a tarot that would be at once a 'work of art and a gateway to truth'.

Boyd Parsons feels the images he instructed Pamela to create were to follow very closely the astrological significance of each suit.[12] Waite's primary focus was on the Major Arcana, allowing Pamela more freedom with the Minor Arcana. Many scholars believe Pamela should have much more credit for her input than she ever received, for she was a core contributor to the mysticism and popularity of the deck, especially the so-called pip cards.

The Golden Dawn influence should not be overestimated, however, for there were many elements at play in Pamela's life development. By the age of twenty-one, she was already well-known as a book illustrator and theatre designer, who W. B. Yeats, knowing her as Pixie, described as full of simplicity and naïveté. Remember, she was later exhibiting her art at Stieglitz's studio (a massive achievement) the very year she undertook the tarot deck commission, but her success was not all down to one fortunate incident. In one of her magazines, *The Green Sheaf*, around this time, Pamela also offered the services of herself as Gelukiezanger, a teller of West Indian folk tales, which she did to amuse friends but also as commissioned entertainment. She was madly busy. Joan Coldwell wrote of Yeats's description from *Where There is Nothing*:

> Last Monday evening Pamela Smith brought round a big sketch book full of designs for the play made by herself and Edith Craig. They were particularly

> pleased because they know Gordon Craig's little stage dodges and are using them rather to his annoyance ... I thought the design for the Monastery scene extremely impressive. The design for Act I was a little humdrum. To some extent that was my own fault, for that croquet lawn and garden path has been the opening of so many plays. Suddenly while I was looking at it, it occurred to me that it could all be made fantastic by there being a number of bushes shaped Dutch fashion into cocks and hens, ducks, peacocks etc. Pamela began sketching them at once.[13]

She was spontaneous, exuberant, proactive, yet also receptive in her work. She enjoyed the Golden Dawn, sharing common ground with Yeats, as she very much enjoyed the pageantry and ceremony without being overly-bothered by the deeper elements. As Waite had noted: 'the one thing she lacked was an interest in the meaning of it'.

Waite, however, saw Pamela was professionally and artistically competent as Yeats had seen; she was imaginative and, in his view, possibly clairvoyant, so she was the right person to produce the artwork for the cards. His guidance was undoubtedly not fully appreciated by Pamela, who was, he said, 'spoon-fed carefully' over the Priestess, the Fool, and the Hanged Man. The Fool is the only card without Pamela's initials, which may be an accident of printing or have some profound meaning. It is the subject of a great deal of debate on Tarot fora. In his preface, Waite wrote: 'They have been prepared under my supervision—in respect of the attributions and meanings—by a lady with high claims as an artist'.

He implies Pamela had little knowledge and understanding of the meanings of the tarot cards she painted, other than what she was told by Waite, but then that is his (male) viewpoint. To her, it was simply an illustration job.

As a jobbing illustrator receiving little recompense, what made Pamela look to the Sola Busca deck? The stunning cards from the Sola Busca deck were from the fifteenth century, engraved on copper, then hand-painted. Pamela's Three of Swords and Ten of Swords are good examples of the similarities between the two decks. Some see the Sola Busca as more artistic, the Waite-Smith as illustrative, which would suit Pamela's artwork. To an extent, the work Pamela did as an illustrator was responding to her client's requirements.

Waite's idea behind the Rider-Waite-Smith tarot was to make them more accessible, and to rectify the symbolism the Golden Dawn found problematic with the Tarot de Marseille, including some of the religious connotations.[14] Pamela, it is felt, would have known about this deck from the Hermetic Order but also from her stage design work. Today, on Amazon, a used set of these repro cards currently costs over £1,000 and a new set, well over £2,000. There is money to be made from tarot.

In modern life, there are many and varied tarot decks, some containing Christian references. The cards are used in many ways, not just for divination,

A fascinating original photograph of Pamela dressed as Gelukiezanger, courtesy of Darren Jones, from his second-hand copy of *The Russian Ballet*. The book was bequeathed by a lady called Claudia Ayton-Lee to a private reference library run by the Old Vic theatre in 1955.

Pamela with Ellen Terry and friends. In her early twenties, Pamela (bottom right) is dressed much more conventionally for her outing to Anne Hathaway's cottage in Stratford-upon-Avon, 1902, with Shakespearean actress Ellen Terry, and women thought to be Christabel Marshall and Lisa Jardine. (*Under licence from the Royal Shakespeare Company*)

Left: Inspired by Darren Jones's photo, Bude artist Lynne Holehouse created a large full-colour painting of Pamela as Gelukiezanger. Lynne's painting portrays her partly in shadow representing the different elements to her character. Never previously published, the image is used with permission of the artist.

Below: Pamela with Christopher St John, Edy Craig, and probably Tony Atwood. Smallhythe curator Susannah Mayor dates this photo of Pamela with Edy Craig and Chris Marshall as 1932. A bespectacled Pamela holds Sappho the cat. If 1932, this was during her time in Cornwall. (*Under licence from the National Trust at Smallhythe*)

Above: A beach holiday in Cornwall with friends, Chris and Edy, around 1932. The photograph was possibly taken by Jacko (actress Vera Holmes, stage name Jack, the chauffeur of the Pankhursts). Pamela is to the left in this image. (*Under licence from the National Trust at Smallhythe*)

Right: Edy Craig and Chris St John. Edy Craig was a friend of Pamela. They shared professional interests in theatre and costume and set design; both supported women's suffrage. Christabel Marshall was one of the two women who lived with Edy. (*The Women's Library Collection at LSE*)

Laurence and Clemence Housman. From 1910, this brother and sister duo founded the Suffrage Atelier with Alfred Pearse. The Atelier, which ceased in 1914 on the outbreak of war, was used by the WSPU (Women's Social and Political Union) for propaganda purposes. (*The Women's Library Collection at LSE*)

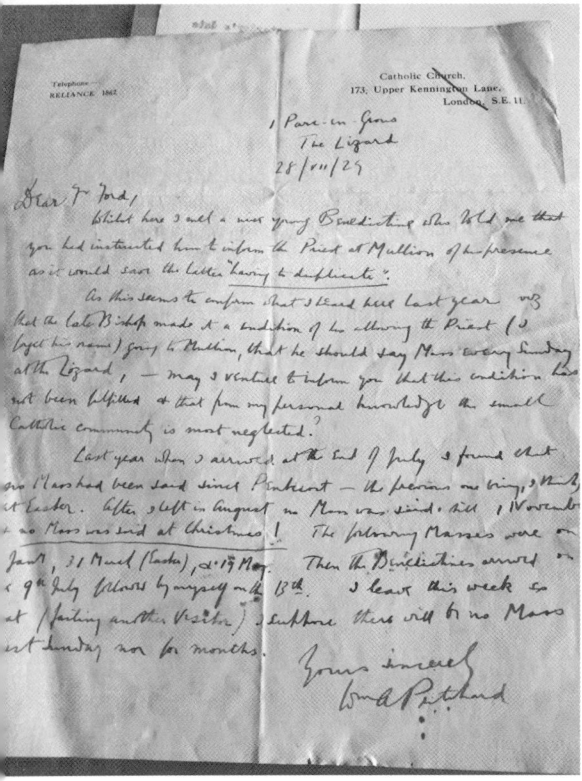

Telephone—
RELIANCE 1862

Catholic Church,
173, Upper Kennington Lane,
London, S.E. 11.

1 Parc-an-Gwns
The Lizard
28/vii/29

Dear Mr Ford,

Whilst here I met a nice young Benedictine who told me that you had instructed him to inform the Priest at Mullion of his presence as it would save the latter "having to duplicate".

As this seems to confirm what I heard here last year viz that the late Bishop made it a condition of his allowing the Priest (I forget his name) going to Mullion, that he should say Mass every Sunday at the Lizard, — may I venture to inform you that this condition has not been fulfilled & that from my personal knowledge the small Catholic community is most neglected?

Last year when I arrived at the end of July I found that no Mass had been said since Pentecost — the previous one being, I think, at Easter. After I left in August no Mass was said till 1 November & no Mass was said at Christmas! The following Masses were on Jan 1, 31 March (Easter), & 19 May. Then the Benedictines arrived on 9th July followed by myself on the 13th. I leave this week so at (failing another Visitor) I suppose there will be no Mass next Sunday nor for months.

Yours sincerely
[illegible]

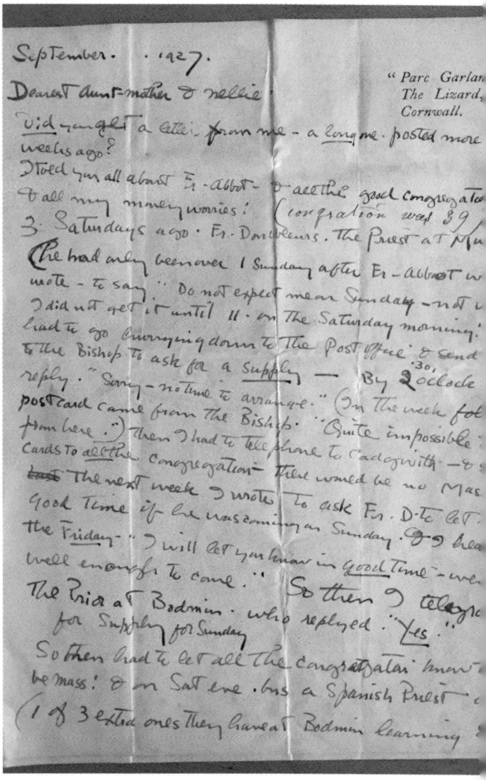

September. 1927.

"Parc Garlan
The Lizard,
Cornwall."

Dearest Aunt-mother & Nellie

Did you get a letter from me - a long one - posted more weeks ago?
I told you all about Fr. Abbot - & all the good Congregation & all my money worries! (congregation was 39) 3 Saturdays ago. Fr. Doubleuns. The Priest at Mu (he had only been over 1 Sunday after Fr. Abbot w wrote - to say "Do not expect me on Sunday - not I did not get it until 11. on the Saturday morning! had to go hurrying down to the Post Office & send to the Bishop to ask for a Supply — By 2 o'clock '30 reply. "Sorry - no time to arrange." (In the week fol postcard came from the Bishop. "Quite impossible from here.") Then I had to telephone to Cadgwith - & cards to all the Congregation - there would be no Mas The next week I wrote to ask Fr. D. to let Good Time if he was coming on Sunday. On the Friday - "I will let you know in Good Time - we well enough to come." So then I telegr The Priest at Bodmin. who replied "Yes." for Supply for Sunday. So then had to let all the congregation know be mass! & on Sat eve. bus a Spanish Priest (1 of 3 extra ones they have at Bodmin learning

Above left: A letter of complaint to the Bishop dated 28 July 1929 about the problems in securing priests to offer mass on The Lizard. By this time, the Catholic Church of St Michael the Archangel had opened in Mullion. (*Plymouth Diocesan Archives*)

Above right: Letter from Pamela to Ellen and Edy, 1927. A letter from Pamela to Edy Craig and a rather aged Ellen Terry written from Parc Garland, The Lizard, during her Catholic mission years, explaining in fine detail her many problems in obtaining priests for services. (*Plymouth Diocesan Archives*)

Right: Letter from Pamela to Ellen and Edy, page 2, 1927. Pamela (calling herself Corinne) is desperately trying to think of some way to salvage her very difficult financial situation and her mission in Cornwall. Her companion, Mrs Lake, appears to be ill, so is being cared for by Pamela. (*Plymouth Diocesan Archives*)

Below: Letter from Pamela. Pamela had a troubled relationship with the priest, Father Dobbeleers, finding him difficult. She expresses surprise at how little money she finds in the collection box and is considering selling her house to buy a little bungalow in Penzance. (*Plymouth Diocesan Archives*)

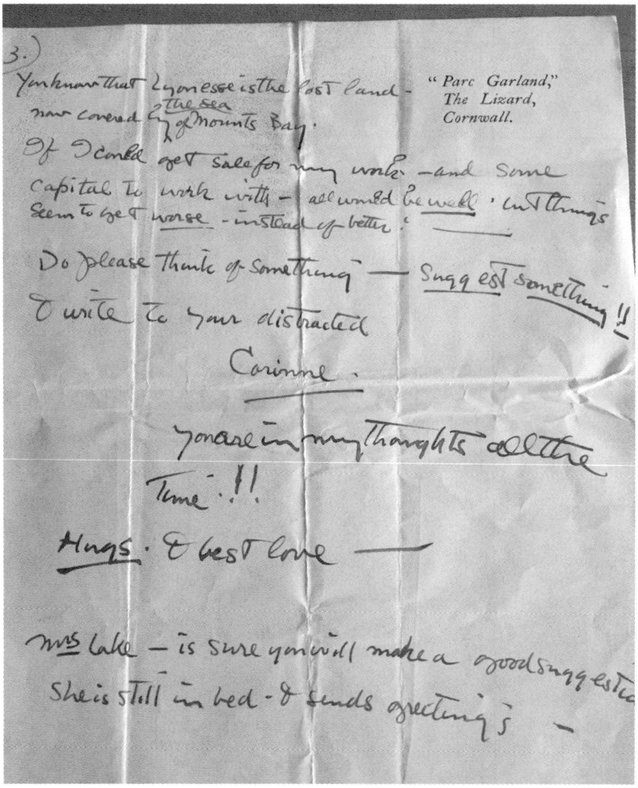

3.)

"Parc Garland,"
The Lizard,
Cornwall.

You know that Lyonesse is the lost land – now covered by the sea of Mounts Bay.

If I could get sale for my work – and some capital to work with – all would be well · but things seem to get worse – instead of better! ——

Do please think of something — Suggest something & write to your distracted !!

Corinne.

You are in my thoughts all the time!!

Hugs. & best love ——

Mrs Lake – is sure you will make a good suggestion

She is still in bed – & sends greetings –

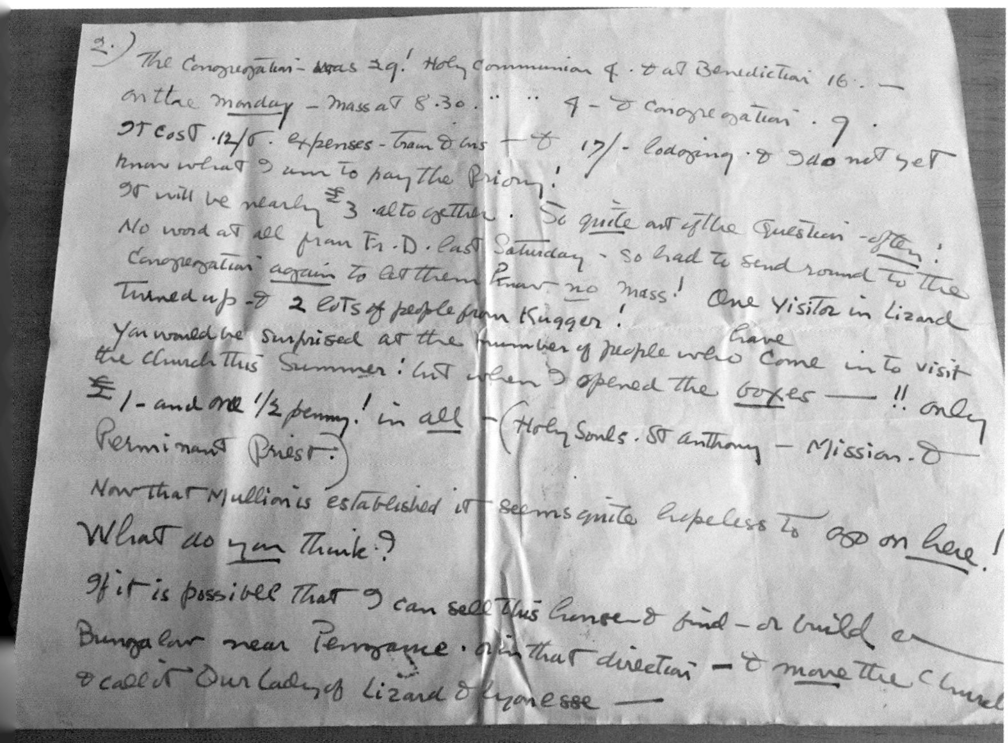

2.)

The Congregation – was 29! Holy Communion 4 · & at Benediction 16. —
On the Monday – Mass at 8.30. " " 4 – & Congregation · 9.
It cost · 12/6 · expenses – train & bus – & 17/- lodging · & I do not yet
know what I am to pay the Priory!
It will be nearly £3 · altogether. So quite out of the question – often!
No word at all from Fr. D. last Saturday – so had to send round to the
Congregation again to let them know no Mass! One Visitor in Lizard
Turned up – & 2 lots of people from Kugger!
You would be surprised at the number of people who have come into visit
the Church this Summer: but when I opened the boxes —— !! only
£1 – and one ½ penny! in all – (Holy Souls. St Anthony – Mission. &
Perminant Priest.)
Now that Mullion is established it seems quite hopeless to go on here!
What do you think?
If it is possible that I can sell this house & find – or build a
Bungalow near Penzance · or in that direction – & move the Church
& call it Our Lady of Lizard & Lyonesse ——

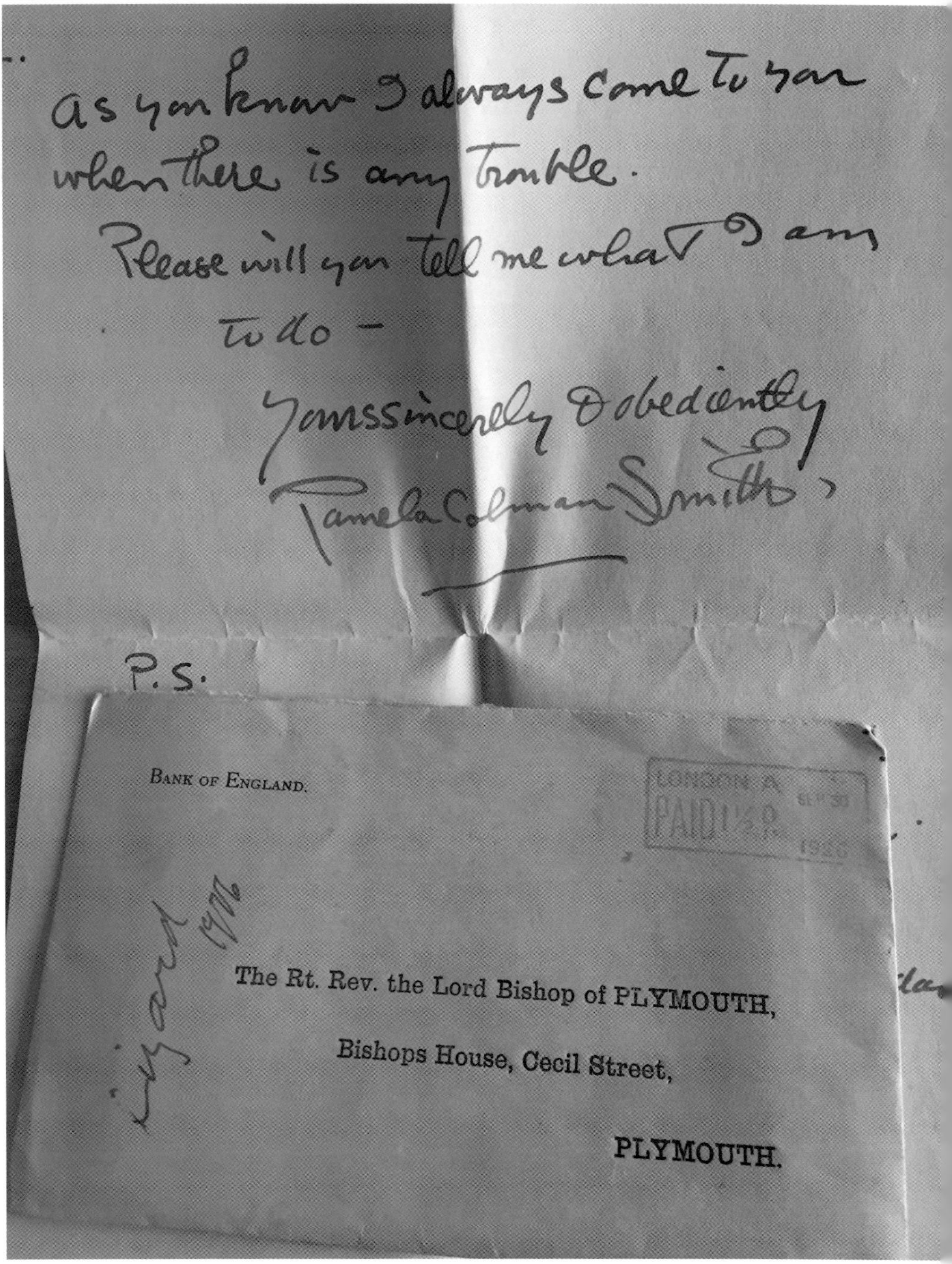

As you know I always come to you when there is any trouble.

Please will you tell me what I am to do –

Yours sincerely & obediently

Pamela Colman Smith

P.S.

BANK OF ENGLAND.

LONDON A
PAID 1½D
SEP 30
1926

The Rt. Rev. the Lord Bishop of PLYMOUTH,

Bishops House, Cecil Street,

PLYMOUTH.

Letter to the Bishop of Plymouth. Pamela here is asking the Bishop what to do at a time when he is beginning to find her very difficult. The situation is not what he had envisaged at all. He later deemed her 'neurotic'. (*Plymouth Diocesan Archives*)

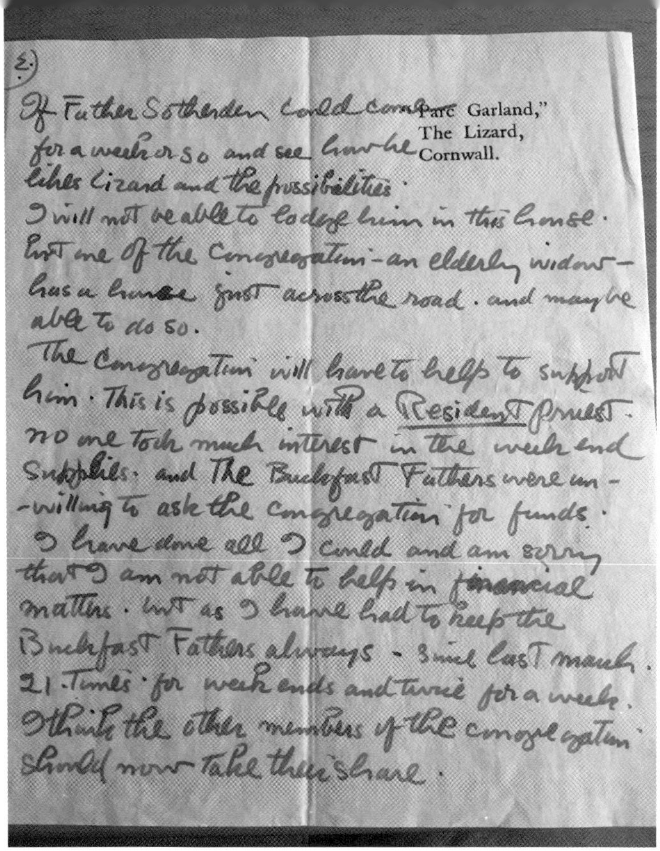

2.)

"Parc Garland,"
The Lizard,
Cornwall.

If Father Sotherden could come
for a week or so and see how he
likes Lizard and the possibilities.
I will not be able to lodge him in this house.
but one of the Congregation – an elderly widow –
has a house just across the road. and may be
able to do so.
The Congregation will have to help to support
him. This is possible with a Resident priest.
no one took much interest in the week end
supplies. and The Buckfast Fathers were un-
-willing to ask the congregation for funds.
I have done all I could and am sorry
that I am not able to help in financial
matters. but as I have had to keep the
Buckfast Fathers always – since last march.
21 times for week ends and twice for a week.
I think the other members of the congregation
should now take their share.

Begging letter. Pamela is beginning to feel the pinch of the cost of priests, complaining that she has an unfair share of the burden of the Buckfast Fathers, which should be shared out among the congregation. She makes the case for a resident priest. (*Plymouth Diocesan Archives*)

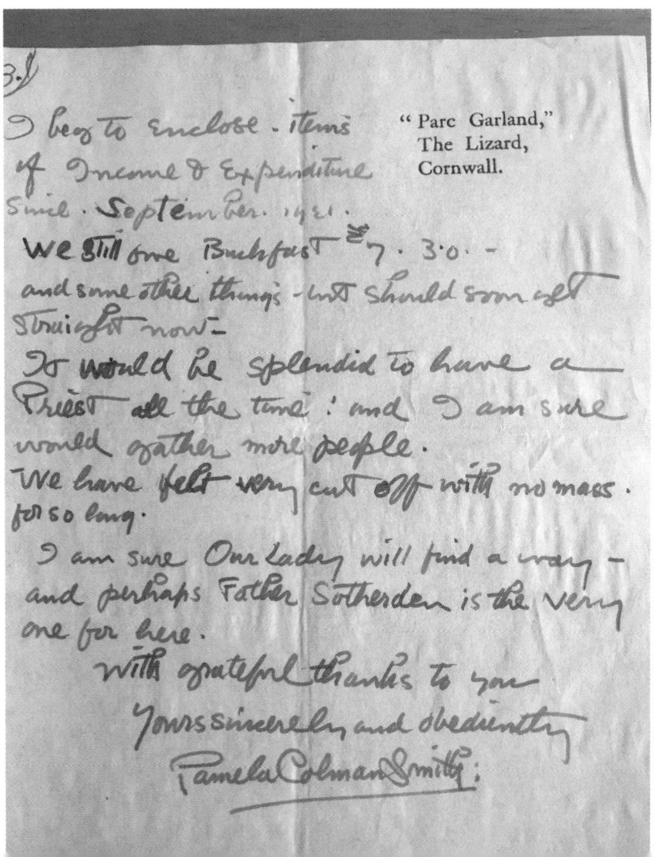

3.)

"Parc Garland,"
The Lizard,
Cornwall.

I beg to enclose. items
of Income & Expenditure
since. September. 1921.
We still owe Buckfast £7. 3. 0. –
and some other things – but should soon get
straight now –
It would be splendid to have a
Priest all the time! and I am sure
would gather more people.
We have felt very cut off with no mass.
for so long.
I am sure Our Lady will find a way –
and perhaps Father Sotherden is the very
one for here.
With grateful thanks to you
Yours sincerely and obediently
Pamela Colman Smith.

Income and expenditure letter. Once again, Pamela makes the case for a resident priest. The cost of a resident priest would be lower than peripatetic ones, and the congregation would increase. (*Plymouth Diocesan Archives*)

The Strand magazine feature, Tchaikovsky, 1812. In this picture of Napoleon's retreat from Moscow, Pamela is described as a 'clever' artist, her gift labelled as 'psychic'. She describes her 'music pictures' as thoughts loosened and set free by the spell of sound. (*The Strand*)

An image drawn to music by Schumann, 1812. It is a stark, solitary work containing bleak, desolate representations of humanity. Pamela is using and promoting her psychic, synaesthetic technique to sell her paintings. (*The Strand*)

An image of actress Ellen Terry, Pamela's 'surrogate mother', taken from *The Story of My Life*, original edition from 1908. The signed photograph is of the famous actress dressed as Beatrice in *Much Ado About Nothing*. The book is dedicated to Edy. Original book borrowed from Dorothy Walsh.

'Our Adventures' silhouette drawings, 1908. Taken from *The Story of My Life*, Pamela comically illustrates one of the last provincial tours of Henry Irving and Ellen Terry. Humorous comic-book style sketches in silhouette highlight a train journey from London where the engine breaks down. Original book borrowed from Dorothy Walsh.

Silhouette drawings, 1908. The second part of Pamela's comedic drawings in *The Story of My Life* as the journey recommences and all arrive worn out and exhausted. Pamela toured with the Lyceum Group, helping with stagecraft and 'bit' parts. Original book borrowed from Dorothy Walsh.

Above left: The Russian Ballet, 1913. Pamela illustrated Ellen Terry's book with black and white pen drawings, not popular with everyone for the ballet epitomised vibrancy and colour. (*Author's own copy*)

Above right: Le Carnaval. The Ballet Russes performed this ballet by Schumann, which captured Pamela's imagination. Set at a masked ball, the melancholy Pierrot unsuccessfully pursues Papillon. Pamela was accused of giving disproportionate space to *Les Sylphides*, *Le Carnaval*, and *Le Spectre de la Rose* in *The Russian Ballet*. (*Author's own copy*)

Below left: Le Carnaval—Pierrot and Papillon. The ballet premiered in 1910. Terry wrote that the comedy in *Le Carnaval* was of a very high order, more acting and pantomime than dance. (*Author's own copy*)

Below right: Schererazade, a ballet by Rimsky-Korsakov, portrays horror and violence. The emotions evoked are of sensuality and cruelty, in a dazzling tale from the Arabian Nights of a sultan and his wives. (*Author's own copy*)

THE SUFFRAGETTE
1d May 2 1913 1d
EDITED BY CHRISTABEL PANKHURST
RAIDED!
THE SUFFRAGETTE
1d May 2 1913 1d
EDITED BY CHRISTABEL PANKHURST
RAIDED!
THE SUFFRAGETTE
1d May 2 1913 1d
EDITED BY CHRISTABEL PANKHURST
RAIDED!
May. 1913

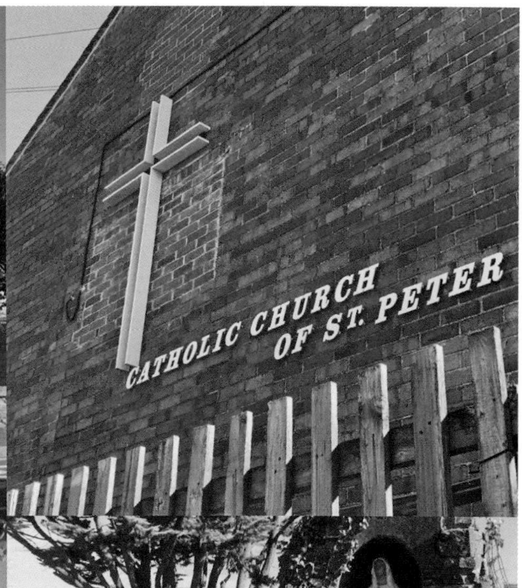
CATHOLIC CHURCH
OF ST. PETER

The Bencoolen Inn

Above: Father Dobbeleers. From Pamela's letters held at Plymouth Diocese, the Belgian priest Father Dobbeleers and Pamela clashed enormously over the provision of Mass at her chapel. His granite memorial stone with carved crucifix remains at St Michael and the Archangel Catholic Church, Mullion. (*Phil Hodges*)

Opposite above: A photo of a WSPU meeting from May 1913. Pamela was not known as an active suffragette, more a suffragist, but she voluntarily contributed to the political art of the Suffrage Atelier to aid the cause of WSPU. (*The Women's Library Collection at LSE*)

Opposite below: When Pamela and Nora Lake first moved to Bude, they lived in Gorseland, at Upton. Their clifftop residence offered stunning views but for two ill ladies, it was not ideal, so they moved to what is now the Bencoolen Inn, once a gentleman's residence, then converted to flats. (*Dawn Robinson*)

The small attic room at Parc Garland, Cross Common, The Lizard, is thought by the current owner to be where Pamela painted and conducted tarot readings. No evidence has yet borne out Pamela's continued interest in the tarot, which would have been incompatible with her Catholic faith. (*Phil Hodges*)

Parc Garland on The Lizard was Pamela's first (and last) real home for around twenty years, where she tried to continue the Catholic mission started by Victorine Roberts. An attractive residence, there is a stone pond and an orangery outside. (*Phil Hodges*)

An image from a postcard of Pamela's Catholic Church on The Lizard. Tiny but appropriately set out, Pamela went to great efforts to create her chapel. A sacristan, she ensured sacred items were properly cared for and displayed. (*Phil Hodges and Hayley White*)

Kynance Village. Close to Parc Garland is Kynance Cove, now owned by the National Trust. Now considered one of the most beautiful stretches of coastline in the south-west, this photograph is from 1920, around the time Pamela first moved to The Lizard. (*Ray Boyd*)

Pamela's chapel is sadly now derelict with permission to convert it to a dwelling. (*Phil Hodges*)

The kitchen of Parc Garland, 2018. In this room, Angie Hodges, of the Catholic History Society, said she felt the hairs rise on the back of her neck and felt close to tears, but it was not a scary feeling. (*Phil Hodges*)

but also for personal growth. The Tarot de Marseille deck contained some Christian references, such as *Le Jugement* (Judgement), *Le Pape* (the Pope/Hierophant) and *La Maison Dieu* (House of God/The Tower), with more controversial cards like *La Papess* (the female Pope), so it is easy to see why the Golden Dawn may have required a 'rectified' version without such religious icons. However, her study of the Sola Busca played a part in informing Pamela about Catholicism; *Le Pape*, for example, belongs within the social context of the Catholic Church as one might expect from a set of Italian cards.

An article by Cody Delistraty suggests a strong link between the tarot and Catholicism.[15] The article mentions Marie Anne Lenormand who ran away from her convent school, aged fourteen, in 1786. She set off, alone, to Paris, where she learned the art of cartomancy, working for forty years as a fortune-teller, advising Napoleon's wife, Josephine, plus Marat and Robespierre on their fates. When she met Frances, Lady Shelley, she read her fortune. Lady Shelley said:

> After about a quarter of an hour of this mummery, during which time she had arranged all the cards in order upon the table, she made an examination of my head. Suddenly she began, in a sort of measured prose, and with great rapidity and distinct articulation, to describe my character and past life, in which she was so accurate and so successful, even to minute particulars that I was spellbound at the manner in which she had discovered all she knew.[16]

When Marie Anne died at seventy-one, her devoutly Catholic nephew inherited her possessions and burned all her wicked fortune-telling paraphernalia but despite this, fortune-telling by tarot cards persisted. Where Pamela is concerned, the link with Catholicism is interesting. Most Catholics despised fortune-telling for it contradicted the idea of an all-knowing God, which suggests nothing is random, for all is ordained by God who keeps things in order. Fortune-telling provided an alternative to established religion so thus challenged its legitimacy.

Yet, the important part is the irony that the apparatus of fortune-telling and of Catholicism are similar. Tarot cards, suggests Delistraty, may be 'viewed as a bridge towards Catholicism. The patron saints and icons of Catholicism, each of whom has defining characteristics, occupations, and symbols, mirror the characters of the tarot'. The author suggests links, for example, between the Archangel Gabriel and the High Priestess. The article discusses chance; it is easy to see the draw of the icons and rituals of both to Pamela.

When Pamela joined the Golden Dawn, what kind of emotional/mental place was she in? Boyd Parsons explains that around 1900, Pamela's life was disorganised as half of her belongings were still in New York, making her restless, feeling unsettled.[17] It felt transient, as if living in borrowed space, not feeling quite at home and established. By 1901, she went to Sussex where she spent time with Edy Craig and Christopher St John, then on to Whitstable in Kent. In all, she spent some months there, maybe trying to build the friendships we all crave, which are built on a shared intensity of experience. She completed her book *Little Charles* but it was rejected by publishers on various grounds, all of which infuriated her. This, suggests Boyd Parsons, is where Pamela lost faith in commercial publishing and began to turn to more spiritual matters. She was therefore psychologically ripe for her introduction to the Hermetic Order of the Golden Dawn, which became part of her new social life.

Of course, we remember when Pamela first met Yeats, prior to joining the Golden Dawn, initially, she disliked him, finding him 'most stupid' and 'affected'. This was Pamela's view of his public persona and façade. He eventually won Pamela over with his shared interest in mysticism and folklore, but she utterly deplored the simpering women who pandered to his ego. By 1901, Pamela was working with his more introspective younger brother, Jack Yeats, on their *Broad Sheet* but also on more remunerative projects, such as bookplates and drawings which she hoped to exhibit.

Serendipitously, it was W. B. Yeats who introduced Pamela to the occult Hermetic Order where she met Waite. She was initiated in 1901 to the organisation whose motto was 'Whatever You Would Have Done to Thee'. The Order was founded by three Freemasons in February 1888. It had over 300 members, attracting many middle-class people, artists, thinkers, and scientists. Part of the backlash against materialism, answers to life's crucial questions, were sought from pagan traditions and ancient wisdom. Hierarchical in structure, the initiated learned basic occultism (such as astrology), tarot, and geomancy; they would then ideally pass from the outer order to the inner.

Not only did the Yeats family introduce Pamela to the Golden Dawn, but they might also have inadvertently sparked her interest in Catholicism. Joan Hardwick mentions how in 1903, Jack and his wife Cottie Yeats, along with Pamela, helped Lily Yeats with a big commission for her Dun Emer Guild by creating designs for banners depicting Irish saints for St Brendan's Catholic Cathedral in Loughrea.[18] Pamela often visited Lily and Lolly Yeats when in Ireland. Hardwick writes:

> The male saints designed by Jack Yeats have a strong peasant quality to them while the female saints designed by Lily Yeats and Pamela Coleman Smith are sweet rather than distantly pious. Pamela is known to have designed St Brigid which Lily then embroidered.[19]

Later in her book, Hardwick explains how Lily made some very derogatory remarks about Catholics due to serious disturbances taking place in Dublin in 1914. She also complained about a Catholic priest who had stayed with the Chestertons, and about Hilaire Belloc, a Catholic 'drunkard', which Lily seemed to see as inevitably twinned characteristics. Lily had regularly enjoyed Pamela's 'pleasant hospitality in her brightly decorated flat near Victoria' but as Pamela became a Catholic convert she was declared dull and boring, so strong were Lily's prejudices. She may not have been alone. At the end of the nineteenth century, there was significant anti-Catholic feeling in England, Catholicism commonly perceived as idolatry; a move from London and such harsh sentiment may have been welcome to Pamela. Her friends and colleagues found her far more exciting when she was a part of the Order.

It was 1901 when Pamela moved into her own flat, where she held her weekly 'at homes' inviting creatives such as writers, actors and artists, with friends and professional colleagues to her salons. Regulars included W. B. Yeats, John Masefield, Arthur Ransome, and Alphaeus Cole. So, what happened at these evenings? Well, there was an exchange of folk tales, and they discussed and criticised each other's art. They also drank 'Opal Hush', a combination of claret and lemonade. They grew slightly merry but also had fun, enjoying good conversation. An enchanting way to spend an evening, especially if Pamela was paid for the reciting she so adored, at such times very much her mother's daughter.

After Pamela joined the Golden Dawn, labelled 'a society of would-be magicians' by Gilbert, Waite's biographer, she stayed there for some years.[20] The organisation influenced people from Yeats and Waite to Allan Bennett, the latter previously a Catholic. It is an order open to all religious persuasions, the idea being to help individuals to know themselves through ceremonial magic.

Whether Pamela was more interested in the Celtic Revival than the Hermetic Order is debatable, but she did draw items from Irish folklore, and her correspondence made mention of creatures from folk lore, such as fairies, mermaids, the Sidhe, and other items of mythology. Her interests were reinforced by visits to the Yeats family. Meanwhile, she continued apace, selling prints and drawings through the Macbeth Gallery in New York, as well as designing scenery. She truly was multi-talented and readily intrigued. Yeats was pleased with her work, which probably benefited from an understanding of his religious philosophy. He was a keen member of the Golden Dawn, his involvement spanning thirty-three years, only leaving in 1923, says Rebecca Beattie.[21]

In 1903, the Order split. Yeats joined the Stella Matutina group while Pamela followed Waite. However, despite the occult schism, she appeared to remain friends with Yeats, seeming to rub along well with men who were members of the literati. Somehow, she tended to rub some women up the wrong way, such as theatre pioneer, founder of the British repertory movement and another 'arty celebrity' member of the Golden Dawn, Annie Horniman (of the tea family). Annie, English theatre manager and creator of the first repertory theatre, consulted the tarot daily to help her with decision-making. A hugely independent and adventurous woman, Annie never married, wore trousers, smoked Turkish cigarettes, and cycled lone across the Alps. She also knew the actress, Florence Farr. Not only was Farr clever, but she also wanted to break through Victorian ideas of femininity, becoming an actress in the attempt to support women's suffrage, equal education and divorce reform—in short, the feminism of the day. Leader of the Golden Dawn, she was also the mistress of George Bernard Shaw. She would have inspired Pamela in many ways. Farr, however, sadly died from breast cancer in 1917 after moving to Ceylon. She was 56.

Pamela, to her credit, stuck with the Golden Dawn for some years, as it was not until 1909 when Waite commissioned her to design the Tarot deck, so we assume she gained something from her association with the Order. Given Waite wanted to create a 'rectified tarot' therein lies a contradiction. If the tarot contains higher esoteric knowledge, then a popular version for everyone is the antithesis of this. How Pamela 'drifted' into the Golden Dawn and 'loved its ceremonies' without pretending to understand them fits rather nicely with her interest in Catholic ritual but low level of intellectual engagement with esotericism. Pamela was a competent artist, but other than the Sola Busca, from where did she find her inspiration? There are suggestions that some of the illustrations on the cards were portraits of her friends, making Ellen Terry the Queen of Wands and adding Florence Farr in The World. She was obviously inspired by many areas of her life.

While Pamela has an immense reputation among tarot readers everywhere, her own interest seemed largely professional. As any freelance artist or writer knows, commissioned works are done to order and completed because one has the skill rather than the desire; they are the stuff of income, not dreams. Pamela was the artistic version of a copywriter. She was busily engaged on other projects, not just the tarot deck, that year. Her limited understanding of the tarot is reinforced by Waite, if we believe his interpretation.

It was the tarot deck that sealed Pamela as an artist, though not in her lifetime. Was Pamela otherwise a great artist? That is open to debate. Her pictures have a basic, comic-book illustrative quality to them; there are also more ornate tarot decks available. However, it seems her approach laid the way open for tarot readers to very much interpret the cards as they wish. An intuitive reading of the cards mainly requires we look very closely at the symbolism, from which enormous amounts of meaning may be gleaned. Pamela's artwork, at first sight, looks simplistic but its use has been surprisingly widespread in modern culture. It was used in the James Bond film, *Live and Let Die*; as a backdrop in Madonna's Re-Invention World Tour; by Led Zeppelin guitarist, Jimmy Page; and more recently in the music video of 'Riptide' by Vance Joy. The deck has thus had staying power in the creative world and popular culture, triggering the intuition.

Her comment in 1909, in her now-famous letter to Alfred Stieglitz, her New York art agent about a big job for very little cash was about this job. Without the tarot deck, it is likely Pamela Colman Smith would have fallen into almost total obscurity, though Pamela was briefly in Stieglitz's circle. Fortunately for her, Stieglitz championed certain types of women, as Pyne explains:

> He selected those whose art he thought revealed the essential woman within, folded them (or tried to) according to his own evolving vision of the woman modernist, and promoted each until he found someone whose 'unconsciousness' fulfilled his needs even better.[22]

Stieglitz was capricious in his preferences, but his role was to uncover new talent, to exhibit promote and sell art.[23] He chose Pamela over the work of Rodin in 1907. His view on art expressed in 1922 tells us why:

> Photography is not art. Neither is painting, sculpture, literature or music. They are only different media for the individual to express his aesthetic feelings ... You do not have to be a painter or sculptor to be an artist. You may be a shoemaker. You may be creative as such. And, if so, you are a greater artist than most of the painters whose work is shown in the art galleries of today.[24]

It is odd that Pamela wrote so little about her time in the Golden Dawn, and of the tarot though she did indicate how people might learn to intuitively read the cards. This is very much how Pamela worked in the theatre, how she created images of people and considered stage design—nothing terribly mystical there.

> Note the dress, the type of face; see if you can trace the character in the face; note the pose ... First watch the simple forms of joy, of fear, of sorrow; look at the position taken by the whole body ... After you have found how to tell a simple story, put in more details ... Learn from everything, see everything, and above all feel everything! Find eyes within, look for the door into the unknown country.[25]

Pamela's later turn to Catholicism is curious as divination is largely at odds with Christianity (and especially Catholicism) as it is perceived as superstition that detracts from the worship of God. It is difficult to reconcile how divination (seeking knowledge of the future using supernatural, non-biblical means) fits with Christianity, implying Pamela was less of a believer in divination than most people suggest, either that or she had a massive major change of heart prior to her conversion in 1911.

15

Pamela the Outsider

We know Pamela mixed in exalted circles as a very popular entertainer and storyteller, but we hear very little about her close friendships. This may be because most of the information available about her life relates to her work. Pamela wrote informative letters about her work, travels, and activities, but few about her true feelings (compared to say, Ellen Terry) nor did she (to our knowledge) keep a diary, so we must piece together her personality from what we know of her work and her movements. She was involved with many people and key movements, yet often seemed to exist on the fringes.

Pamela's artwork falls into two main categories. Pre-1900, she was very much an illustrator. From 1900–1912, she was more involved in her so-called 'visionary' work, via her 'musical paintings', and it is here where she achieved some success in New York. In 1912, Pamela had enjoyed another successful show in New York, sponsored by the Berlin Photographic Company. Yet she somehow still failed to feel at home in America, returning to England shortly after. She spent a little time at Smallhythe, where she enjoyed the tranquility, entertaining children and adults with her *Annancy Stories* and games. By now, her studio was near Westminster Cathedral in London, which is still used today for the Rite of Christian Initiation of Adults' Rite of Election, all part of the process of becoming a Catholic.

As war broke out, and money presumably became even tighter, she began to devote herself to more charitable concerns, likely influenced by her religion, holding bazaars and donating money to the Red Cross and other organisations. She made intricate toys, such as mermaids. These were detailed, with silver scales, holding real combs and mirrors in their hands. In 1914, she also designed posters concerning the plight of war victims. This involvement fits nicely with what Tony Edwards later said about her disapproval of him joining the army.

She was keen to illustrate the written work of others, especially women. Feminist interpretations of *The Green Sheaf* suggest Pamela poked a fair bit of fun at patriarchy and men in general.[1] This was an aspect to her character most men then would not like or find attractive. The content was broad and loose, which also created its own problems. At whom was it directed? Who was the target audience?

It is this that some people think gives us a clue about her feelings at the time, that she lacked clarity about the way her life should go. After all, she had tried many enterprises, never finding one that sustained either her interest or her finances.

The fourth issue of *The Green Sheaf* contains her stark illustration of a woman walking by herself in a field barren except for two leafless trees standing watch. It is complemented by the poem 'Alone', in which the speaker laments that she feels alienated regardless of the setting: 'In cities large—in country lane,/Around the world—tis all the same;/Across the sea from shore to shore,/Alone—alone, for evermore'. The full poem is discussed later.

Was this Pamela's own isolation or merely writing in the tradition of the day? To be honest, it is not great literature, either way.

O deary me
how idle is / is great and weary
town. / For people talk and never
do / As they go up and down.[2]

Her poem about city life (above) gives some indication that her life is empty of anything meaningful. It describes a mild anomie. It may simply be Pamela was not a great poet, and was making the words rhyme, which is highly likely. It was not until some years later, in 1914, the year of the outbreak of war, that Pamela announced she did not care for people any more, when she may have felt the loneliness of having no close friends or family nearby or it may have been a wider comment on the state of a world careering towards a terrible war. She had lost many of her high-profile friends when she converted to Catholicism, mixing with what Lily Yeats believed to be dull, ordinary, and not terribly bright people whose only common ground was religious belief. Yes, of course, she felt she did not quite belong.

If Pamela was searching for meaning, had tried mysticism and not found her answers, this may be where religion filled a gap. Regarding her magazine, Pamela was considered strange and fanciful; she was vilified, once again not taken seriously. She obviously failed to fit the conventions of the day and had ruffled a few feathers. Pamela probably realised she would never be allowed to achieve her creative aims—perhaps she was no longer even able to—thus, she gave up on the whole idea, seeking solace in religion. An experimental writer and artist, Pamela sadly never had the resources to do exactly as she pleased; perhaps, she deluded herself that some of her skills were greater than they were. Fashions also changed.

Earlier, in 1908, she had written her famous phrase to Stieglitz about her disappointment with the publishing world:

> The publishers are as dull here as elsewhere! Except for the usual harmless dull insipid stuff by feeble females! I know plenty of 'em who are living well by the inanities! We disgruntled devils don't please anybody![3]

Humour, anger, and resignation? Were publishers, and women writers, truly dull or was it the 'playing safe' inane drivel produced that she felt was dull? Either way, Pamela seems at no time to have been driven towards producing the same herself. In her essay, Elizabeth Foley O'Connor suggests, like Virginia Woolf's heroine, Judith Shakespeare (imaginary sister of the famous playwright), Pamela had few of the advantages trailblazing men had.[4] It is the failure after her moderate success that O'Connor, like others, attributes to her retreat from public life and descent into almost three decades of anonymity and poverty. There may be something in this, but where is our certainty, and how does this ally with her adopted and beloved Catholicism? On the one hand, O'Connor suggests Pamela's letters demonstrate an irrepressible spirit, but on the other, we are told her spirit was very much repressed, so much she totally changed her lifestyle. The impact of rejection, of being an outlier of modernism, may have taken their toll. The evidence is far from convincing but all seem to agree that she lived on the margins, failing to feel a sense of belonging, constantly searching, and failing to find what she sought until she found God.

O'Connor suggests Pamela's artistic integrity and refusal to conform led her to retreat from public life. In her earlier years, she was prolific, multi-talented, and multi-faceted, which should have been positive but which diluted her reputation. She exhibited in the US and Europe, while her Green Sheaf Press focused on women writers. O'Connor writes:

> Her venture into publishing appears to have emerged as both a calculated business move and a reaction to the frustration she encountered when dealing with the publishing establishment, which at the time was overwhelmingly dominated by men. She … vents her frustrations over not receiving royalties to which she considered herself entitled.
>
> … Colman Smith's letters to friends, patrons, publishers, and gallery owners reveal an irrepressible spirit committed to rooting out all types of hypocrisy and prejudice, including classism, sexism, and racism—she was of mixed race, and her letters often recount the inability people had in 'placing' her.[5]

Cariann Colman, distantly related to Pamela on her mother's side, believes that Pamela was not mixed-race, for she knows of no racial mix in her family of that time.[6] A feminist, Pamela had some impact on many groups, but always from the margins. The 'Pixie' identity is thought by some researchers to have been developed specifically as a strategic device to tackle and confront prejudices pertaining to her questioned ethnicity, sexuality, and appearance, yet Pamela merely suggested she was called it by Ellen Terry and it stuck.

O'Connor suggests the difficulty in placing or situating Pamela lies in this exoticising of her and contrastingly seeing her as naïve and simple. Despite her well-known relatives, Pamela was, as Kathleen Pyne notes 'a woman of mysterious origins, who to contemporaries seemed part Asian or part African or of some indeterminate "mixed blood"'.[7] Perceptions of her and who she was may well have been different.

Pamela wanted to tell some Jamaican folk tales but did not do so in *Green Sheaf*, as it is suggested she would wish to tell them in the local patois, which may be common now but was rarely a literary device then. Her *Annancy Stories*, published by R. H. Russell (New York, 1989) were said by Thomas Nelson Page to be 'the most original contribution to negro folklore literature since the day when "Uncle Remus" gave us his imperishable read of Brer Rabbit'.[8] It is uncertain whether Pamela wrote the stories herself or merely related them. Some of the tales are said to bear traces of Aesop, combined with Arabian Nights, and certainly some fairy tales. Mother Calbee, for example, reminds us of many a wicked stepmother and other step-sibling rivalries (Snow White, Cinderella, etc.). The illustrations are, of course, original.

Visiting her other work, Ellen Terry writes of Pamela's drawing of Schehererazade in *The Russian Ballet*:

> Miss Colman Smith's drawing gives a very vivid impression of the effect produced by the first appearance on the scene of the Lover and his companions. Here is a very good example of the amazing influence that colour and shape of mere garments can have on the imagination.[9]

She mentions elsewhere:

> Miss Pamela Colman Smith has given what some may think a disproportionate amount of space to her studies of '*Les Sylphides*', '*Le Carneval*' and '*Le Spectre de la Rose*'. I think she was, perhaps unconsciously, more strongly attracted by these three dance poems because of their greater wealth in the immaterial.[10]

While her sketches do sometimes seem a little naïve , they manage to create accurate impressions. In Rachlin's book, Pamela is mentioned as having a room in the haunted house in Smith Square mentioned earlier, previously used by a spiritualist.[11] A smell of stale incense was noted, believed to have been used by Catholics who used the room as a small chapel. Did this spark an idea in her head that later took root? Pamela was said to 'see and hear all kinds of things' as did anyone else who stayed there, so was she psychic or was the place simply haunted?

Refreshingly in *The New Yorker*, Bebergal indicates occultism may not help an artist's reputation:

> Secular readers may forgive an artist's Catholicism, say, because organized religion is serious and cultural, the writer and critic Jessa Crispin told me

recently—but the occult, she added, is just someone who spent too much time in their room alone and went to a weird place.[12]

Yet, writer and critic, Jessa Crispin says: 'Smith is an uncelebrated illustrator, who took the original tarot imagery and refined it into something that really does resonate'.[13] Great store is set by the poem, 'Alone', yet she seems to have written this many years before she departed for Cornwall. There is some suggestion that within *The Green Sheaf*, through poems and illustrations, Pamela presented how she felt about her contemporary world. A good deal of poetry does not necessarily reflect reality, yet women's poetry, in particular, is often viewed as an expression of the personal. Pamela's poem 'Alone' is often thought, therefore, to suggest she felt terribly isolated and lonely but it may simply have been a poem, or inspired by someone other than herself. Poetry does not always reflect the self, but may be an observation of others or of life. However, where gaps in understanding exist, it is human to try to fill them.

It seems from this poem, if it is autobiographical, Pamela experienced isolation and loneliness in whatever setting she found herself. Who can know the true motivations behind any poem? It was useful to 'vox pop' a few people for their interpretations. Some knew of Pamela, others did not, but all interpreted in a broadly similar fashion:

> She must have been very lonely. I wonder whether a part of her was afraid to love and lose ...
>
> I feel she's talking from the heart here of her love lost. It feels to me she's disconnected from the usual world around her, but like a rudderless ship or a homeless soul, she's left to wander, seeking and searching but feeling despair that never again will she find love. And that no one understands her loss and therefore the inner Pamela
>
> For me this speaks of the existential aloneness—Moustakas carried out a heuristic inquiry about 'loneliness' and I think this poem captures that sense of inner aloneness. The loneliness of being, of birth of living and of death - we seek out connection, we drink, we spend, we constantly do to separate ourselves from this aloneness and our inevitable existential angst that is so much a part of being human.
>
> It is a poem straight from her soul. She is despairing. My guess is she has lost her love.
>
> Initial thought in the poem is that she feels alone regardless ... almost like she feels she is a misfit.
>
> Sounds like alone means lonely and wherever she goes or whoever she's with, that feeling doesn't change. So she's travelling around, trying new things, constantly seeking something, but never finding it – and never really expecting to. In other words, she's feeling that no-one understands her (which they probably didn't).

> What a moving piece of poetry! Speaks to me of a kind of spiritual disconnect maybe stemming from the irrationality of depression. The brain recognises that the world isn't necessarily malfunctioning but that the writer is fundamentally unable to grasp it and pull herself into that world. She doesn't want to stand aloof or isolated from it but she is simply unable to find the doorway into a world she once participated in. Possibly written after the death of a life partner (or secret longstanding lover about whom she cannot speak) and will never recover from the loss of?[14]

All assumed it to be a personal cry from the heart. Pamela was full of ideas; she did not struggle with them. She thought of several book-length projects, such as her Shakespeare heroine book. While this sounds inspired, there were no takers to publish it, so she had similar problems in the writing world as the art world, which explained her attraction to self-publishing. She thus attempted to gain more control over the process. In the extracts from letters included in O'Connor's article, we see once again that Pamela was a blunt speaker, lacking social subtlety, again not making her universally popular.

O'Connor also suggests her departure merely foreshadows the 'bleak turn' of modernist poetry at that time, so Pamela was simply keeping up poetic fashion.[15] While we are kidding ourselves if we consider Pamela much of a poet, the content is interesting. In 'The Town', the focus is less on the sheer volume of people in urban settings but on the low levels of authenticity, the empty talk, and the failure of people to do what they say they will. This might also have been heartfelt or merely an observation, but within it, if we believe it to represent her innermost feelings, we begin to see a sense of disenchantment with society. It was also, however, a common theme of the time that cities lacked meaningful community and interpersonal relationships. In 1887, a sociologist called Ferdinand Tonnies had coined the phrases *Gemeinschaft* and *Gesellschaft* to describe rural communities compared to industrial society.[16] Communities were traditionally formed of real social ties, emotion, and obligation, with some form of moral code underpinning the interrelationships within. Society concerned more rational, indirect and impersonal interactions. It was a common cry accompanying the advent of industrialisation, that with the growth of urbanisation and cities, grew a decline in authenticity and real meaning. It was people fearful of this who clamoured for family, kinship, religion, and the rural idyll to provide true meaning.

The descriptor 'strange' indicates Pamela's underlying unconventionality and free spirit, which would ruffle (male) establishment feathers, for her free spirit was also a wandering one, where she tried venture after venture without much economic success. Her persistence was admirable, shifting from publishing and illustration, card production through to acting, storytelling, and back to fine art, even instruction in hand-colouring, but maybe her lack of focus dissipated her talents, and led to her being a 'jack of all trades', necessitated by financial considerations and the need to earn a living as a single woman. She seemed to strongly dislike traditional, conventional women, especially those who churned out 'harmless' material, so obviously felt artwork should be doing or saying something rather than be trivial; it should have purpose. It is odd then how some of her writing projects lacked exactly that quality.

When Pamela had written to Stieglitz and Bigelow Paine about publishers, she was having a rant. Pamela loved her exclamation marks, emphasising her sense of drama, but her letters could drive people close to literary meltdown. Her writing style was not great. It denotes impatience, excitement and excitability, perhaps even desperation, and a rushed, at times amateurish grasp of English. Indeed, her later letters are dashed off, spewed out, and strewn with spelling and grammatical errors. She wanted a life less ordinary, more idealistic and certainly meaningful, hence, her impatience with the mundane, for she seemed to lack patience with ordinary folk and even simple sentence structure. Why was she in such a hurry?

16

No Brooklyn Belle

In Brooklyn, when Pamela attended the Pratt Institute, she was considered something of a wild child by her father's side of the family, her education severely disrupted by travel. She was something of an 'outsider'. She was absolutely no Brooklyn belle but instead considered loud and raucous. Akela Reason advises how young ladies of Brooklyn were usually demure, often chaperoned by their mothers or a servant.[1] Chastity was a virtue, as presumably was marriageability. Pamela did not fit this demure conservative stereotype, for she had no pretty manners, though she appears to have been chaste.

She gelled with Arthur Wesley Dow, her tutor at Pratt, who encouraged Pamela in her work, especially her use of line and colour. It is here she realised she was a natural storyteller, cutting her teeth on her Jamaican tales. Some found Pamela intriguing, while others found her irritating, which happens to anyone who puts their head above the parapet. Ambitious, Pamela was to become hard-headed in the pursuit of work but she also quickly captured the creative imagination. Greatness did not impress her; indeed, she would poke fun and be a little irreverent in the face of it, as seen in her letters, one of which indicates her during one social situation, sniggering in her handkerchief like a schoolgirl. Was this juvenile humour or social ineptitude?

Enjoying a pun and wordplay, she had a fantastic memory for recital; she could focus and impression manage. Her life was lived front stage, yet she was considered eccentric. We can tell little of her level of true emotional engagement with others from her letters or her work. Certainly, she was perceptive and highly competent in her accurate observations of people. Caricature was one of her many skills but it is easy to see how she might have vexed those with influence, maybe taking her at times caustic observations a little too far or too strident for some.

She travelled often, both with the Lyceum during her earlier years, and to exhibit her artwork both in Britain and abroad. With the Yeats family, Pamela often visited Devon and Ireland. In her later years, however, it seems she rarely ventured outside her Bencoolen flat. Her world in Bude was extremely small and very close to her home—St Peter's Catholic Church towards Stratton, a few shops, and the Conservative Club (most recently Oceans Community Centre) on The Strand. She was not known to walk up the hill along Belle Vue, instead having her groceries delivered. Nor is there any great evidence she walked the short distance to the sea at Summerleaze beach. Her health was extremely poor by her late sixties, which may explain why she moved from clifftop Upton to the centre of town, less of a challenge to someone with the heart condition that ultimately killed her. She certainly wanted to attend church. She had downsized dramatically as her flat at The Bencoolen was small, implying limited resources, but she retained her crucifixes. Her Bude life appeared extremely sedate compared to her earlier life, but her time on The Lizard would have prepared her well for such obscurity, and she appeared to remain cheerful. However, it was a far cry from the social whirl of her early adult years.

Earlier in life, Pamela was very proactive and persistent about finding work, not readily deterred. She contacted W. B. Yeats about a possible book on Gaelic mythology and Bram Stoker about staging performances of her miniature theatre. Stoker, a mathematician, was relatively unimpressed with the commercial viability of her miniature stage (which at this point was still in New York), but Henry Irving was keen so they talked about a permanent job for her as a costume designer, though this never came to fruition. She visited Ireland with her father, meeting, among others, the Reverend Sabine Baring-Gould, who was linked with Bude through his celebrated but controversial biography of the Vicar of Morwenstow, Reverend Stephen Hawker (who, curiously for a Church of England vicar, converted to Catholicism on his deathbed). She managed to regularly collaborate with Edy Craig, pushing herself forward unashamedly for whatever work was available. Her art was her currency rather than an ideal. She was only as good as the next sale. Thus, she largely painted to order, or with a view to selling rather than painting for posterity.

In 1907, Pamela met Florence Farr (of the Hermetic Order of the Golden Dawn) at the Martha Washington Hotel in New York, says Mary Greer.[2] She was twenty-nine, working as an artist and theatrical designer. Greer wonders who helped Pamela create the tarot, implying it cannot have been entirely her own idea. We know Waite felt he guided her, certainly relating to the Major Arcana cards. Some felt W. B. Yeats or his close friend, Florence (who claimed Romany descent), worked with her, too. One thing is certain—most people do not work for nothing and she would not have wanted to share her meagre earnings for the job.

Not many years later, Pamela's professional collaboration with the Yeats family was over, though they remained friendly for a time. In 1913, Lily Yeats, with and for whom she had previously completed illustrations, stayed over with her in London when attending a craft sale at Londonderry House. Lily by now remarked Pamela was an 'ardent and pious' Roman Catholic, noting it made her less interesting as a friend but (importantly) added to Pamela's own happiness. She wrote, rather unpleasantly, as a friend who feels abandoned, might:

> She now has the dullest of friends, selected entirely because they are R.C., converts most of them, half-educated people, who want to see both eyes in a profile drawing. She goes to confession every Saturday—except the week I was there—she couldn't think of any sins, so my influence must have been very holy.[3]

Coldwell notes one 'so eccentric and unpredictable became conventionally staid and pious', or of little interest to anyone once she grew zealous. Sadly, it seems Pamela was only of interest if she was giving out, offering service, providing something. Once this stopped, interest in her dwindled to nothing, her early friends distant both geographically and emotionally.

17

The Woman Question

Boisseau's PhD thesis focuses on the women of the Abbey Theatre, Dublin, part of the Irish Cultural Renaissance to produce indigenous Irish drama using Irish actors, with which Pamela was involved through the Yeats family.[1] The thesis explains how historians focused much more on the men involved in the venture than the women. This is, of course, nothing new. There were tensions between the politically minded and the artists, but also the men and the 'women did not flourish at the abbey because their roles in the theatre were consistently diminished as the theatre itself became a more commercial enterprise'. It seems while Pamela designed sets for early plays, for example, no mention of any female contributions occurred before 1924, long after she had moved to Cornwall. Irish politics were, of course, inextricably linked to religion. However, women did play a vital part:

> Pamela Colman Smith, 'Pixie' to her friends, was asked by Yeats to design the set for the first production of J. M. Synge's *The Well of the Saints* in February 1905. She readily complied, with the assistance of her friend, Edith Craig.[2]

Not only was she artistically talented yet versatile, Pamela possessed a keen sense of humour, along with an understandable enthusiasm for politics and women's suffrage. Understandable, for it is easy to imagine how this young woman living during a time of social and political upheaval felt passionately about votes for women, equal rights, and certainly as her friend, Edy Craig, was actively involved in the movement. Edy was described as a mover and shaker, someone who liked to stir things up without necessarily wanting ownership. Not precious in that sense, Edy was an activist who inspired or provoked change, yet did not seek the limelight. She grew interested in women's suffrage as a child after meeting Elizabeth Malleson. Maturing, she organised suffrage petitions and addressed envelopes, but later sold the magazine, *Votes for Women*, though she was forever being moved on. She was also critical of the non-consultative methods of the Pankhursts, viewing the vote as social justice, but not necessarily transformational. She did not anticipate revolution but Pamela was known to have been arrested for her suffrage protests.

Winning the vote was a major democratic issue for women. Pamela had surely already accepted she could rely on no man to provide for her, and why should she? She needed (and wanted) to be self-sufficient. It was essential for her to work and be taken seriously, at a time when women, especially married ones, were largely considered irrelevant. She not only supported women's suffrage ideologically, but practically, as Pamela was kinaesthetically minded in some ways. Abstract theorising was not her *métier*; she wanted to have a hands-on impact. She was thus a political activist in her own preferred way, using her drawing talent, providing humorous cartoon artwork for the movement as part of the Suffrage Atelier. This was a publication collective formed on 21 June 1909, founded by Laurence and Clemence Housman with Alfred Pearse. Clemence was a respected member of the WSPU (Women's Social and Political Union). It was an ideal outlet for Pamela as it needed illustrators who could work quickly and whose work could be readily disseminated. Her style and way of working neatly fitted the bill.

Tara Morton explains that the Atelier was a group of artists producing propaganda (artwork and plays) for the suffrage movement from 1909–1914; it ceased work on the outbreak of the First World War.[3] Their work was conducted in the domestic, private sphere of people's houses, so it had a cosily sociable feel to it, a sense of community, of belonging, despite wider societal outcomes. There was a strong feeling throughout her life that while Pamela was self-sufficient, she enjoyed being part of a community, whether among the creatives at Smallhythe or the politicos at the Atelier, which was an arts and crafts society working for the women's franchise. Work for publication was offered first to the Atelier, the sale of which would afford a percentage of the profits to the artist. Its focus was posters, cartoons, and postcards.

The Atelier was associated with militant suffrage societies but worked mainly with the Women's Freedom League. It also had a training function to train artists and craftspeople in the skills and techniques of production, so they would produce items but also learn from others within the group. It was one of those dynamic self-sufficient groups of (mainly) women who worked together to effect social change. Weekly meetings were held, the focus very much on 'turning out' material, at which Pamela was very talented.

Cockcroft and Croft suggest Pamela was a close friend of the Smallhythe household, borne out by other evidence.[4] This, along with her membership of the Golden Dawn with people like Florence Farr, meant she saw 'social and spiritual transformation as intrinsically linked'. She contributed to the hand-printed *An Anti-Suffrage Alphabet* compiled by Laurence Housman, which contained purple and green illustrations documenting female subordination and lampooning opponents of women's suffrage, such as the following:

W is for washing
Which women must do
Day in & day out
& on polling day too
If she wants a day off
You had better say bosh
And tell her such fanciful notions
Won't wash.

Whether she was more actively a suffragist is hard to say. A suffragette she was not. Suffragists, led by Millicent Fawcett, campaigned for the vote using peaceful means, while suffragettes, led by Emmeline Pankhurst, finding suffragism too slow or ineffective, advocated direct action, attracting greater working-class involvement. The impact of this early feminism was immense, as historical photos impart. Ellen Terry (1847–1928) was not only the most famous actress of her day, but she was also a founder member of the AFL (Actresses Franchise League). This gave kudos and weight to that organisation. In one fundraiser, she played actress Nance Oldfield. Yet, in Terry's own memoirs, she questions the suffrage issue seeming rather uncommitted. However, Cockcroft and Croft assert that Smallhythe became a safe house for radical suffragettes lying low from the police.

While Pamela contributed artwork, there is no evidence she was actively involved in any of the radical actions associated with the suffragette movement such as breaking windows or enduring hunger strikes; nor by vandalising artwork, as did the militants for the cause; suffragism was probably her limit. It is hard to imagine an artist like Pamela feeling sympathetic to militants like Anne Hunt, who attacked with a meat cleaver a painting of Thomas Carlyle by Sir John Everett Millais in 1914, or indeed the action of Mary Richardson in 1914, who in the National Gallery, slashed the *Rokeby Venus* by Diego Velázquez, again using a meat cleaver. Yet, she was linked to the suffragettes. Helen Farley suggests through her association with the Atelier, Pamela would almost certainly have known Sylvia Pankhurst, who attended The Royal College of Art at South Kensington, and perhaps met artist and psychic Austin Spare, a close friend of Sylvia's, creator of another tarot deck, though the two decks have little in common.[5] Art linked to tarot was linked to women's rights. The middle classes seemed incredibly interlinked whatever their cause.

The propaganda posters of the Suffrage Atelier were often in the form of cartoons. Cartoons are a bold, unconventional format, for they often caricature or challenge the *status quo*. This is their purpose and a method that Pamela used in her Lyceum drawings. The artwork was very stark and visual, often simple to convey a message, which of necessity invariably involved stereotypes. The aim was to reach a large audience by subverting anti-suffrage stereotypes. Pamela did not come across as intensely generally political; however, in later life, she gave her errand boy, Tony, the impression she was not keen on his aims to join the military, and he, a lifelong Liberal Democrat, classified her, with some disdain, as a Conservative. When checked, he was convinced by her Conservatism and anti-radicalism. However, by this time she was in her sixties, so her youthful idealism may well have run its course, and anyway, by then, women had the vote.

Cockin mentions the tensions that existed in the roles for women available at a time of war, for they were juggling feminist principles with 'war work', work which often reduced them back to 'helpers'.[6] This issue appears in Radclyffe Hall's 1928 novel *The Well of Loneliness*, where women ambulance drivers struggled with the expectations of their gender. In her book, Cockin says Pamela beautifully illustrated the tensions of juggling these roles for women in her design for a play programme cover, using a visual metaphor of women carrying unfeasibly high piles of plates.

The period between 1899 and 1907 was the age of the 'new woman', which challenged the *status quo*. Women were rejecting Victorian confines in all its guises, such as restrictive clothing, thereby unveiling the mysteries of femininity. Controlling their own sexuality was an important part of this movement, the breaking of boundaries at every level. This was a time when middle-class women were ridiculed for walking out alone in the street. It was a time of reviling. Stereotypically, the 'new woman' wore masculine dress, which both Edy Craig but especially Christopher St John and war artist Tony (Clare) Atwood (the third member of their so-called *ménage à trois* relationship) appeared to enjoy (though not always) but Pamela did not favour in photographs from the time. On the literary front, women often masqueraded as men to publish things. O'Connor mentions, for example, Christabel Marshall, a noted campaigner for women's suffrage as well as a playwright and novelist, contributed a range of fiction and translations on almost every issue under the pseudonym Christopher St John.

It was also increasingly common for unmarried middle-class women to leave their families and live apart, which was another bid for independence. Pamela, of course, did not have close living family, so she had to make her own way in life anyway, undoubtedly not easy. This was important, as living either alone or with other women was deemed to deny the importance of marriage, but in other ways denoted economic necessity. In one way, it was a marginal existence; in another, it was independent and alternative—non-conformist. Such unorthodox living arrangements often included vegetarianism and same-sex relationships, a breaking down of preconceived differences between genders. Cockin says Christopher St John's written representations of life with Edy Craig dispel any myths they were just good friends, although Clare (Tony) Atwood appeared to be on the fringe of the relationship, rather than central. The author also suggests Edy's dalliances with men were 'experimental', an aberration. For whatever reason, it seems Edy wanted to achieve a heterosexual love affair but was browbeaten by the suicide attempt of Chris St John and the overbearing response of her mother.

It seems, from Cockin's book, that not everyone in the family was overly-impressed by Edy's woman-centred existence, using descriptors such as 'aggressive' and 'troublemaker' as character traits. Her brother, Gordon Craig, for example, felt her unmarried status was due to a hatred of men (a criticism often directed at feminists) probably stemming from hatred of her father. Gordon Craig was himself controversial in many ways; some may say misogynistic. This was, of course, all part of the marginalisation of women at the time. By the 1890s, Cockin notes: 'antipathy towards spinster feminists and their push for social change created a climate in which love between women became the subject of condemnation'. Previously, passionate relationships between women appear to have been acceptable if not actively encouraged. Now, lesbians were perceived as 'mannish' because if sexuality was congenital, then a feminine lesbian was a non-starter; likewise, the effeminate male was stereotyped.

Edy had earlier (1898) fallen 'deeply and passionately in love' with married actor Sydney Valentine before living with St John and had a dalliance with composer Martin Shaw, leading to a marriage proposal in 1903. *Hungerheart* by Christopher St John, however, focused on 'unfulfilled' desire. Cockin writes 'the "hunger" driving the protagonist is fulfilled partly by her relationship with "Sally" (assumed to represent a thinly disguised Edy) and by her conversion to Catholicism.' There is a manuscript of Christopher St John's diary in the library at UCLA, USA, about her feelings for Edith Craig. Otherwise, there seem to be no documents which explicitly refer to any of their relationships. While heterosexuality places undue emphasis on sexual acts and practices, lesbianism focused more on a commitment to women and a political alternative to male supremacy. Sheila Jeffreys wrote: 'It is more than likely to include a sensual component, which may or may not take a genital form'.

There is no evidence that Pamela was lesbian, but she knew exactly what she was doing in constructing her own image and persona. In creating ambiguity, no one could quite pin her to a cause or belief system. O'Connor mentions a 'personal mythology' created by Pamela to encourage this ambiguity but also, taking it a step further, to root out hypocrisy, describing some of her work as having a 'feminist bent'. She adds as a reminder of Pamela's prolific output:

> While Colman Smith has seemingly vanished from our current understanding of modernism, she was far from invisible during the approximately thirty years that she was active (1896–1927). While this is not an exhaustive list, the communities Colman Smith was involved with include Arthur Wesley Dow and the American Arts and Crafts movement in *fin de siècle* New York; the

> Yeats family, as well as writers and artists associated with the Irish Literary Revival in Dublin and London; Arthur Edward Waite and the pre-World War I London occult community; the Trans-Atlantic little magazine and small press network; the post-Impressionist art world in London and New York; Alfred Steiglitz's circle in the 1910s and teens in New York; Ellen Terry, Henry Irving, and the Lyceum theatre scene as well as the more radical theatre groups associated with both Gordon and Edith Craig (who were Terry's children and Colman Smith's longtime friends); scarcely to mention the Women's Suffrage Atelier in London.[7]

That list makes impressive reading. Pamela achieved so much while intriguingly knowing that living on the margins encouraged ambiguity about her origins (including her age, as did her mother), adopting her androgynous Pixie persona to tackle and confront inherent prejudices. If this is the case, it makes Pamela obviously, if not overtly, political. Yet, we must remember that Pamela wanted work so would do whatever was needed to promote whatever persona people wanted at the time. She could be all things to all people. O'Connor also mentions that by the age of twenty-four Pamela had been on many long voyages, twenty-five, in fact, starting at three months of age. She lived in Jamaica on and off for seven of these years. There is little wonder she felt as if she existed on the periphery; she was a bird of passage.

18

Pamela's Love Life

Why did Pamela, who seemed to love children and was loved by them, never marry, so she could be a mother? There are many suggestions, mainly that she preferred women to men, but we only need to look at the social norms of her time to know that, while this may be the case, there were alternative scenarios. Maybe she was lesbian, but if so, there is very little hard evidence to suggest Ellen Terry's 'red-haired devil' was actively so. Indeed, her love life reads rather like a barren desert with no oasis. For someone who was very public and 'out there', Pamela's romantic life appears to have been a well-guarded secret, or there was nothing much to share. Not all women, then as now, wished to marry. Lucy Bland's book came recommended by Professor Katharine Cockin, an expert on the life of Pamela's friend and professedly 'adoptive mother', Ellen Terry.[1] Bland mentions an 1888 article in *The Telegraph* which revealed 'discontent and sometimes profound unhappiness' among women stuck within the institution of marriage. Feminists also criticised its many injustices, in terms of coverture (being under the 'protection' of the husband') property and infant custody rights; 'feminists felt that gains for married women were lagging somewhat behind those of her single sister'. They were right.

Pamela was a known feminist. Her Suffrage Atelier work was voluntary. Her views were not something she hid, so she mixed with many women in the movement, some more radical than others. She wholeheartedly felt the immense impact of their ideas, so it may simply be she chose not to be under the jurisdiction of a husband. Bear in mind Pamela had seen her mother following her father everywhere he went with his work, regardless of whether she truly wished to or not. It was expected. Meanwhile, Susan Yeats, the mother of her friends, was dreadfully unhappily married, resulting in debilitating depression, and Ellen Terry, who had given it a fair try, was no keen advocate, either. Few around her would have promoted it as a way forward for an independent and creative woman. The bohemians she entertained as 'Gypsy' also largely led unconventional love and sex lives, which may or may not have appealed; starving in a bohemian paradise was not for everyone.

For some, marriage equated to possession. The feminist Mona Caird portrayed marriage as akin to prostitution, a contractual arrangement, an idea since revived by Carol Pateman.[2] Marriage required reform, the debate continuing until the late 1890s, or Pamela's early adulthood, and onwards.

Pamela may have liked children of her own for she seemed to enjoy their company, finding it easy to enter their secret, magical, and imaginative world, but she was raised largely by servants as a youngster so surely had no illusions about motherhood. Children were more of an expectation for women than necessarily desired. If a woman married, she had little option other than to be a mother, presuming her body played ball on reproduction. Pamela often told children stories. There are pictures of her interacting with and enchanting children at Smallhythe, so marriage would have been an obvious opportunity to have some of her own. Marriage was primarily for this purpose, rather than to pursue emotional or sexual satisfaction. Attitudes to married women were highly questionable. The following well-known tale gives some idea of how women were regarded, indicating why some may have been thoroughly deterred from the institution.

Bland cites the case of Edmund and his wife, Emily Jackson. Edmund moved abroad then returned in 1888, but she refused to see him. He applied for restitution of his conjugal rights. By 1891, he and two accomplices grabbed Emily at church in Clitheroe, Lancashire, and locked her in. Her sisters applied for *habeas corpus*, and the Court of Appeal deemed her free to leave. She was booed on her return, and her sisters' houses were stoned, all for defying her husband. *The Times* wrote 'marriage in England was abolished'. This was hardly so, but it was hailed as a great victory by feminists that married women had at last gained a charter for personal liberty. Marital rape, however, remained an issue. None of this made marriage a particularly attractive option for anyone with viable alternatives and funding, and certainly for someone with limited sexual desire. It may be Pamela simply did not meet a man she wanted to marry; we have no evidence she ever fell in love, unlike Edy Craig.

Women did not always want to live alone, nor could many afford to long term, so alternatives to marriage were available. Free love (free unions) was a limited option or preference for most women, so the key alternative was predominantly spinsterhood. Some consciously opted for it, but for others, there was no choice. There was a surplus of women. By 1911, there were 1,068 women for every 1,000 men, and this had risen dramatically by 1918. While Pamela was too old to have been affected by the shortage of men due to the First World War, an Oxford University educational resource post mentions the loss of life, tragic in so many ways, severely impacting upon women in the 1920s.[3] By this time, Pamela was in her forties, although many women married later than we might think.

> The middle classes were especially affected with a higher proportion of officers killed than those in lower ranks. The 700,000 deaths resulted in a particularly large gap between the male and female populations of people aged 25 to 34 with 1,158,000 unmarried women and 919,000 unmarried men, according to the 1921 census.[4]

However, even prior to the First World War, women often remained unmarried, but if she had not met a husband before the war, it was even less likely to happen afterwards. Even before Pamela was born, close to a third of women were unmarried. One possibility is the option simply never arose.

> The 1851 census showed that 30 per cent of English women aged 20 to 40 were unmarried. By the late 19th century, around a third of British women between the ages of 25 to 35 were unmarried, and census records show that an imbalance of men and women continued in the Edwardian years.[5]

Additionally, there was a higher male death rate and emigration rate. For many, marriage simply was not possible, though the institution does not seem to be something Pamela mentioned having any expectation of, or desire or strong feelings for in her communications. Her considerable energies were directed elsewhere. She was always terribly busy with her own money-making schemes and her attempts to publish and sell, too focused on her own life to take on someone else's. For someone unconventional like Pamela, who had many professional irons in the fire, who was peripatetic, and who was unlikely to do any husband's beckoning, then it was seriously unlikely to be a success if it happened.

Single women like her, therefore, had to redefine themselves in roles where they could maintain their lives, while also enjoying what they had. Bland writes they did this by transforming the passive labels of purity and goodness into active spirituality and passionate social service. Indeed, a spinster who could stand alone and make her own way was respectable and respected. The associated chastity was viewed as a positive redirection of energy. Some women actively sought out and regretted not finding a husband, Lily and Lolly Yeats being rather odd cases in point, given their poor experiences of men within their own family, amply demonstrating that spinsterhood was not something most aspired to.

Another option, however, was 'romantic friendship'. For those who ideally wished to marry and avoid the potential loneliness of a spinster's life, long-lasting emotional ties with other women were often the answer, be they supportive sisters, cousins or non-related friends. Romantic friendship, even among married women, included declarations of love and sometimes physicality. Such romantic friendships sometimes also involved kissing, hugging, and even sharing a bed. This was perceived as a normal benign practice until the late nineteenth century. Clearly, there were also lesbians involved in erotic relationships with other women, though they did not tend to define themselves as such at the time. Sexuality was largely viewed as heterosexual; therefore, eroticism between women was perceived as something else altogether different. The big issue was less about sexuality and more focused on the breeding of children, for there was little perception women may actively enjoy sexual activity, even or especially with each other.

A huge problem for some women was the real impact on their independence if they married, of which many were only too aware. Marriage often rendered an independent career and personal freedom impossible, so no matter how attractive the man was, there was a price to pay for marriage; this also applied to bohemian women, much to their chagrin, who often thought they were marrying free thinkers, but found their men to be traditional on the 'woman question'. In the early twentieth century, the debate shifted a little, but the issues remained. There has been a modern tendency to assume any woman who did not marry and who socialised with other women (especially known lesbians) was herself Sapphic, but anyone who has completed any serious research on Pamela has found no evidence she was. Indeed, there is little indication of any kind of sexual relationship with anyone, only guesswork.

Among some of her modern followers, there is a firm insistence and agenda that Pamela preferred women. Not only is there no substantial evidence of this but Melinda Boyd Parsons tells of a letter from Lily Yeats to one of her cousins saying Pamela had fallen in love with a male doctor who ran a 'fat farm' in Cornwall, which is why (said Lily) Pamela moved to The Lizard.[6] Lily was ambivalent, at times spiteful, towards Pamela, despite earlier being good friends. Religion definitely caused a distance between them; a converted Catholic was not an ideal friend for an Irish Protestant. Lily thought all Catholics were alcoholics, and Pamela had 'unearned income'; she was also unmarried with no opportunities arising. So, Lily was a little bitter in her comments about Pamela, despite at times working closely together and enjoying her hospitality. The 'fat farm' suggestion is presumably unproven nastiness, possibly a comment about Pamela's weight, though the house Pamela bought on The Lizard was previously built by a doctor.

Pamela mainly received mentions in memoirs and biographies for professional, not personal, reasons. As Pamela was friends with Edy Craig, it is often assumed to have been a lovers' relationship. Ellen Terry expressed some jealousy about her daughter, Edy, spending time with the two other 'old trouts' in her life, as she called them, Chris and Tony. Pamela did not earn the nickname 'trout'. There is no indication Pamela was encouraged to join this polyamorous relationship of Edy, Chris St John, and Tony Atwood, though she visited the three women (and Ellen) often at Smallhythe, seemingly unperturbed by their living arrangements.

One of the *ménage*, Clare (later Tony) Atwood helped with set designs for the Pioneer Players. She was a calm, gentle, and accomplished artist. Edy got on very well with her, inviting her to live with her and Chris, with the proviso that if Chris did not like it and thought she was interfering with their primary friendship then she must leave. This was a very unusual scenario. Chris liked her though and found she acted as peacemaker between Chris and Edy. Each had their different roles: Chris was literary, Tony was busy working on props, while Edy would produce pageants. They moved in the same creative circles, enjoying each other's work. They also visited concerts, galleries, theatre or played games like Mahjong. Edy earned the nickname 'Boney' (Bonaparte) because she directed events and was so bossy. Meanwhile, by the early 1920s, Ellen began to lose her grip on reality as all became 'puzzledom' and old age kicked in. Edy later devoted her life to creating a shrine for her late mother. She also became something of a tyrant in her own way. Her two closest friends would say things like: 'Edy has bitten off more than we can chew'.

It is sad so many memoirs, letters, and writings pertaining to their lives were destroyed by Christopher St John. One wonders why, but maybe because Sapphic love was becoming controversial. Vita Sackville-West described Edy as a 'tearing old lesbian' though was not above a little sexual experimentation herself. It was when Vita invited the trio to her home and showed them her bedroom that Chris St John fell violently in lust. If she had a sexual love relationship with Edy, this was bizarre, to be so openly infatuated with Vita, so openly sexually promiscuous. It was not the norm, but then bohemianism had subverted many social mores.

Chris enjoyed one night of passion with Vita (who was possibly intrigued) but while Chris remained infatuated, Vita clearly was not. Melville suggests there were tremendously volatile scenes at the cottage following this. Edy, it seems, was not immune to jealousy after all, and what started as friendship had presumably become rather more to her. They all remained friends for some years, until death in Edy's, Tony's, and Christopher's cases.

So, Pamela never married and died childless, whether by choice or circumstance. When she died, she was sharing a flat with Mrs Nora Lake, about whom little is known. Given the 'Mrs' status, there was once a Mr Lake, thought to be a handyman at Parc Garland, who later passed away. There seems to be no conclusive evidence that Pamela had a romantic relationship with Nora, not that her sexuality is terribly important now in more enlightened times, but women then were hidden from history and lesbian women more so than others.

Pamela may have been celibate, maybe asexual, or she may have desired someone, male or female in her life and failed to attract them or have a relationship with them; perhaps love simply did not happen. She would not have made a compliant partner for any man or woman. We hear little told of Pamela having feelings for anyone, despite her friendship with Edy Craig. There are no laments for lost love or declarations of affection.

Her artwork, however, contains a good many drawings of women characters. Edy, by comparison, despite her later *ménage*, had already received a marriage proposal from the composer, Martin Shaw, in 1903, which she accepted, though was thwarted from carrying through; she had also previously fallen in love with a married man and been very close to a male friend who died. So, at the very least, one might assume Edy liked men (enough to marry one) or both sexes and was surely bisexual or bi-curious, but we never hear anything like this of Pamela. There seemed to be no major love interest mentioned in her life. Most of her comments about men were made in jest. She caricatured anyone, male or female.

The reality is none of us will ever know the full detail of Pamela's life, her thoughts, or her predilections unless something amazing comes to light. While her sexuality is not crucial to our understanding of her as a person, outside certain circles, same-sex relationships were not condoned at that time. There was stigma and taboo attached, which may have impacted upon her life decisions, indeed her conversion to a pious life of Catholicism.

If she was attracted to women, it is easy to see how marriage to a man would have been unsavoury but while the impact of marriage upon her career would have been little short of catastrophic, a husband would have provided some financial security, something with which she struggled throughout her life. If she was ambivalent, it may have been tempting. She was always desperate for money. While Edy Craig, with a steady maternal income, could live a life without too much scrutiny, someone making their own way probably had to play very much more by the rules, though this was not something Pamela seemed to find easy. Pamela had to forge her own path in life and probably preferred it that way, though would have appreciated more support along her journey.

She did not appear to attract a life partner. It was not uncommon at the time for two women to share accommodation and expenses, for good friends to live together. Nora and Pamela both struggled with their health in later life, so it may well have been a mutually supportive partnership, or even a romantic companionship, a common non-sexualised way of avoiding the tribulations of marriage but of enjoying tremendous friendship, and caring for each other, especially in later age. When Pamela mentioned Nora, it was usually as 'Mrs Lake'.

Of course, if lesbianism was her sexual orientation, does it matter? In her early, more bohemian circles, probably not, or it might have been a bonus, but it would have been at odds with the leanings and beliefs of the Catholic Church she adopted so fervently, for even in 2016, over a century later, Pope Francis opposed same-sex relationships, saying these can never be considered the equal of heterosexual marriage. Therefore, it would have been a strange religion to wholeheartedly embrace at mission level if she was actively and convincingly lesbian. However, Christopher St John seemed to fervently embrace the faith, too. Religion was often used historically as a form of 'hair shirt' for alleviating guilt and paying penance for homosexuality or other 'sinful' traits. For some, it was a step towards asceticism, including celibacy, whereby a conventional and structured belief system acted as a very real constraint in maintaining bodily purity. If Pamela was a lesbian, maybe her belief system helped her to remain celibate, though the same is unlikely to hold true for Christopher St John. Certainly, during some of her later time in Cornwall, Pamela seemed to live a relatively lonely life, befitting the area she chose to move to.

Smith-Rosenberg examined ways in which women fought to break free of the rigid Victorian sex roles they were allocated.[7] Women's lives in Victorian times were radically different to the current day. Female friendship was long-lived and intimate, yet little has been written about it, she claims: 'eighteenth and nineteenth century women routinely formed emotional ties with other women (in America) ... it was a world in which men made but a shadowy appearance'. Romantic friendships should not necessarily be viewed as libidinal as they were post-Freud, but should be placed in their contemporary cultural and social setting. Smith-Rosenberg's own study included an analysis of correspondence and diaries ranging from the 1760s to the 1880s, the latter at a time when Pamela was a young girl. She describes two typical friendships:

> These two friendships, intense, loving, and openly avowed, began during the women's adolescence and, despite subsequent marriages and geographic separation, continued throughout their lives. For nearly half a century these women played a central emotion role in one another's lives, writing time and again of their love and of the pain of separation. Paradoxically to twentieth century minds, their love appears to have been both sensual and platonic.[8]

In the case of Sarah and Jeannie, the women adopted *nom de plumes*, one female and one male, which they kept as secret names until old age. Marriage did not alter the frequency of their correspondence, nor their desire to be together or motherhood. Despite marriage, they wanted closeness. Perhaps closer to Pamela's situation, she also mentions Molly and Helena, who studied together, visited each other's families, and formed part of a social network of other artistic young women. Both expressed their love physically (writing of sending many kisses) but both eventually married. The women were lovers, maybe not physically, but certainly emotionally. It was a twentieth-century (and post) approach to the question of whether such relationships were genital, lesbian, or platonic. The focus on sex undermines the emotional attachment many women felt towards their close friends. The author suggests the women, their husbands, and their families all very much accepted female friendship and love was socially acceptable and compatible with heterosexual marriage, that such women were in complementary heterosocial and homosocial worlds.

The author also questions the romantic rhetoric of the day. If we remove the sexual, though not the physical (hand-holding, hugging, etc.), what function did such relationships perform within society? Well, there were severe social restrictions placed on interactions between young men and women, so supportive female networks were useful in every important event during a woman's life. The world was very clearly socially segregated into male and female spheres. What is positive about this hypothesis is that it perceives women as not merely 'an isolated and oppressed subcategory in male society', indicating such relationships grew out of sincere affection and supportiveness. 'Entire days, even weeks, might be spent almost exclusively with other women'. Sometimes, husbands were temporarily displaced and women would share most aspects of their lives. Vacations were often based around friendship, such as Pamela's visits to Smallhythe. So, the system was incredibly integrated, often through groups of kin and among friends. If we think of Smallhythe, it seems a community of women lived very well and largely harmoniously together, becoming emotionally central to each other's lives, and attracting many female visitors. Women would share joys and troubles no man could understand. Mothers and daughters were also often very close, though we hear little of Pamela's mother, but Ellen Terry presumably fulfilled that role to some extent.

At school, girls sent away from home would regularly sleep together, as well as kiss and hug each other. So, there was an emotional proximity that had been the norm for many years, centuries even. Girls would often love each other, but not in the sexual way we would probably automatically assume today, but in a form that approved mutual dependency and deep affection. In the twentieth century, such homosocial ties were cut short, as sexuality entered the fray. Individual needs were ironically less likely to be fulfilled in a sexualised era than during a culture of feminine friendship.

The other aspect of the book of interest to us during Pamela's earlier years is the gender crisis from 1870–1936, alongside the growth of the New Woman. The New Woman eschewed marriage, aimed for professional status and visibility, and was generally socially and politically radical. Indeed, the New Woman was a challenge to the old order, linked with the growth of women's colleges and the ensuing education, later marriage, upward mobility, and growing literacy. Women were moving outside the traditional domestic setting, and some men, like Pamela's father, were encouraging them, as he did with his daughter.

Interestingly, while the more radical of these women rejected patriarchal family structures, they embraced alternative single-sex families. Were they lesbians? Undoubtedly some were, but not all. Therein lies the rub. We cannot assume Pamela was, but whether she was or not, the supportive culture of feminine friendship was admirable. Often, these women worked together to forge social reform. As we know, Pamela, Edy Craig, and friends were involved with the suffrage movement.

Another aspect of this was these women needed to find alternative careers for themselves than motherhood. Mary Evans wrote:

> It is in this sense that I see her as a perennially liminal figure - a figure always outside of the existing social structures and with no way of coming in'[9]

Pamela was not quite part of things, she was often on the threshold. This sense of independence and distance frightened men, and when we later see the Bishop of Plymouth describe Pamela as 'neurotic' we see it as part of the general derogatory male framework used to deal with women who 'favored her mind at the expense of her ovaries'.[10]

19

The Sapphic Rumour

Why do so many people think Pamela preferred women to men?

By the 1890s, unmarried women, especially political activists, constituted an 'intermediate sex' considered to be 'mannish lesbians'. Some women responded to this label by doing just that, entering the male sphere and realm by dressing like men, androgynously, engaging in 'unnatural sexuality'. Rejecting conventional feminine behaviour was perceived as a symptom of sexual perversion. As time passed and the new sexologists grew in popularity, charges of perversion became a popular way to discredit professional women, since Havelock Ellis unhelpfully linked education and feminism with lesbianism. Sexuality was used to keep women in their place.

The introduction (by Keith Carabine, 2014) to the Wordsworth edition of Radclyffe Hall's novel *The Well of Loneliness* sheds some light on this whole curious categorisation.[1] The story is of a 'mannish woman', Stephen, who finds comfort in 'a branch of Christianity which has been most insistent that sex be confined to heterosexual marriage', Catholicism. He writes 'homosexuality was recognised by the Vatican in 1975 as innate, so without fault, but the Catholic response is to state men and women who are gay should live in a state of celibacy'. Hall was a Catholic convert, who had a private audience with the Pope in 1913. Chris St John, Pamela's friend, also underwent her conversion in Rome.

The label 'lesbian' was not used at that time. The main character in the novel is what was called an 'invert', women who were more mentally and physically masculine than 'normal' women. Where women sexually desired other women, this was perceived as inborn, rather than environmental. Inversion was considered an inherited degenerate condition, not punishable because it could not be helped. The sexologists believed a woman was born an invert, yet it could also be encouraged socially within the family, Stephen a case in point whose mother could not bear to touch her, and whose father wanted a son, with a resulting confused identity arising.

In the novel, Stephen feels an attraction to 'normal' women, not simply other inverts, so love is doomed. The suggestion Carabine makes is that inversion went with a craving for religion. The church turned this love into 'repentance, self-suppression and suffering'. Hall herself was flamboyantly masculine. For many women, masculine clothing was the norm, though Hall tended towards skirts to accompany her severely cropped hair. Many women wanted to break down injustices and emulating men was believed to be a way to do this. Basically, for a woman to want the privileges of men, she had to be perceived as freakish.

Pamela was certainly not mannish like the 'inverts' within the group who met at Smallhythe. Like many of her contemporaries, she perhaps joined the Catholic Church to escape or confine her sexuality. After all, as so many people were attracted to Catholicism, discussions about why must have been rife. Pamela was certainly no wearer of masculine shirts, ties or smoker of cigarettes. We never see her dressed that way, for her figure was rounded, not boyish. If anything, she was the antithesis to masculinity, and maybe that was part of her perceived identity as very much a womanly woman or at times a woman-child. Edy Craig, by comparison, had a confused love life.

Ballet dancer Moira Shearer suggests:

> There are accounts that Edy, in her early twenties, had two heterosexual love affairs which were brought to an end by Ellen's disapproval. All that is certain is that Edy's natural feminism became more strident and her attraction towards women stronger; she met the writer Christabel Marshall, who called herself Christopher Marie St John, and they set up house together in 1899. Later, in 1916, they were joined by another woman, Clare Atwood, called Tony, and this so-called *ménage à trois* (until Edy's death in 1947) became the part-support, part-harassment of Ellen's last years.[2]

The trio lasted; it was a durable, complementary relationship, however it worked, even to the death. Joy Melville stated the ashes of Edy's mother, Ellen Terry, had been stored enshrined in a specially blessed oratory in Edy's flat before being taken to St Paul's.[3] Conversely, Edy had asked for her ashes to be buried with Kit (Christopher St John) and Tony (Atwood) but she died well before them (Tony was in her early nineties when she died) and they were forgotten, only found twelve years later by her niece, Olive Chaplin, in a tin box. Chris and Tony, however, were buried side by side in the little graveyard at Smallhythe. In their last years, Chris and Tony had become reclusive. In her nineties, Clare Atwood went into a nursing home and Chris went to Tenterden Hospital, where she was said to have been an insufferable patient.

In all, Edy had three relationships with men in her earlier years. Katharine Cockin writes of thirty-seven letters that survived from Joe Evans to Edy between 1888 and 1896, and one telegram back from Edy to him, writing of travels, friends, and plans to meet. They exchanged gifts, including a Tiffany glass given to her in 1884, and a bookplate designed by her brother, plus a picture containing clover, sent to him in 1885. Ellen seemed to communicate with him, too, in one letter, sending Edy's and her love, as well as giving him a substantial gift. The American landscape artist Evans, who was said to be lifelong disabled, died at the age of forty in 1898; he was missed by Ellen and presumably Edy. He was very fond of Ellen, who perhaps pursued him overzealously on behalf of her daughter. This relationship was followed by her infatuation with married actor, Sydney Valentine, perhaps in reaction to Joe's death. Ellen dealt with this ruthlessly, threatening to send Edy (by then aged twenty-six) home, giving her no comfort about the end of her affair or crush. Martin Shaw's marriage proposal came in 1903, so during her young life, Edy appeared to like men. Melville writes about her fixation with Valentine:

> Used to her mother receiving all the adulation, she felt she had at last been loved for herself. The abrupt cessation of the romance, with no advice or understanding, or cooling-off period allowed, could hardly have helped her feelings to heal.[4]

Ellen had already decided it would take a bold man to win Edy over. Until this point, Edy had been cocooned inside Ellen's house with its constant stream of women visitors. However, Ellen struggled with Edy, describing her to Shaw thus:

> Edy looks a tragedy, and is about the most amusing, funniest creature living, a casual wretch. Oh, she is odd.... She says that no one would put up with her but me ... She's high, she's low ... She loathes emotional people, yet adores me. I scarcely ever dare kiss her, and I'm always dying to, but she hates it from anyone. It 'cuts both ways' I assure you, the having an impersonal person for a daughter ... Edy says she'd never marry because she would not stay anywhere where she was not entirely happy ... She's such a baby ... and yet so clever.[5]

The focus on Edy is important in understanding how and where Pamela fits in. So, Christabel Marshall (who took part of John the Baptist's name on converting to Catholicism) had originally fallen in love with Ellen, like many others. Edy was asked to look after Chris on one of her meetings with Ellen. They liked each other from the start, it seems. Chris adored Edy's nearly black hair and wide-set brown eyes. By now, Edy was nearly thirty. Edy was happy to chat but would always busy herself doing something else rather than give Chris her full attention. While Ellen was away touring for eight months in 1899/1900 Edy joined Chris in Smith Square, Westminster, with Ellen's blessing, in an undomesticated setting. Here they were nicknamed 'The Squares'. Ellen had a line in unkind nicknames, saying it like it was. Edy was not overly-demonstrative as both her mother and Chris St John complained.

Edy enjoyed living independently of her mother. Chris had not previously had a serious relationship. She was well built, rather plain, with a slight limp and a speech impediment. Their friendship meant a great deal to her. Ellen was less impressed on her return, assuming Edy would live with her mother forever, but eventually overcame her feelings. Whether she approved of the unorthodox living arrangement is hard to say, but she certainly did not want to lose Edy to a husband now Joe was no longer a contender. Chris St John explained how she became treated as a son-in-law might, becoming the 'willing slave' of both mother and daughter.[6]

With the later move to Smallhythe, Ellen allowed Edy and Chris to live in the Priest's House, one of the cottages there. In 1901, Ellen went on American tour again as the money was a draw. She had to (on her £300 a week) support her son (who seems to have regularly requested money, to which she commonly responded angrily) and daughter and other dependents while also maintaining her homes in London and the countryside. While Edy was a reputed theatrical costumier, she never made any money from her atelier. This was the story of many women of the time, which makes Pamela's efforts appear more successful.

Ellen enjoyed regular flirtations, but Edy seemed to quietly do as she was told, though she was like steel in other respects. Ellen, it seems, was a real force to be reckoned with, commanding and domineering in the most manipulatively charming ways. While Edy's brother, Gordon Craig, escaped her clutches, Edy had enjoyed little company of men. Melville suggests an unhealthy interdependency between Ellen and Edy, a symbiosis almost to the point of parasitism, writing: 'Men as devotees were accepted, but the possibility of one becoming a husband threatened their own dependent relationship and was always violently opposed'.[7] This may explain why she accepted Christopher St John.

In 1903, Edy had received and accepted a marriage proposal from composer, Martin Shaw, who had fallen in love with her as they worked; Gordon Craig wrote:

> My friend Martin Shaw seems to have proposed to my sister Edy. E.T. was greatly disturbed and came to see me about it, as though it was any of my business. She said it was to be prevented and I must help her to prevent it. Well, all I could do was do nothing except agree dutifully with E.T.—but the matter seems to have been pretty soon forgotten. For they did not elope—and real lovers always do that if any obstruction is encountered. So E.T. was right after all.[8]

Martin was disfigured (Edy's weakness was for physical imperfection) but was said to be a brilliant pianist (a talent Edy had enjoyed before rheumatism stopped her playing) and immensely kind. His talent was attractive, intriguing, and delightful. Ellen had already 'lost' Edy to Chris, so the variable is there was a man involved. However, he had little or no money, and Ellen's financial threats, along with Chris's histrionics, sufficed to break up the relationship. In *Hungerheart*, it seems the Edy character felt she cared for him, wanting to marry him, caring little for his deformity. In response, outside the world of fiction, a manipulative Chris made a statement by frenziedly drinking cocaine lotion, commonly used at the time for various ailments like toothache, and nearly killed herself.

Edy looked after her while continuing to see Martin. The romance fizzled out, and Edy never spoke of it again. It is unclear whether Ellen ever realised Chris and Edy then lived as lovers rather than casual flatmates, but she was not unworldly, so she probably did. In *Hungerheart* again, Chris suggests she was a 'congenital lesbian' but Edy liked men 'if they behaved well'. Edy is portrayed as sexually reserved with physical contact confined to hand-holding. There may have been some sexual contact, or that may have been why Clare Atwood joined them. Maybe she provided the physical element Chris needed in the relationship. Bear in mind Chris also had her night of passion with Vita Sackville-West. Melville suggests that is not the kind of topic Edy and Ellen would have discussed.

In response, Chris's attempted suicide was a remarkably powerful, calculating attention-seeking reaction. She was obviously a woman of strong emotions and reactions as later seen in her stalking of Vita Sackville-West. Chris wanted not only companionate and even romantic love but sexual love; Edy, it seems, wanted only friendship, if we believe Rachlin, whose book barely mentions the women's sexuality. To Chris, Martin Shaw's proposal was a total bombshell. She reckoned the only thing sublime about him 'was his conceit'. She was exasperated, felt Holroyd, that Edy wished to marry him, complaining of his facial disfigurement, unaware that Edy's previous attachment, the safely married Sydney Valentine, also had a facial blemish. It has been suggested that Edy, more than falling in love, was using it to irritate her mother, whom she enjoyed throwing into chaos, a form of interdependency again. However, all this raises questions about Edy's sexuality and in turn the labelling of Pamela by association.

Holroyd felt Edy 'responded emotionally to people whose marks of disadvantage were clearly visible'.[7] Maybe she was like her mother and enjoyed collecting waifs and strays, or maybe it was linked to her own sense of self-worth. He indicates Edy was in love with Martin, while Chris (also markedly unattractive, it is reported) could only think of the 'grossness of matrimony'. Intimate relations with a man were obviously a horrific concept to Chris.

Edy saw Martin constantly though never mentioned him to Chris, understandably, so they obviously gelled very well as a couple. Ellen, playing the role of domineering matriarch, in opposing the match, threatened to stop her daughter's allowance (if she married) and let Edy's company fall into bankruptcy. So, the relationship ended. Edy never explained it. Chris wrote: 'I still loved my friend, but my ideal of friendship had been tarnished. I saw that I was never to know a human relationship in which I was to be the "only one" to the "only other"'. This is a bit rich when Chris was known for her infatuations. Holroyd says she hints at a few episodes with other women, then, as a convert to Catholicism, she embraced the ideal of surrender to the love of God.[9] It seems Edy was not heartbroken by her broken relationship, so continued with her working life as before. Edy rarely seemed heartbroken about anything. Her heart was rarely worn upon her sleeve.

Certainly, photographs and her paintings suggest Pamela and Edy were very good friends and workmates for a while. The circle at Smallhythe was openly Sapphic, Chris very stridently so. It was a place of safety where they, and others, could be themselves. Susannah Mayor, curator at Smallhythe, explains how the women were not openly 'mannish' for much of the time, often wearing bucolic smocks, dancing around like carefree children.[10] Of course, it was an untroubled, insouciant world there in the Smallhythe enclave. Ellen Terry was a celebrity and, while she became poorer later in life, she had grown from rags to riches through sheer endeavour and talent. Her children may have moaned about money but they never truly had to worry too much about it, nor did Chris by association. Therefore, having free licence to live the lives they wanted, both artistically and sexually, was not too difficult. Bohemianism and free love were much easier if you had an income flowing in.

Pamela had also been born of reasonably affluent parents. However, their deaths meant she had to make her own way, despite being one of the many people in need Ellen picked up along her lifetime, being quite fond of her. Whether Pixie was lesbian or not, we have no way of knowing, but she did seem to enjoy her time (presumably holidays, including one in Cornwall) with Edy and her crowd (including Sappho the cat), which is understandable given the shared levels of talent, creativity, and interest in women's suffrage. Again, it does not necessarily mean she had or indeed wanted a physical relationship.

Smallhythe also sheds light on the biracial question. Seeing Pamela's drawings at Smallhythe, pictures where she is characterised with varying shades of skin tone, from pink to dark, from a large palette of colours, we can only assume artistic licence. There are also photographs of Pamela by Edy who was a keen amateur photographer (rare snapshots from 1904). There, Pamela looks pale, dancing around bonfires, wearing smocks, and entertaining children. A selection of smocks was kept for visitors. There was a great deal of emancipated dressing, too, with photos of some women in their ties. There are also Pamela's costume drawings. She was designing for Edy when Edy had her costumier role. Susannah Mayor says she imagined them all round Edy's flat in Covent Garden 'getting stuck in, being really busy'. Susannah added: 'I think she obviously came down here for holidays or whatever, but there is nothing much here after 1929' (after Ellen's death, implying the link was more Ellen than Edy). That said, she had stayed with Edy and Chris a good deal. They also visited their friend, Jacko, in

Cornwall. Jacko (Vera Holme) was a militant suffragette, cross-dressing actress, singer and chauffeur to the Pankhursts, whose stage name was Jack.

Joanne Glasgow suggested since Christopher St John's religious faith never mentioned lesbianism or such sexuality, it was 'seen as innocent by the church. Lesbian sexuality did not exist as a Catholic reality'.[11] So, omission was seen as permission, though omission is, of course, also considered a sin.

Susannah Mayor added:

> Her group here in London was still going into the twenties, so she was the one who left her social circle. It would seem something happened in her life. Things are not always as they seem. Edy, for example, died alone in her bed with no candles, which was rewritten by Chris St John as almost a full-on Catholic ceremony, so available information is not always accurate, anyway. We've got Edy Craig's archive and a massive Ellen Terry one. In Edy's, most isn't inventoried, but we have a whole load of drawings from 1900 done on board ship. There are lots of self-portraits of Pixie and Edy.
>
> That's in Katherine Cockin's book but they have never been published and are mainly unseen. They had quite an interesting friendship and are referred to as 'the little devils' all the way through. One of my favourites is of Laurence Irving. The image is so full, so detailed. The pictures are so charming. One of the pictures is of Ellen Terry with her plate of clams and her cocaine. I looked into this. Sarah Bernhardt was a great advocate of cocaine. If you worked in the theatre, working quite late, a little pick you up in the afternoon was needed. It wasn't made illegal until 1910, so these pictures are all about 1900 ish with poems by Edy. Some of Pamela's costume drawings are not brilliant, but these are something else. They are really good cartoons and it shows them all having a laugh. They performed a concert on the ship to pass the time, Bram Stoker, and Ellen dressed as a saloon girl. Edy wasn't on the ship but was included anyway. Pamela was a pretty amazing artist, really.
>
> I don't know if Edy and Pamela were lovers but Edy was with Chris St John who was described as a "mule-faced harridan". Chris wrote about Vita Sackville-West, about how she'd been at the barn and hadn't looked at her. It's very teenage although she was in her late 50s at the time; Vita became an obsession. She says that Edy and Clare told her just to get over it, which is quite interesting coming from her partners! I don't think we will ever really know about the full extent of their relationships. Edy didn't seem to have any kind of dalliance with any other women. She was very faithful and she was always so busy. Ellen had a lot of friends who were gay. Edy's circle of friends were just about all gay, and very creative.
>
> Edy started her theatre in 1929, and I've never come across any evidence of Pixie being here for any of those productions, which were big, with Gielgud, etc. I haven't seen much of her in our materials after 1910, so her Catholicism

> probably largely ended her associations with Smallhythe. Ellen Terry had this whole thing going on of not liking corsets. They took, when they were here, to wearing smocks pretty much. There was lots of flowing stuff going on and I wonder whether Edy got that idea from her.
>
> Chris St John, Clare Atwood with Pixie feature in one photo. Pixie is wearing a turban, but isn't particularly dark, Chris St John is in a bathing outfit, with a picture of Cornish rocks. Pamela's legs are so pale, she is not naturally dark. After moving to Cornwall, she maybe [*sic.*] returned to Smallhythe to see her old friends but we do not know.[12]

For some women at this time, as we have noted, romantic companionship was a way out of heterosexual marriage. With women like Ellen Terry, however, Nina Auerbach explains: 'she was never educated single-mindedly into the infantilising dependence of a proper Victorian marriage', which would have brought with it respectability—an unconventional approach that surely passed down through her family.[13]

A love of Smallhythe was understandable, for it is utterly charming, though required much renovation at the time it was purchased. It was an idyll two hours away from London by train then (much harder to reach now by public transport) and would have been very rural (now a fairly busy road runs past the front of it). The gardens are beautiful with spring flowers (violas, hyacinths, and daffodils in March) amidst the incessant call of birdsong. In one of Edy Craig's photo albums, however, Pixie is listed merely as a 'visitor' rather than one of the household. There is one delightful picture of her playing with children in the garden close to the nearby church. One photo shows her chatting animatedly with Edy, with a group of other women, most of whom wore ties. Of course, at the turn of the century, women wearing men's clothes was making a statement, an act of defiance against the constraints experienced by women, but later, it was ridiculed. These women wanted to be thought of not as women but as successful. The roles they played dramatised their transformed natures, in the mode of the Ladies of Llangollen, two aristocratic ladies who eloped to Wales in 1778. Lady Eleanor Butler and Sarah Ponsonby were known as 'the two most celebrated virgins in England'. Allegedly, they wanted a quiet life of gardening, reading, writing, and drawing but attracted many well-known visitors, such as William Wordsworth, Lady Caroline Lamb, and Josiah Wedgwood. The two spinsters were a sensation, a *cause célèbre*, but probably not lesbian.

Victoria Glendinning describes Chris St John as 'very ugly' (photos show her not to be a great beauty) indicating she was 'without charm or great intelligence'.[14] This seems unbelievable as, hailing originally from Exeter, she studied Modern History at Somerville College, Oxford, becoming secretary to Lady Randolph Churchill. Christabel Marshall converted to ascetic Catholicism in 1912, in Rome, a year after Pamela. Pamela did not wholeheartedly change her name but added in Mary. Atwood was also a Catholic. If they were ascetics, they would abstain from sensual pleasure. Emily Hamer wrote: 'She once gave Radclyffe Hall a piece of the True Cross, the one Jesus was crucified on, for safe-keeping'. She adds, however, that Chris struggled with asceticism: 'In 1932, Chris fell passionately in love with Vita Sackville-West; this caused huge rows between Chris and Edy, with Tony unsuccessfully trying to act as peacemaker.'[15]

Edy's energy was said by Auerbach to go into her work.[16] While she spent her life with Chris St John, whether she was ever wildly and passionately in love is pure conjecture, although she was obviously extremely fond of her. In St John's book *Hungerheart*, Edy, portrayed as Sally, is described by Auerbach as 'there is no consummation in a loving retreat with Edy "Sally"'.[17]

In the book, Chris's character, John-Baptist, is devastated when Sally later embarks upon a relationship with a man, describing the pain of Sally's betrayal as 'a bomb hurtling through the serene air of my Paradise ... even the touch of a hand would penetrate to my soul when words left me unmoved'.

The desire from Chris was certainly there but whether it was ever fully returned by Edy lies very much open to question. In all photos, the women appear to avoid touch. Did their Catholicism purge the women out of physical love? Tony Atwood later added energy to the household at a time when Ellen's was fast fading. On a different note, it is worth reading Hamer's book, which notes on the literary front about women masquerading as men in order to publish things.[18]

The British Library contains various letters from Pamela Colman Smith to Edy. In them, she calls herself 'Picky' or 'Pick'. They date from 1913, along with a letter of contract between Ellen Terry and Pamela agreeing to be joint proprietors of *The Russian Ballet* and to equally divide the returns, so there was certainly a business contract between the two. By 1928, Pamela responds to newspaper reports of Gandy's (Ellen Terry's) illness and mentions picture postcards for Miss (Christopher) St John. She offers prints of Gandy with a price list, presumably exploiting the demand for all things Terry-related, which again seems more of a contractual than a friendly relationship. She mentions in correspondence she had turned a room of her house on The Lizard in Cornwall into a shop but had sold nothing that year.

Certainly, there are many mentions of Pamela in the company of Edy Craig and Christabel. In an undated letter, from 'Awful Ellen Louisa' (Ellen Terry) to Chris Marshall, it mentions she is obliged to postpone the visit of Pixie since there are problems with servants leaving because of illness. If Pixie was an honorary family member, this would not matter. She is obviously seen as a visitor.

Nina Auerbach raises more interesting points about Ellen Terry, Edy, and the entourage of which Pamela at times formed a part.[19] If we accept her comments, then we need to rethink the questions about Pamela's sexuality, among other issues. Edy was good friends with Pamela. Their lives were teeming with women, some of whom Ellen liked and some she did not. None of them could quite match up to the leading charismatic light that was Ellen Terry, and by comparison, Edy seemed dull; even her letters (she was a hesitant speller) failed to flow with the life the exceptional Ellen's simply had. Auerbach mentions the suffragist, Emmeline Pethick-Lawrence (one of the thirteen children in the days when women were worn out by excessive childbearing) recalling the changes relating to women coming of age in the 1890s, living in a life of destabilising change, but also religious and intellectual challenge. It was a time of great promise for women.

Ellen and Edy's relationship was an odd one—prisoners of each other, yet unable to release themselves. Ellen controlled Edy's life, dwarfed her, and Edy later turned the tables as Ellen grew older, weaker, and more vulnerable; love–hate probably sums it up. There was an oddly deep love and this seemed to be the prime relationship for both, clinging to each other, all else secondary. On the plus side, the advantage of their living arrangement was a community of women, what Auerbach terms 'woman-controlled space'.[20] This meant in practice, Edy and her friends, to some extent including Pamela, were less oppressed by the domestic duties than they would otherwise have been, despite Ellen Terry being largely indifferent to women's suffrage. Marriage offered domesticity and economic dependence, tied down by the selfless, sacrificial roles of wife and mother. Marriage was an alliance, often unsatisfactory, as in the case of Susan Yeats.

Edy had been willing to embrace marriage to escape her mother when she fell in love. Yet, Auerbach suggests Edy was frankly indifferent to love, rather as she had been to playing the piano, acting, and school, but she really did rather enjoy throwing her mother into turmoil.[21] By 1898, Edy made another half-hearted attempt to leave. Christabel Marshall entered their lives in 1896. Auerbach describes her as 'the woman who could take on the roles no man had been able to manage'.[22] She described Marshall 'as the person who could act as a husband to Edy and sanctify the marriage between mother and daughter', for despite Christabel loving women, she reckoned she had the soul of a man.

Ellen was happier about the idea of union between Edy and Christopher than she was about any heterosexual marriage. In any case, Auerbach suggests both loved Ellen more than each other.[23] By 1899, Edy and Christopher took a flat together. During the First World War, they were joined by Clare (Tony) Atwood which prevented them being a couple. Effectively, they were Ellen's support network. In 1903–4, when Edy made her final break for freedom, in falling for Martin Shaw, her brother's collaborator with the Purcell Opera Company, she was once again brought to heel with few complaints and lived (presumably) contentedly thereafter in her community of women. However, her dalliances with men were surely no aberration, not if she had three relationships.

Curiously, her antagonistic feelings on marriage did not stop Ellen remarrying, as she united with James Carew, effectively herself fracturing her 'marriage' to Edy; the rules were different for Ellen, who overshadowed her daughter.

Who then was Pamela's companion, Nora Lake, who lived with her for many years in Cornwall? Nora Lake is herself an enigma, whose information is based on unverified local knowledge. She and her son, Freddie, used to live at the bottom of Valley Road, Bude, in a bungalow, close to The Bencoolen flats where Nora had lived with Pamela, though we hear no mention of Freddie then. She was a spiritualist as was the father of a Bude lady, Jackie Adams, who believes Nora used to attend spiritualist meetings at the old Women's Institute in Bude.[24] She also played the piano (a piano case is mentioned in the list of contents sold after Pamela's death). Freddie, her son, worked in Lloyds Bank. When his mother died, he moved out of the house and lodged in Bude with a Church of England Christian family. Apparently, a creature of habit, he always used to walk across the golf course to work, and he always kept to the footpath.

Nora had white hair, described by Jackie Adams as 'a bit "tubby" but smartly dressed'. Freddie was locally considered a little odd. He always wore a suit and did not always reply to a greeting so was not very outward looking. The fact Nora had a son proves nothing but it seems unlikely she was lesbian or that she was close enough to Pamela to wish to adopt her faith. However, the two were companions for around thirty years. Genealogical material explains that Nora and her husband Alfred came from Devon, he from an agricultural family. Alfred (39) is listed on the 1921 census as living at Parc Garland with Nora (40), where Alfred was the valet and Nora the cook. The two married in 1905. In the 1911 census, Nora(h) is listed as single, aged 27, working as a servant in Surrey. Their son, Freddie, is not listed in 1921. Head of the household Pamela is still listed as an artist/painter. By 1939, Pamela and Nora were living in an Exeter boarding house at 24, New North Road. Alfred is not listed, presumed deceased.

20

Once a Catholic: The Mission Years

Pamela's conversion to Catholicism has largely been glossed over almost as an aberration, yet she was not remotely alone in this; there was a minor flood of conversions among her older companions and friends. Edy Craig's female partners, Christabel Marshall (Christopher St John) and Clare (Tony) Atwood, both converted to Catholicism around the same period, along with lesbian writer, Radclyffe Hall. Why this popular conversion among creatives to a faith that has traditionally been opposed to same-sex relationships confuses the modern mind.

Frontain mentions Hall's biographers who believed she sensed no dissonance between Catholicism and lesbianism, suggesting many women joined the Catholic Church to 'ensure that they might be together in heaven'.[1] He suggests this was due to the primary pre-Freudian sexology discourse of the day which saw same-sex desire as a naturally-occurring biological 'inversion' and possibly a self-protection strategy. If lesbianism was a choice, then it was perceived as immoral, thereby requiring action to amend it. If it was due to childhood trauma, a cure would be expected to be sought, but if it was 'God's creation', albeit considered 'freakish' at the time, then no one could argue with it, and no man could amend God's work. If Pamela was lesbian, though there is no evidence she was, this was no hindrance to her embrace of Catholicism.

Both challenge and travel were familiar to Pamela. Her decision to move to the outer reaches of Cornwall would have alarmed her friends, though not her newer Catholic ones; it was certainly not one that promised an easy future, nor one she would have undertaken lightly. Cornwall promised a life far removed from the salon society of London she knew, the city of bohemian storytelling evenings. It was the antithesis to life in the capital where she enjoyed the company of the enormous creative and theatrical talents of her time, though The Lizard was also renowned for its artistic communities.

Her relocation stemmed not only from her disillusionment and frustration with her working life, but also, more importantly and positively, a true sense of mission, a devotion to her faith that is hard for an irreligious outsider to understand. It is this aspect of her life few understand or try to comprehend, dismissing it as a retreat into herself. Yet, Pamela had always wanted to belong somewhere, to be a part of something, to be on the inside rather than the periphery, so helping the Church that had embraced her strange and troubled soul made perfect sense.

British society changed in the aftermath of the First World War. Pamela undoubtedly experienced patriotism at its most extreme. Some 300,000 children never saw their fathers again, while 160,000 wives were widowed during the horrific carnage. Morale sapped and people felt understandably fearful. Outsiders were objects of suspicion. Work on suffrage was halted by the greater external threat, and post-war, almost 25 per cent of working women were back in domestic service as their days as a reserve army of labour came to an abrupt close.

Such ongoing turmoil was enough to make anyone feel uncomfortable. Her previous work surely now seemed frivolous. She would have known people who suffered the loss of loved ones, seen women receiving the dreaded telegrams telling of lost husbands and fathers on distant battlefields. The war meant fear, curfew, censorship, and containment. The major cities, including London, suffered riots, especially after the sinking of the Lusitania by a German submarine in 1915.

While Bohemia still existed, life had become a serious business; fear, xenophobia, and additional concerns about women 'stealing men's jobs' resurfaced while the men were away fighting, creating a deep sense of social unease especially in the urban areas. Post-war, while women had taken on jobs at the docks and in the munition factories, there was huge concern among men that wages were depressed and their jobs deskilled as a result. They were understandably resentful. Women, however, had experienced the workplace, they smelled the scent of emancipation, yet even the radical, militant suffragettes in the WSPU had united with the war effort with their more moderate suffragist sisters. We know Pamela was displeased and tight-lipped when her Bude errand boy, Tony, told her about his plans to join the armed services. For whatever reason, the war had an adverse impact on Pamela, who had been actively involved in creating propaganda in the fight for suffrage, but whose only work for the war effort was for the Red Cross.

Times were hard when the nation was at war. There was little money available for frivolous artwork or professional storytelling. During the war, paintings were war-themed while the terribly realistic poetry of the war poets was a far cry from tales of ballet, sprites, and fairies beloved by Pamela. By this time, Pamela was also an established Catholic, leaving behind the seamier bohemian scene of her younger years. Romantic love, the grand passion, had been replaced in some minds by casual sex and licentiousness, a subverting of previous norms and mores, and a freeing up of people, both emotionally and physically. Art itself was enmeshed within the commercial world, a world which rapidly grew less frivolous, at a time of catastrophe and monumental losses, not least of life. It may seem strange that Pamela decided to leave London but post-war London was very different to the pre-war city.

Clive Emsley suggests there was a post-war moral panic.[2] The pervasive idea perpetuated by the press was of men so brutalised and inured to violence by their dreadful experiences in the trenches that violent crime would result; it was terrifying. Newspapers eagerly filled their pages with tales of often wildly exaggerated violence perpetrated by sex-starved men returning from France. It was little surprise then that women with any sense of choice might prefer to avoid the cities and men in general. Moral panic as a sociological concept was developed by Stanley Cohen in the 1960s but this reality occurred long before he put a name to it. The press exaggerated incidents, amplifying deviance that threatened society, thus creating scapegoating, with massive public outcry, concern, and ultimately crackdown on certain groups in a new wave of social controls. The panic extended to groups of young women. During wartime, 'khaki fever' was a new concern, where adolescent girls, many aged thirteen to sixteen (thirteen was previously the age of consent), in the cities immodestly flocked towards the military for sexual attention; this was widely perceived as a sign of disorder, with middle-class volunteers attempting to control such exuberance through interventionist 'rescue work'.[3] It was yet another huge social change for people to deal with. Pamela was not alone in thinking the world had been turned alarmingly upon its head, becoming increasingly unpleasant in the process.

Pamela's new location choice, however, was intriguing, and probably suggested by the Church; after all, while she had visited parts of north Cornwall and Devon, there is no indication she knew much at all about The Lizard, which has a uniquely Cornish identity. What could she possibly achieve in Cornwall that she could not do in London? Well, her real motivation was religious devotion, for Cornwall needed missionaries to spread the true faith in its non-conformist enclave.

Even by 1993, the Bishop of Plymouth explained:

> Without doubt Cornwall today is the least Catholic part of England, but nevertheless, in at least 35 churches and chapels God is honoured by the celebration of Sunday Mass, and for about half of these chapels and their attendant flocks the Canons Regular of Bodmin Abbey are responsible.[4]

He adds Bude's Catholic Church, where Pamela worshipped during her time in the town, 'dedicated to St Peter, was ready for use on 29th June, 1926'. It is a mystery how Pamela later happened upon Bude as a location, via Exeter, yet there are some clues. Her errand boy, Tony, suggested she was sent to Bude by the Catholic Church; he may well be right, given the links between the two areas outlined here in Father Whitehead's book.

> Miss Catherine Saunders, a native of Week St Mary, proved a very generous benefactress to the Mission … Bishop Kelly, unable to be there at the opening, wrote 'I am so glad. It is a grand thing you have done and what you went for'. The building of the church in Bude was the fulfilment of a hope expressed by the Bishop when he handed over the Launceston mission to the Bodmin Chapter.[5]

Given Pamela's later links to Bude, it is interesting soon after his appointment in 1920, the prior of Bodmin, George McGregor informed:

> We are purchasing a site in Bude on the main road for £150 … Money seems likely to be forthcoming from Mrs Thynne, a non-Catholic … The land was on the Acland Estate and sites were selling at £700 per acre.[6]

The site was secured at £150 for church purposes.

They were also donated a little altar from the private chapel of a Mrs Howell of Rose Hill, Penzance, along with some furnishings. She had been advised of the new church by her brother-in-law. So, there were some links between the far west of Cornwall and Bude, which may (tenuously) indicate the Catholic Church eventually sent Pamela to Bude.

According to Father Ambrose, there are reasons why Catholicism struggled to take root in Cornwall, where numbers of Catholic worshippers were terribly low in the early 1900s. In Penzance, home to a beautiful medium-sized Wesleyan Methodist church on Chapel Street, Catholic worshippers numbered around 150 out of 150,000 (around 0.1 per cent). In the lean times of the 1840s, economic conditions in the west of Cornwall, as elsewhere, were dire. Thousands of miners and their families understandably left for America. The decline of mining and problems with harvests led to depopulation and desperation. In 1898, the editor of the *Cornish Magazine* asked readers for their ideas on how to turn the duchy into a holiday resort, such was the level of hopelessness among the traditional industries that were at starvation levels.[7] Meanwhile, priests struggling with their Cornish mission suffered 'disheartenment and despondency because of the smallness of numbers and the pressure around of public opinion'. In 1882, there were riots in parts of West Cornwall but partly this was a dislike of the Irish Catholics believed to be disturbing tradition and taking jobs. The Cornish anti-authority reputation was an additional obstacle.

This detail is important because Pamela struggled with these very problems in her mission to grow Catholicism on The Lizard, a place priests were reticent to attend to provide Mass. Wesleyans, conversely, were represented throughout the county, despite splintering into various non-conformist groups, for Cornwall was and remains a culturally distinctive region. The 1920s, when Pamela had arrived in Cornwall, was an important decade for the mission of the Canons

Regular of the Lateran (CRL) based in the area. The commission (received in 1880) explained the duty: 'where the houses of our Order have been destroyed, they shall be restored to the Glory of God and for the good of souls'; gradually, Bodmin became the centre of the Cornwall Catholic mission. Such was the abhorrence for Catholicism in parts of Cornwall, Whitehead mentions a Catholic priest from Liskeard attending the dying William Hocken, Rector of St Endellion, considered to be so High Church he was almost Catholic.[8] The priest said: 'He has been a Catholic at heart for many years and should be received into the Church', but he was turned away by Hocken's foster-daughter who said 'he shall die as he lived'.

During the First World War, Catholic missionary work had taken a tumble. Five of the Bodmin community, for example, offered their services as chaplains during the war, so they lost priests, some forever. Mass became both periodic and peripatetic, a distressing development for Cornish Catholics. Mass was and is of the utmost importance for Catholics to express devotion and receive Communion, the ritual being a way of prioritising God and belief.

The New Canon Law of 1918 effectively meant missions were transformed into parishes, stable communities of the faithful, within a particular church and under the care of the parish priest, who was within the authority of the diocesan bishop, whereas 'missionary work' would take place at stations where there were surplus personnel to use. Pamela's work was missionary in nature with a view to establishing a permanent place of worship; however, this is when her problems started. Pamela's aim to help spread Catholicism on The Lizard was laudable, but the practicalities were difficult. She had no experience of mission work, nor of Cornish isolation. By 1920, at the start of her mission, the Prior of Bodmin had a community of twelve priests but seven of these were externs, so were on the move, not permanently based there. This made them less reliable and we certainly see, through her letters to the Bishop of Plymouth, Pamela's struggle to maintain regular priests to administer Mass in the area. People soon grew tired of having no Mass in a Church that set great store by it.

Bodmin, one of Cornwall's oldest towns, set on the edge of bleak moorland, was not a popular place, seeming very remote for student priests. By 1926, six priests were out on mission, and one Spanish priest was in residence. The novice numbers had declined with students of theology going to Rome but philosophy students staying in Bodmin. By the mid- to late 1920s, numbers at Bodmin had declined and most who were left were from Europe, so language barriers created additional problems.

Angie Hodges of the English Catholic History Association said:

> Pixie converted to Catholicism in London, then later moved to Cornwall. I don't think Pixie would have moved to that southern tip of Cornwall unless she knew she would be able to go to Mass every Sunday. Apparently, Miss M.

> Balfour, niece of the Earl of Balfour, built the church in Mullion in 1925 but before that she had Mass said in her own home. There was no other Catholic church on The Lizard at the time. Pixie arrived on The Lizard in 1918. I think she must have made enquiries first to make sure there was somewhere she could go to Mass—even though she built her own chapel at Parc Garland, there was no regular priest there.
>
> Did Pixie meet up with Miss Balfour in London? The Earl of Balfour was A. J. Balfour, the Prime Minister—the title was invented for him. His brother, Gerald, had a daughter—Mary Edith Balfour—born in 1894 in London—who would therefore have been the Earl of Balfour's niece. Gerald was the President of the Society for Psychical Research in 1906–7. That sounds like something right up Pixie's street. Could Pixie have become friendly with the Balfour family? She would have been sixteen years older than Mary. On the other hand, she could have decided to come to Cornwall just because of the art there, and been introduced to Miss Balfour by the Bishop of Plymouth. Or perhaps both Mary Balfour and Pixie were encouraged to evangelise Cornwall by the Bishop.[9]

There are so many questions, but the most promising idea is Pamela seeking to be part of an evangelical Catholic movement in Cornwall, perhaps spurred on by Mary Balfour. It is often assumed once Pamela became a practising Catholic, her artistic career was effectively over as if religion and creative endeavour were incompatible, but this is not so. Indeed, the Church has patronised and thereby supported many arts; religious buildings contain many beautiful items of artistic merit, from paintings to iconography. Pamela's last exhibition was in 1914, so her full-on artistic (painting rather than book illustration and publishing) career was fairly short-lived, but this probably had more to do with changing artistic fashions and the growth of modernism than her conversion to Catholicism.

Nothing she painted after 1920 seems to be in the public domain, but this is precisely the time when she changed her life forever. Again, because we do not fully know her reasons, we can only surmise whether her geographical move coincided with some major unfortunate life event. Maybe she just lost her zest for selling pictures and the people associated with the art world; perhaps opportunities were less forthcoming as she no longer mingled with London creatives in a post-war world; possibly her work simply stopped selling, for out in the wider art world, a change was also afoot. The 1920s was a period of a significant shift. Art Deco design grew in popularity, with expressionism and surrealism growing in stature in artistic circles. Dada, characterised by nihilism and randomness, was also a strong influence. Compare Pamela's work to Edvard Munch's *The Scream* (1893) or the abstract works of Kandinsky. Pamela's work, by comparison, appears from another, earlier, naïve age. She did not grow artistically as quickly as she needed to keep up, or maybe she simply remained true to herself.

Her final step in her conversion or acceptance into Catholicism occurred in 1911, but she would have started working towards this one or two years earlier, when exhibiting with Stieglitz in New York, while creating her tarot deck. It is not an immediate process. People convert for many reasons: a sense of belonging, universality, not being judged by one's talent or wealth, and feeling important to a community; these are all very good reasons why Pamela may have embraced her new-found faith. She still painted and illustrated after her conversion; Catholicism did not draw a line under economic activity, but the focus changed. Post-war, when she moved to Cornwall, she was collecting religious cards and pictures for creative inspiration. In 1917, six years after her conversion, she illustrated a set of cards, *The Way of the Cross*, with verses by Paul Claudel, a French author. This is the journey of Jesus Christ on the day of his crucifixion—something very meaningful to her as a Catholic.

Additionally, she met William Rowland, with whom she worked collaboratively. He was another ex-Golden Dawn member, initiated on 20 March 1895 (Pamela initiated in 1901), though they seem not to have met while at the Order. He never followed up his initiation and later was demitted for non-subscription of dues. Was joining the Golden Dawn a fashionable thing to do? People seemed to come and go, tried it out, and maybe found it wanting. Rowland was never in the Theosophical Society nor was he a freemason (both good recruiting grounds for the Golden Dawn) but he may have been interested in spiritualism. They were obviously both seeking something in the Golden Dawn but found that 'something' elusive. The organisation was, compared to Catholicism, very complicated and intellectual. Roman Catholicism, by comparison, seemed straightforward and easy to follow; not a sect, it is universal, with massive global appeal.

In 1916, Rowland and Pamela cooperated on a forthcoming book to be called 'music drawings'; with drawings by Pamela and *Notes by Rowland Thurnam*, possibly musical notes. Also in 1916, Pamela contributed a drawing of *The Passion* for a book in which Rowland was involved. Rowland, another convert, had a good knowledge of French; hence, his focus on the work of Claudel. He translated Claudel's *The Exchange* into English and from it a single performance was given by the Pioneer Players (founded by Edith Craig) at the Little Theatre, presumably through Pamela's links. It seems Claudel had undergone a conversion experience from non-believing to Catholicism, deeply affecting Rowland who clearly identified with it.

It is astonishing the number of people in Pamela's circle who converted to Catholicism, some progressing from occult fringe organisations—a strange leap but impactful. Nonetheless, both the Golden Dawn and Catholicism employed symbolism and ritual so maybe the leap is somehow logical. Divination is largely at odds with Christianity, especially Catholicism, perceived as superstition which detracts from the worship of God. How do we reconcile how divination (seeking knowledge of the future using supernatural, non-biblical means) fits with her faith? It strongly suggests Pamela was less of a believer in divination than most people like to think; either that or she had a major change of heart prior to her conversion in 1911, perhaps sparked by producing her tarot deck.

Pamela's conversion represented a major shift in her later lifestyle choices. Conversion to Catholicism was for some an intellectual choice; it gained popularity among many creative and intellectual people of this time as a growing faith. Lincoln Mullen, describing conversion in the USA, says missionary priests between 1870 through the early twentieth century converted thousands, the reasons mainly being a yearning for catholicity, universality, inclusivity, and 'unity in a visible, orthodox church'[10] People had a need to conform, to be part of a greater whole, to feel a part of a community, to belong, contradictorily when other people were trying to differentiate themselves through bohemianism. Maybe a collective identity was more important than rampant individualism, after all.

Pamela had mingled with the bohemian set though (as usual) appeared more on the fringes, exploiting their emotional and artistic needs rather than fully embracing its philosophy. It was bohemian followers who enjoyed her Gypsy sessions, but did she want to embrace the lifestyle (which was still not terribly open to women, even talented ones) or simply use it to make a living? Probably the latter. Virginia Nicholson, granddaughter of artist Vanessa Bell, wrote a rich description of how life was for those who felt or elected to be different between the turn of the twentieth century until the outbreak of the Second World War.[11] Bohemianism was a wave of thinking that included artistic modernism, feminism, spiritualism, pacifism, and freedom of thought, in sharp contrast to the Victorian mores accepted by the masses. It was a spiritual home for artists who often found themselves on the fringes of society. A peek at bohemianism helps us to understand Pamela, who, unfettered in her youth, later embraced the structure and boundaries of the Catholic Church. Many bohemians idealistically wanted to live the lives of artists, people who rejected materialism and expressed contempt for wealth. Arthur Ransome, who attended Pixie's soirees, believed to be bohemian meant to be materially poor within this life of bliss.

Nicholson wrote: 'The bohemian is an outsider, defines themselves as an outsider and is defined by the world as an outsider ... A lot of people regard them as subversive, elitist and possibly just a little bit immature'.[12]

The problem with bohemianism was that it was hard to maintain on many levels. In the late nineteenth century, it related to unorthodox, non-traditional lifestyles of artists, poets, and musicians, free to follow an anti-establishment line. However, the downside is that they were also often drugged and impoverished. The uniqueness of the individual lauded by bohemians led to their underappreciation. Life was a pursuit of hedonistic merriness, fun, and colour. Despite a dislike of all things bourgeois, bohemians relied very much on education and a comfort blanket of wealth provided by others. Taken from Rodolfo of *La Bohème*, here is a summary:

I am a poet!
What's my employment? Writing.
Is that a living? Hardly.
I've wit though wealth be wanting,
Ladies of rank and fashion
All inspire me with passion;
In dreams and fond illusions,
Or castles in the air,
Richer is none on earth than I.

Pamela was only too aware of tales of creative people starving (literally) in the garrets of Chelsea, living hand to mouth. Many of the middle classes lived extremely frugal lives but also subverted convention by giving up on (or seeking handouts of) necessities like food while retaining luxuries like books and entertainment. Seeking lives outside the rat race, the tales of ruin are many. This dislike of materialism and yet the need for money partly explains Pamela's contentious relationship with her publishers. In terms of love and romance, free love was also embraced, yet many a woman fell in love and had the misfortune to marry and bear children only to be dumped when parental responsibility kicked in. Arthur Ransome wrote: 'The door into the registrar's office was the door out of Bohemia'.[13]

By comparison, Catholic converts were mainly people who enjoyed ritual which simplified their lives and thinking. Converts, of course, could not just join the church, they had to be received into it. An Oxford Movement convert, John Henry Newman, described the benefits of the nurturing nature of Catholicism: 'you feel as if you had gone back a long way and turned baby again, and it is very nice to be a baby when you have such a grand thing as the Church to take you in its arms and carry you along'.[14]

An Almighty Father, a clear set of rules and promises of better things to come felt very attractive, especially at a time of great personal, social, and global change. The early 1900s were a time of great transition—a fledgling democracy was on the way, with universal adult male suffrage and votes for some women aged over thirty. Politically, a good deal was at stake as Britain moved towards the most horrific and wide-scale war.

What Catholicism seemed to offer many people in a rapidly changing world was security and authority, so who can blame Pamela or others for wanting it? Converts simply had to believe and have faith. Conversion was not so simple; indeed, it often alienated people from their peers, as it seemed to for Pamela (Lily Yeats a case in point, for Pamela the Catholic was not feted for her entertaining company). Newsome explained:

> The convert became, as it were, an exile in his own land ... In addition to the humiliation of social ostracism, the pain of severed friendships and the torment of past memories, there was the inescapable problem of beginning life again within an alien community, while recognising that all one's past distinctions and achievements counted for nothing.[15]

That last sentence relates strongly to Pamela's experience. It is difficult to find an example of an intellectual or creative person who derived either social or monetary gain from a conversion. For many, on the contrary, the material and prestigious losses were considerable. For those who felt Pamela chose an easy way out of her previous society, think again. Her friends appeared most bewildered that her new pious life dulled her, those previous accomplishments counting for little or nothing; her status was clearly diminished. She certainly derived no pecuniary benefit from it, so one can only hope she attained salvation. No one loves a convert because its very nature suggests a dissatisfaction with what went before, often perceived as a criticism of the others known in a pre-conversion life. Joan Coldwell wrote of Pamela's relationship with the Yeats family:

> We can see how Pamela, once well ensconced with the Yeats family, very quickly fell out of favour. She had worked with the Yeats sisters, contributing designs to their Dun Emer Industries.
>
> The few known details of Pixie's later life confirm the impression that she, who was once so eccentric and unpredictable, became conventionally staid and pious ... This altered lifestyle (on The Lizard) no doubt contributed to the early decay of her reputation.[16]

Yet Pamela is described by Coldwell as hard-headed in her youth when pursuing W. B. Yeats for her own advancement, cultivating his friendship and influence for her own ends. Well, if she did, she succeeded, for her success was closely allied with the fortunes of the Yeats siblings; Pamela also admired his younger brother, Jack Yeats, and wife, as artists. Her working relationship with the Yeats family drew to a natural end but she remained on broadly friendly terms. As late as 1913, Lily Yeats stayed with Pamela in London after attending a craft sale at Londonderry House, but as Pamela mixed with more mundane, ordinary people, she became less extraordinary and important to the lives of her previous high-profile friends.

Boyd Parsons has indicated Lily (Susan Mary) Yeats was spiteful and disliked Pamela, but it is also worth remembering the importance of the Catholic question.[17] The Irish Yeats family was raised as Protestant at a time when the Catholic Home Rule movement was gaining momentum, so there was some political and religious incongruence. W. B. Yeats originally shared a fascination with the occult in common with Pamela; after all, it was he who had introduced her to the Hermetic Order of the Golden Dawn. He did, however, have serious issues with Catholicism at many levels:

> If you show that this country, southern Ireland, is going to be governed by Roman Catholic ideas and by Catholic ideas alone, you will never get the North ... You will put a wedge in the midst of this nation.[18]

Without dipping too far into Irish politics and the great religious divide, it is not difficult to see why members of the Yeats family may have been dismayed by Pamela's conversion. Yeats's mother, Susan, came from a profoundly Protestant family, who had considerable influence over its members given John Yeats's inability to or dislike of providing for his family.

The Catholic Church itself was ambiguous in its pleasure of conversion. Intellectual people who converted to the Church of Rome would question key tenets, like the infallibility of the Pope. However, we must not underestimate the genuine sense of religious conviction underlying conversion; it was not undertaken for fun. Converts often became seriously attached to and passionate about their church, as in Pamela's case; she liked to do things properly. When Pamela converted to Catholicism, she was understandably boring to some of her friends, for suddenly, her interests were not theirs. That might be enough to dissuade many people from following it through. She obviously saw things differently, once or twice describing her faith as fun, encouraging others to join, though this may have been her mischief-making coming to the fore again, or maybe she was truly something of a missionary—evangelical—which her later activities on The Lizard imply. If you find what you believe to be true faith, it must be hard not evangelise.

Why Catholicism? At a wider level, many prominent artistic people, and intellectuals turned to Catholicism in the late nineteenth and early twentieth centuries. A rather personal, stumbling hypothesis is that artistic characters like the ritual, flourish, and beauty. The Catholic Church is packed with this. Why would an artistic and dramatic person opt for the simple, non-ornamental, and uncertain (in salvation terms) approach of a Calvinist?

In Pamela's case, Catholicism drew her to Cornwall. Suggestions why range from bowing out of public life to, oddly, wanting to go to the land of the pixies (as per her namesake) or being closer to America. Yet move she did, but she also stayed in West Cornwall until the outbreak of the Second World War in 1939, implying some sense of enjoyment or belonging, or maybe just little other option once she had done it. However, it was a massive geographical and social change, again not one that would have been lightly undertaken, and where she remained for around twenty years.

Her late-life conversion is absorbing, especially as peculiarly Arthur Waite was a lapsed Catholic. So many links remained throughout her life to the Catholic

Church through people she knew from different situations. How does the tarot link with Catholicism, a religion that is, after all, rich in imagery and symbolism, yet does not consider itself occult? To Catholics, the very first commandment is vital. It states: 'I am the Lord thy God. Thou shalt not have any gods before me'. To trust in God means, to some extent, to have no fear for the future. Certainly, people should not try to tell or predict it, and should realise to summons occult power is a mortal sin, gravely wrong, leading to eternal damnation unless absolved from it. So, Pamela is surely unlikely to have looked back on her work as a tarot artist with much joy once she turned to God. Did she celebrate her tarot art? Probably not. Yet, if we believe Tony Edwards, her errand boy, and we have no cause not to, then she still had similar paintings around during her senior years in Bude, and Hayley White, who bought the house, is convinced Pamela still used her deck of cards at Parc Garland.

Her circle of friends and acquaintances, apart from Christopher St John and Tony Atwood did not share her passion for the Church. Lily Yeats, who employed a keen turn of phrase, exclaimed when Pixie had converted: 'I heard the other day of a priest who said that confessing nuns was like being eaten alive by ducks'.

Lily Yeats, wrote to her father, John B. Yeats in 1913, reporting the religious change had sorely affected Pamela's social circle. Pamela would have been on the receiving end of a good deal of taunting for her conversion by her fashionable, intellectual friends. Yet, for many people keen on mysticism, a return or a switch to Catholicism made sense. The sacraments seem to have magical aspects to them. Evelyn Underhill says:

> Those who have observed with understanding, for instance, the Roman rite of baptism, with its spells and exorcisms, its truly Hermetic employment of salt, anointing chrism and ceremonial lights, must have been seen in a ceremony far nearer to the operations of white magic than to the simple lustrations practised by St John the Baptist.[19]

Pamela's artistic associates were not amused, especially as she gradually cut them off from her life, whether on purpose or by default. Perhaps they withdrew from hers. Little saleable artistic work seemed to materialise after 1918, but then the economic effects of the War undoubtedly affected production and sales. However, it is as if she also had some private crisis of conscience. In 1918, she received some money, a legacy from a deceased uncle, perhaps Theodore E. Smith (Teddy), which enabled her permanent relocation to Cornwall.

We know Pamela was heavily into ritual from her storytelling activities, but she also spent many painstaking years learning about the ceremonial aspects of her beliefs to get them right. Virtually everything in the public sphere says she opened a convalescent or holiday home for priests, which appears in letters held by the Diocesan archive to be incorrect; odd then, it has never been questioned. Why would Pamela even do this? What was in it for her? She had never shown any great patience with men, and tiresome elderly priests were no exception, though she would have been keen to hear regular Mass, for to not do so was a mortal sin.

Pamela's attempts to develop a Catholic flock on The Lizard succeeded, for a while. However, not many years later, a church was established at nearby Mullion, leaving Pamela's ad hoc attempts scattered in the breeze. Father Dobbeleers from Belgium was the priest in charge of the widespread parish of Mullion, The Lizard and Ruan Minor. After various hiccups, on 5 April 1925, the church at Mullion opened, was solemnly blessed, and the first Mass celebrated. Ten years later, an extra wing was added to the Church; it included the lady chapel and the little tower. The Sacred Heart Chapel was added in the 1950s. Much of the Church furniture was purchased in Belgium in 1924, giving the interior a continental flavour, enhanced by paintings from the St. Croix Studio, Bruges. Pamela's little makeshift chapel at her home in Parc Garland literally fell by the wayside.

This was no holiday home for priests. While she undoubtedly understood the importance of priests, trying to secure their services on many occasions, she truly wanted a permanent one for The Lizard. She had the building, so if she had a permanent priest, people would worship at Parc Garland and a largely self-funding church could develop. This was her belief, her aim, her mission, to continue what Madame Victorine Roberts had started in bringing Catholicism to this Cornish outpost. In practice, it did not happen. If she ran a holiday home for priests, then someone would surely have been regularly available to take Mass.

Her letters to the Bishop of Plymouth suggest she was often rather less than accommodating of some of the elderly and unhealthy or foreign priests scraped together and sent out to her remote mission at Parc Garland, considering them an expense, a bother, unreliable and not worth having.[20] To reiterate, they were not resident, they were peripatetic, else priests would have been at hand to administer regular Mass. Given the importance of the Mass, she might have been more hospitable, a point which was made in communications with the Bishop. They were certainly not sent to this wild and unwelcoming part of the country for hospitality, and most were not keen to go; it was a hellish trek, sometimes by rough sea, with poor transport links, all for a very small congregation, so it was hardly welcoming, beneficial, or even especially useful. Evangelising was hard work. For this aspect of Pamela's life, the very helpful Diocesan archivist Sister Benignus not only holds many beautiful church vestments in Exeter but also a folder full of correspondence from Miss Smith, as prolific at spurts of letter-writing as she seemed to be at everything else. The correspondence gave some clues into her later life change.

The English Catholic History Association offers further insight into why Pamela may have chosen Cornwall.[21] The revival of Catholicism in Cornwall in the nineteenth century onwards coincided with the arrival of the Canons Regular of the Lateran from France in 1881, due to anti-clerical legislation there; they were asked by the Bishop of Plymouth to remain in his diocese, and, based in Bodmin, to re-evangelise Cornwall, so this was not in any way incidental, rather a proactive Church mission to bring the faith to the far west. The Canons used to spread out during wartime to take Mass, and but also worked similarly before, for peripatetic priests were delivered to hear mass around The Lizard. They established many missions in Cornish towns, setting up what became permanent Catholic churches. If Pamela expressed a desire to help the church, to do something innovative and thereby make a difference, might a Cornish mission have been suggested, especially as she had the funds to make the move and buy a house with the space to start her quest?

Additionally, the Molesworth family (from the eastern shires, not Cornwall, but linked to Helston) played a significant role in this mid-nineteenth century faith expansion, becoming significant benefactors of churches in Penzance, Newquay, Liskeard, and Plymouth. If there was a big push on the 'true faith' in Cornwall, then Pamela's move to The Lizard begins to make good sense, especially if she wanted to make a difference, to be a part of the evangelisation, and to have an impact. From what is known of Pamela, she wanted to make her mark, a quality that persists in a person over time. She lived her life in the public eye. Having exhausted the fields she had trained in, the Church offered new opportunities to make a success of something and do something meaningful. Pamela was skilled at moving on and seizing opportunities. Additionally, the attraction of this property-ownership was a no brainer to the Catholic Church; she was a pious woman who came with good references and a house and chapel. Pamela's artistic career was waning, and her friends were fading fast as she adopted her new way of life, so inspired by religiosity. Life was cheaper in rural Cornwall than in London, given money was forever an issue for her.

Parc Garland on The Lizard peninsula in Cornwall was not in the more sheltered area around Helford but, for anyone who knows it, the desolate middle section down to Lizard Point. If the war had an impact, escaping from the city was welcomed. The Lizard (*An Lysardh* in Cornish), raw in its beauty and power, is surrounded by dramatic seascape, extremely rugged yet stunningly beautiful, with coves like Kynance (now under National Trust ownership) nearby, and the wild, savage, Church Cove with its seriously strong, dangerous, noisy seas even closer; it was (still is) very isolated, probably too isolated for most people to live there for too long, especially those moving from cities, even those utterly stricken by its desolate beauty.

Pamela used her inheritance to buy a house and two acres at The Lizard, an area known of artistic reputation due to the light quality, but where she devoted herself to religion, not art, bearing in mind she always painted in artificial light anyway. Seascapes and the natural world were not the subject of Pamela's painting and illustration. She had once been to Devon with the Yeats family but we know little of any time in Cornwall prior to her period at Parc Garland, apart from an earlier letter from Tintagel. The Celtic spirit of Cornwall was like a foreign land, cut off from mainland England. Of course, by the time Pamela arrived, so had the railway.

Pamela was rather lonely in London, despite her adopted outgoing persona. Her group of intimates enjoyed her amusing, childlike qualities and talents, yet she felt alone, different, and excluded. Her poem, 'Alone', if taken literally and at face value, certainly suggests this sense of dislocation from everyday life. She was well travelled but did not quite fit in and never settled, so perhaps she began a slow retreat from the world. People did not appreciate her, so she felt unrecognised. Kaplan says: 'For a time, art was an escape, a way for her to express herself, but it could not carry her into a happy life'.[22] Art could not carry her to a happy life, but religion perhaps could. It is not likely, based on her past, that she drifted down to Cornwall in some kind of despair, like some tragic heroine. Instead, it was very much a decision proactively made upon faith and action, as she quickly busied herself trying to create a place of worship, thereby creating service and purpose in her life, the stuff of spinsterhood.

This general low-level of satisfaction from people, her work, and her art partly explain her ongoing dissatisfaction with her life and a search for greater meaning, but also her decisiveness. Catholicism has a long history of tradition. A highly structured faith, it strongly differentiates between good and evil, offering less discretion on how people live their lives than other churches. Is it that large a leap from mysticism to Catholicism? Was Pamela ever truly mystic, anyway? Before her conversion, Pamela lived an unconventional life. Smallhythe was a sanctuary for creative people and those of varying sexualities. The place was tremendously woman-centred. To those within, it was like a cocoon from the rigours of society. The enveloping arms of Catholicism, although different, similarly swaddled its believers.

Her conversion is a crucial question about Pamela's life. What made other writers and artists of the day do the same? Also, what made Pamela's conversion different, making her turn her back on the others? The answer is belief. It seems Pamela actually believed in her faith rather than simply saw it as a new form of artistic endeavour, something to try out, an adventure. She may have been enticed by ritual and ceremony but she really seemed to take the whole religious conversion seriously, more so than many contemporaries. To Catholics, the sacraments were vitally important, whereas Protestants relied more on scripture, an importance she focused upon even during her London years.

David Ross suggests there was a wave of Catholicism in Ireland which may have affected W. B. Yeats, and thereby, Pamela.[23] The Ancient Order of the

Hibernians was a secret society, a ban on which was lifted in Ireland in 1904. Ross writes, 'it was a force to be reckoned with in the south, where it was closely related to a contemporary wave of triumphal Catholicism'.

Pamela and Arthur Waite also had some similarities. He was born in 1857 in Brooklyn, to which Pamela had strong family links. His father, a sea captain from Connecticut died, so his mother, Emma Lovell, returned home to England, where Arthur was raised, attending a Catholic boys' school. Waite was illegitimate (his father died at sea) and his mother never married. Resulting from the social ostracism, Emma was obliged to raise her children in very difficult and straitened circumstances. It was her family's rejection that led to her conversion to Catholicism in 1863, perhaps to find a wider family or support from a community. However, after the death of his sister, Frederika, in 1874, Waite began to lose his faith in Roman Catholicism, though he still enjoyed the ceremonial aspects and ritual. So, Waite was born Catholic and lapsed, while Pamela conversely embraced it as a convert.

In the last decade of the nineteenth century, a significant number of English writers converted. Part of the Decadent movement ('art for art's sake'), its many conversions included the poet John Gray, Aubrey Beardsley, and Oscar Wilde, who received the sacrament on his deathbed in 1900. Some converts were openly homosexual or had leanings, so how did they dovetail this with Catholicism? The answer seems again to have lain in ritual and asceticism rather than as an expression of living faith. Catholicism was believed eloquent and expressive. There was an escape from scepticism and a return to spiritual certainty. The artistic tradition was a source of inspiration, rather than a theology. A British Library article by Carolyn Burdett tells us: 'mainstream Victorian culture saw art and literature as a means of self-improvement or a spur to good works'.[24]

Faith was romanticised against a dreary backdrop of Victorian reality. The Church was highly respected yet also a hotbed of scandal, with many people converting late in life. It is questionable whether a sense of shame and sexual guilt played a part in their embracing of the faith, hedging their bets before death. John Gray, for example, was possibly Oscar Wilde's lover. He converted to Catholicism, endured a breakdown after his 'life of sin', and ultimately entered a seminary to train as a priest. Radclyffe Hall was another Catholic convert, whose 1928 lesbian novel is packed with Catholic imagery. Where to Protestants the word was important, to Catholics it was the ritual, imagery, and symbolism that made it accessible to all. Its celebratory beauty was a barricade against the ugliness of modernity, bearing in mind theatricality does not emulate nature, but oozes artifice.

The growth of scepticism and disbelief led to nostalgia for the sacred and for religious fervour. The attraction of the Decadents was not only to Catholicism but also to mysticism, the occult, esotericism, spiritualism, and even Satanism. Basically, science was too harsh and dry for these creatives. They wanted a sense of certainty and authority in a time of rationality and change. The continuity of the Catholic Church was comforting in a time of non-conformism and conflict within the Church of England. Catholicism was stable and unchanging, asserting the superiority of faith over reason. The cult of saints and the sacraments all served to produce a sense of mysticism. Realism and common sense were less attractive. In this spiritual utopia, the impossible becomes possible, the symbolism of the church linked to the search for the ideal. Today, if you enter a Catholic church, you are drawn to the symbolism and beauty in a form of escape from the dreary outside world. It evades mediocrity.

21

Her Cornish Exile

What attracted Pamela to Cornwall? She certainly spent much more of her life on her Catholic mission than she ever did on mysticism and possibly, just about, even her artistic career, so it is her hidden later years that are the most intriguing. Her life was dramatic, and would probably make good film material, being of the riches to rags variety. Her move to Cornwall was itself mysterious but additionally, no one knows why she left The Lizard (in 1939, staying a few years at Exeter) for Bude in 1942. Bude is the Cornish town nearest to the Devon border. It has always welcomed new people so she would not be the first or the last to settle in the beautiful seaside resort. She began her new life in Upton, near the cliffs with sea views, on the road out to Widemouth Bay—rather out of the way in the 1940s. She ended her days at what is now The Bencoolen Inn, nearer to town.

In Bude, Pamela lived a very quiet life, mainly because of failing health, though in 1946, in her late sixties, she made her last journey to the USA to visit New York artist Alphaeus Philemon Cole and his English wife, Peggy, who were close friends. There is no mention of Nora Lake accompanying her. The Coles had met in 1902 and married in 1903, so it is good to see Pamela retained contact many years later despite her life changes, given so many others had dropped from her life. They were originally frequent visitors to Pamela's open house parties and appeared regularly in her visitors' book.

They relocated to the United States in 1911, the year Pamela coincidentally converted to Catholicism. Her visit in 1946–7 was one of the occasions where she described Catholicism (exhorting Peggy to embrace it) as fun. Cole was born in 1876, son of the noted engraver, Timothy Cole, not too many years before Pamela. He lived to be an amazing 112, then the world's oldest verified living man. A portraitist and still-life painter, a friend of Whistler, and certainly no fan of modernism, he painted the popular trademark oil artwork of Pamela in 1906, dressed as Gelukiezanger, her storytelling stage name. She had dressed the part, with braided hair scarf and gypsy style clothing—a far cry from how she dressed in Cornwall.

Most information about Pamela's Cornwall years comes from Plymouth Diocesan archives. Archivist Sister Benignus summarised from documents held at the archives:

> The original owner of the Little Chapel at The Lizard (Our Lady of The Lizard) was Madame Victorine Roberts, who for many years kept an open Chapel, and employed the *Abbé* Edward L. Julién. It would appear that this Little Chapel was a rented converted small building owned by a 'Landlord Hill'. Madame Roberts had financial concerns in France and was obliged to return. In August 1919 she wrote to the then Bishop of Plymouth (Bishop Vaughan) to ask if Miss Colman Smith could look after the Mission of Our Lady of The Lizard and to transfer it into her own freehold property. It would appear that the offer to maintain a Chapel in the garden of a newly acquired property was accepted by the Bishop. Miss Colman Smith wrote that she would not transfer the Altar and other furniture until the deeds of the Freehold of land were signed.
>
> In November 1920 Rev B. Wade (from Penzance) reported to the Bishop that the new set up was suitable for the celebration of the Sacraments, and all was in good order and would hold 30/40 people. Miss Smith mentions, in her communication, an elderly priest from Scotland, Monsignor Barns, who would minister there. She now reports that there are 31 Catholics in attendance.
>
> By 1922, they seem to be having difficulties. Priests in attendance were irregular. Buckfast Priests could no longer attend as they were owed money which was not forthcoming. By 1926, letters of complaint were reaching the Bishop from parishioners about the unsatisfactory state of affairs. Many of the Catholics were now instead attending the Church at Mullion.
>
> In a letter to the Bishop in October 1926, Miss Colman Smith complains of the dire financial straits in Church funds. She is unable to pay the priest as the collection is only meeting the cost of Church supplies and heating. The number of regular Catholics is now down to 21, and Mullion gets all the visitors as well as regulars, consequently the gifts and donations. She asks the Bishop for advice on what to do. As there is no record of the Bishop's reply we can only assume that it is about this time that she decided to leave Parc Garland as the next document is a letter from Miss Balfour to her mother from the same address, Parc Garland, in September 1927. She is writing about similar difficulties. It appears that she (Miss Balfour) owned the property containing the Chapel at Mullion, for in 1931 she transferred it to the ownership of the Diocese.
>
> You will see that Pamela Colman Smith (sacristan) did not run a retreat centre for Priests, but made an attempt at continuing the Mission/parish that was begun by Madame Roberts.[1]

This is crucially important. Pamela was not running a holiday home; it was not just a job. She was on a mission. The most southerly part of Cornwall including

The Lizard Peninsula had no Catholic church until the 1920s. In 1925, a tiny church built on private ground owned by a parishioner was built at Mullion. In January 1925, the mass was celebrated at Kenabos, the home of Miss M. Balfour. There are photographs of Father Dobbeleers and Miss Balfour on the btsarnia website.[2]

Kaplan suggests various aspects were at play in Pamela's move.[3] She was misunderstood, perceived as simple, perhaps even primitive. She appeared to lack business sense and cynicism (her childlike nature is often mentioned) so she was taken advantage of (certainly payments for her work were slow and small). Furthermore, her gender and her exotic features may have compounded discrimination. During that time, she became lifelong friends with Nora Lake, with whom she later moved to Bude. Alice, the sister of Nora, wrote during the Second World War of Pamela's care of her sister at that time, calling 'Miss Pamela ... an administering angel' for nursing her from 'the shock'. 'Miss Pamela' is formal, an old-fashioned English way of addressing an employer. The letter sent in February 1942, also enclosed sleeping tablets for Nora. Did she lose her husband during the war? Maybe this explains why they moved to Bude.

Pamela was for a time the sacristan for Our Lady of The Lizard Church. It began regular services in February 1919, after being moved from the other end of the village to her stone building at Parc Garland. Such was the strength of anti-Catholic feeling in Cornwall, that on 5 March 1921, a petition was brought against the building stating the pictures of the Madonna and crucifixes Pamela painted outside, presumably promoting her chapel, were an eyesore. This was despite the fact Parc Garland was then relatively isolated. There were growing problems fitting in with those around her, which was not too surprisingly in a Methodist area, as while Catholics used crucifixion imagery to represent the healing from Christ's suffering and death on the cross, Methodists used a much plainer cross to symbolise the power of resurrection and overcoming death. The chapel eventually fully closed in 1943.

During 1927, we know she did not sell any art at all. Additionally, Ellen Terry died in 1928. Pamela wrote to Edith Craig describing her straitened financial circumstances and her social isolation. No one appears to have rushed to her aid as Pamela, while still a friend, was distant. In 1934, Pamela was still at Parc Garland but her health was poor, with developing heart problems. On 15 February 1939, Alice Lake, expressed sorrow for her 'feeling so poorly with your heart'. She was ill for some time as she did not die until 1951. If Pamela and Nora were ill, this may explain their move to Exeter where Nora had family. In 1942, however, she moved with Nora Lake to Gorseland, Upton Cliff, Bude, perhaps to start afresh after the loss of Nora's husband. In a probate notice, a Nora Lake lived in Heavitree, Exeter. Dying on 23 May 1962, at Swinton Nursing Home, she left her effects of £823 19*s* 9*d* to Alice Sandford (wife of Wilfred Potter Sandford). Was this the same Nora Lake? Little is known about

Pamela's companion but it is likely after Pamela's death, left with nothing, she moved back to be with her sister. What became of her son, Freddie?

Gorseland was situated on the cliff edge on the road from Bude to Widemouth, with wonderful views but undulating, even hilly. Pamela later moved from here to Bencoolen near the Strand, closer to the town and flatter. Pamela was in poor health, overweight judging by earlier photos, though we are not sure by how much; her heart condition deteriorated. Her errand boy, Tony, noted she suffered with her chest. In the last years of her life, she was ill and at times bedbound, yet not without good humour. Bude was a strange place for Pamela to end her days, but no one is sure of the reason behind her move to Upton. We know of Pamela's financial problems on The Lizard where the rumour is that an unscrupulous employee syphoned off her money, but there was a large gap between her raising concerns with the Bishop and finally leaving Parc Garland. However, she had sunk her money into buying her home so perhaps had little alternative than to stay there.

What inspired her to turn her attention to The Lizard in Cornwall if not mission? It was not the quality of the light, which brought many artists to West Cornwall, as she preferred artificial light. The Lizard, even now, is a wild, desolate, and beautiful place that cut off and very isolated. Transport was difficult there; parts are relatively inaccessible even today by car. The population is scattered and limited, still predominantly non-conformist. Trying to create a Catholic mission was a real job in such circumstances, as there was a deep suspicion, but there were also deeply practical issues, especially given the distances priests would need to travel and the cost of accommodating them. A trip to The Lizard would have been low priority for any peripatetic priest, given its location and the small congregation, so Pamela's enthusiasm, fervour, or even zeal was naïve. The bishop suggests she was not sympathetic to the issues suffered by often elderly and unwell priests, so the mission became an unattractive place for them to attend. Nonetheless, Pamela appears to have been a devoted convert and remained Catholic until her death. She obviously felt it to be the true faith, advantageous, and presumably wanted to spread the word. Was this to encourage ministrations to others or simply to ensure she could participate in Mass?

The books suggest Pamela was childlike in many ways; certainly, she seemed to wear her heart very much on her sleeve in her communications with the Bishop of Plymouth. Pam could talk her way into most things, but here she bit off more than she could manage; her letters sounded whiny and complaining. She was at a loss to know how to cope when things did not go to her plan, a little lost and inept when being herself and not playing a role. Getting things right was of utmost importance to her.

It is easy to see how what looked initially an attractive proposition to the Diocese turned into a veritable nightmare. Pamela lacked business acumen, but also the Gelukiezanger confidence she once had was no longer in evidence. In the early Cornwall years, she was uncertain and lacking initiative, which was not the Pamela of her youth. This was all new to her—confusing. She ran tiny details past the bishop and struggled to understand his lack of support and interest in the day to day struggle. From his few responses, we see the bishop attributes neurosis (stress, hypochondria, anxiety, and obsessiveness) to Miss Smith. This was a common male response at the time to women who could not be controlled, but it emphasises the interactive difficulties between the two, and to be fair, her letters were taxing.

Parc Garland was very much out on a limb, though it is now surrounded by much more modern housing. With its hotels and harbour, Mullion is a much more attractive proposition, both for holidaymakers and locals. It is hard to imagine many tourists going the way of Parc Garland at Cross Common, as most would head to the coast, the cliffs, and the harbours—the places with tourist attractions and hotels rather than the raw, untamed hamlet of Church Cove. Pamela, whose artistic skills lay in illustration rather than tourist souvenirs, also seemed surprised few tourists bought her artwork or, indeed, added money to the collections, but she was in the wrong location.

So, how did Catholicism gain a foothold on The Lizard in the first place? Sister Benignus was, of course, right. A John Roberts married a French lady from Lyons, who lived on The Lizard. Madame Roberts, a devoted Catholic, needed priestly ministrations but Camborne was her nearest access, or Falmouth or Penzance, all quite a distance, and even so, not on Sundays. In 1899, she therefore employed *Abbé* Edward Julien who resided at Beacon House from 18 June to 4 November 1900, saying Mass at a coastguard cottage and photographic studio. At her invitation, Bishop Graham visited Maenheare in 1900 and on 7 June had morning and evening services in the little chapel, where he confirmed three people and blessed a statue, Our Lady of the Wave. It had begun.

22

The Catholic Correspondence

Once again, we rely on primary sources—namely, letters—to give a taste of her life in Cornwall. Throughout this chapter are extracts from letters held by the Plymouth diocese.[1]

On 5 September 1919, *Monseigneur* Henry O'Brien, of the Church of the Holy Apostles, at Claverton Street in Pimlico, expressed his high opinion of Pamela:

> Miss Coleman Smith, an old friend and penitent of mine is, as you know, buying a house at The Lizard and I believe undertaking the welfare of the mission there.[2] I must congratulate your Lordship in having her in your Diocese, because what she undertakes to do will be done. I am very sorry to lose her because she has been a staunch and faithful friend for many years ...[3]

In 1919, Pamela's handwriting is far neater and less agitated than in her later letters, perhaps indicating a calmer state of mind. Her letter written on 29 August from Kynance Cove, explains:

> I have recently bought a house here at The Lizard and shall be moving into it shortly. I am a Catholic and would very much like to help the mission here. Madame Roberts, who used to support and look after the chapel at The Lizard, has now returned to France.
>
> She is willing that I should take over and look after all the furniture, etc., of the chapel and move it to a building in the garden of my own house (the building has stone walls and floor, slate roof and walls and roof lined with wood).
>
> If you will grant me permission to do this and re-erect the stations of the cross.
>
> If it is desirable to move the things, as the present building is in a very bad state of repair and very damp. The building in my garden is convenient for such use until a permanent chapel can be built, which I hope one day to be able to do. As I am buying the freehold, the chapel will be safe from interference.

> I am aware that there have hitherto been difficulties in the way of the suitable conduct of the chapel, but it would be my care to improve this for the future. If your Lordship would give me permission to have the chapel in my garden as I wish, and to act as sacristan myself, I would see that the necessary expense was borne locally.
>
> I have been taking care of the chapel for the last 5 weeks, and there have been four masses daily ... I feel sure that if the chapel were cared for that more Catholics would come to the district.
>
> I have lived near the cathedral at Westminster for seven years and am a member of the Confraternity of the Blessed Sacrament (a prayer group raising funds for the enhancement of sacramental vessels) and a Child of Mary.[4]

The Confraternity of the Blessed Sacrament was founded in 1862, part of the Catholic Revival, a brotherhood of men and women praying and working for a greater devotion to Jesus in the Eucharist and in the Sacrament of his Body and Blood, so very much a missionary movement. Pamela was heavily involved in the Catholic Church in London before moving to Cornwall, living a useful life as an efficient church helper, hence her reference. She offered her services. She also promised the bishop to bear the expenses locally so we can see the attraction of her proposal, plus her conviction that the idea would work, rather like many of her previous ideas.

On 15 September 1919, we see Pamela's attention to detail and her desire to get things right; she is trying her hardest to succeed. Pamela wrote:

> I have been in London moving my furniture from my flat there to the house at The Lizard.
>
> I shall not move the church furniture, altar, etc., until the deeds of the freehold of land are signed which may be a few weeks yet. When setting up the white marble altar again, I will fit on it a new steel safe tabernacle which The Art & Book Co have just arranged for me. It has a wooden roof to fit on top with a ball and cross on as I believe, according to the new canon law, the crucifix must not be standing on top of the tabernacle but on a shelf over it.
>
> The steel safe has a silver plate on the door and I wish to know if it is necessary to have a veil to cover it or if a veil over the top and sides (as I have seen in the Diocese of Clifton) is sufficient.
>
> I had a letter yesterday from Canon Burns of Falmouth who said he was coming to The Lizard by boat yesterday but the weather was so rough that the boat did not come.
>
> ... I do not wish to trouble you with all these details but thank you greatly for the interest that you have taken in my poor endeavours to make this mission a worthy resting place for Our Lord.[5]

All is still looking good by 1920 in this report of the Dean:

> Everything is in fine order. Miss Smith is hoping for the restoration of a priest. She has a fine house and the prospect the freehold will come later on. The chapel will hold 30 or 40 to hear mass. Miss Smith talks of building a stone church, putting the place safe in the hands of her Catholic relatives (unsure who these were). I think it will end the troubles on The Lizard for many years to come. She talks of a friend, an old priest, who wants to come to Cornwall.[6]

On 1 November 1920: 'There are now 31 Catholics in The Lizard and neighbourhood—all residents—and I am glad to be able to tell you that … there have been over 200 masses said at The Lizard since last February'. These were halcyon days.

By 28 February 1922, in a letter to the Bishop of Plymouth, we see Pamela's problems have started:

> My Lord,
>
> Thank you so much for your letter of the 27th inst.
>
> So far, I have only seen one member of the congregation since receiving your letter this noon …
>
> We have had Mass here for four Sundays. The Abbot of Buckfast suddenly wrote and said he could not send a supply again till we paid up what we owed Buckfast. His letter came just after you sent me the £15, so I sent £7 at once to him, as we were overdrawn at the bank (church account) we could not pay him more then, so we still owe Buckfast £7.3.0
>
> I have got in another £3.10.0 since then from the circulars and hope some more will come soon …
>
> If Father Sotherden could come for a week or so and see how he likes The Lizard and the possibilities, I will not be able to lodge him in this house, but one of the congregation—an elderly widow—has a house just across the road and may be able to do so.
>
> The congregation will have to help to support him. This is possible with a resident priest. No one took much interest in the weekend supplies, and the Buckfast Fathers were unwilling to ask the congregation for funds.
>
> I have done all I could and am sorry that I am not able to help in financial matters, but as I have had to keep the Buckfast Fathers always—since last March, 21 times, for weekends and twice a week, I think the other members of the congregation should now take their share.[7]

So, Pamela offered some grudging hospitality to visiting priests but not to convalescing ones. By now, she is growing tired of the demands on her purse, but there is also a weariness with the ebbing and flowing of non-resident priests.

I beg to enclose items of income and expenditure since September 1921 …

It would be splendid to have a priest all the time, and I am sure would gather more people. We have felt very cut off with no Mass for so long. I am sure Our Lady will find a way—and perhaps Father Sotherden is the very one for here …[8]

The Plymouth Diocesan Record of 1923 mentions that near Lizard Light exists a chapel in an 'out of the world spot, not much known except to summer holiday folk'. It adds generally there are some thinly scattered Catholics as far up as Helston and adds 'communications on Sunday are impossible and there are no resources for a resident priest'. She persisted on 21 October 1926:

My Lord,

Enclosed you will find receipts for candles, oil, and the car from Mullion for Father Dobbeleers up to the end of September … £2 went to Buckfast Abbey for supply in June, 1925. This is all out of the £25 you kindly sent on June 1st, 1926.

Father Dobbeleers came today and demanded £10 of the collections money for his supplies (26 times). I urged him before he began to come every Sunday to wait until I got some funds with which to pay him, and also wrote to him to this effect on April 23rd, 1926. On April 24th, he sent me a telegram: 'Saying Mass on Sunday at Lizard. Bishop's orders'.

Of course, I thought everything was getting on quite comfortably and he seemed pleased to come. The congregations have been quite good. There are 24 people at Lizard and Cadgwith who come here to Mass.

Father Dobbeleers now refuses to come until he is paid the £10. I have given him breakfast each time and also the lad who comes with him to serve. Also, the last two times, the man who drives him, as well. He has done 3 or 4 Holy Souls masses from offerings in the box.

I should love to be able to pay him each week as I need to pay the supply but I have explained to you before that I have not the means now to do so; and lately my difficulties have been greater than ever.

Mullion now gets the gifts and donations from those who stay at the hotels there, when they used to come here to Mass and give it to Our Lady of The Lizard.

During the summer, a young woman staying at Lizard was asked by Father Dobbeleers to collect from visitors at Lizard for the Mullion mission and he asked her not to let me know.

But she was so troubled about it (she was an invalid and I had tried to be kind to her) she felt she must tell me about it before leaving, as she thought it so wrong when this little church—which they all seem to like—was in need.

> I have a copy of the letter to Father Dobbeleers of April 23rd, and the details of collections (roughly £12) and numbers of congregations if you wish to see them. As you know, in the winter there is nothing to carry on with, and the little place has to be kept warm and clean—washing and repairs (come) from the collections of the summer.
>
> As you know, I always come to you when there is any trouble. Please will you tell me what I am to do.
>
> Yours sincerely and obediently ...
>
> PS: I do want the congregation to hold together as they have been doing since he came. There is a baptism waiting for Sunday.[9]

Pamela struggled with Cornish seasonality, the source of most Catholics being visitors, but especially once the chapel at Mullion, 5 miles away, opened, competing for congregation and funds. She also struggled immensely with Father Dobbeleers.

In a letter dated 6 October 1927, sent to Madame Roberts, the Bishop of Plymouth explained:

> Of course, I have tried, and with very slender means, to keep the number of places, but I have had a good deal of trial about The Lizard.
>
> Ever since the chapel at Mullion has been opened, Miss Smith's position has greatly changed her. I am only saying my conviction. Miss Balfour managed to get an invalid priest who does all he can but Miss Smith has not been too pleased with his help or too considerate when he is not well enough.
>
> The whole position is rather irregular—and more I shall not do because I cannot.
>
> Many of The Lizard congregations have no business to be there and a bishop in my state cannot afford to supply them with funding ... if they go where there is none.[10]

He describes a letter received from Pamela that explained her 'neurosis which explains much'.

Exhausting the Bishop, in 1927, Pamela wrote to her 'aunt-mother' and Nellie for advice, where we sense her growing levels of desperation with her situation. Would they be interested in such detail?

> Three Saturdays ago, the priest at Mullion wrote to say do not expect me on Sunday—not well. I did not get it until 11am on the Saturday morning, so had to go to the post office to send a telegram to the Bishop to ask for a supply. By 2.30, I had a reply: sorry, no time to arrange.
>
> In the week following, a postcard came from the Bishop: quite impossible to supply from here.

Then, I had to telephone Cadgwith and send postcards to all the congregation. There would be no Mass on Sunday. Congregation = 39.

The next week, I wrote to ask Father D to let me know in good time if he was coming on Sunday. I heard back on the Friday: I will let you know in good time when I am well enough to come. So, then I telegraphed the priest at Bodmin who replied 'yes' for supply on Sunday.

So, then had to let all the congregation know there would be a Mass! On the Sat evening bus, a Spanish priest arrived (1 of 3 extra ones they have at Bodmin learning English). Congregation = 29. Holy Communion = 4, Benediction = 16, Monday Mass at 8.30 = 4, Congregation = 9

Cost 12/6 expenses train and bus. 17/- lodging and has to pay priory.

Then no Mass, had to let a lot of people know. [Poor Pamela.]

One visitor on The Lizard turned up.

2 lots of people from Kugger (near Helston)

You would be surprised at the number of people who came to visit the church this summer, but when I opened the boxes only £1 and 1 penny in all.

Now that Mullion is established, it seems quite hopeless to go on here. What do you think? It is possible that I can sell this house and find or build a bungalow in or near Penzance - or in that direction - and move the church and call it Our Lady of The Lizard of Lyonnesse. You know that Lyonnesse is the lost land now covered by the sea at Monts Bay.[11]

Even now Pamela is keen to have a church involvement, a mission, but is aware that the success and proximity of Mullion makes a church at Parc Garland a non-starter. Her life in London is well and truly over, while life on The Lizard is also not working, so what next for Pamela?

She signs off: 'you're in my thoughts all the time!! Hugs and best love'.

Why on earth she thought they could help or would have much interest in all that detail is curious. It is almost as if she wanted someone to make her decision for her. Once again, Pamela writes self-obsessively.

Pamela obviously knew the myth of Lyonnesse, a beautiful stretch of bay from West Cornwall (St Michael's Mount) to the Scilly Isles, stuff of legend. It was said to have 140 churches and a beautiful cathedral but was lost one terrible night when it was swallowed by the ocean during a dreadful storm. If you listen carefully, you can hear the church bells in the sea, off the Cornwall coast. Only one man escaped: Trevelyan; he rode his white horse furiously before the waves and managed to reach the higher ground at Land's End. It is a myth of Arthurian standards, Britain's very own Atlantis, which may have been created by fishermen who saw submerged bronze age settlements between Cornwall and Scilly. Lyonnesse is mentioned in Thomas Mallory's *Morte d'Arthur,* allegedly the place of King Arthur's demise.

So, Pamela had plans to move on. She added, indicating she was still drawing and painting:

> If I could get sale from my work—and some capital to work with—all would be well but things seem to get worse instead of better. Do please think of something, suggest something. I write to you distracted, Corinne.
>
> Mrs Lake is sure you will make a good suggestion. She is still in bed and sends greetings.[12]

Nora, a married or widowed woman, also seemed to be ill. By now, Pamela was calling herself Corinne.

By 1929, there were numerous complaints that the Catholic community on The Lizard was neglected, with masses only occurring on 1 January, 31 March (Easter), and 19 May rather than every Sunday, but her troubles had started well before. Meanwhile, in 1927, Miss Balfour of the Mullion Chapel also had her problems. She seemed to have malicious talk against her spread by a Mrs Emery. Miss Balfour supported over fifty priests, with the same objective as Pamela of building the faith on The Lizard, but some suspected more alarming motives, for there was nastiness among the women of the area, questioning her activities in housing priests. It is uncertain what, if anything, Pamela had to do with this, but certainly there was rivalry for congregations.

Miss Balfour was described in a letter to the Bishop of Plymouth by Father Dobbeleers:

> Well over 50! and when that age is attained it might be considered a suitable age and a good work to help a poor priest in the right way…. Her one object is to build the faith in this place … I know there has been wicked talk about her started by an evil woman and so-called Catholic, Mrs Emery.[13]

Catholics remained unpopular it seems:

> All last summer, Miss Balfour had to put up with most insulting things that were said by that woman. This all in spite and jealousy when she turned upon Miss Balfour who would not be guarantor for some money Mrs Emery wanted.
>
> There is no poisonous talk in the village except what Mrs Emery tried to make without success! The curate of the Church of England speaks to me sometimes. He comes from Jersey (where Mrs Emery has lived before) and his friends there told him last summer that she is the most dangerous and evil woman. Have nothing to do with her, she does mischief wherever she goes.[14]

The same curate talking of the wicked agitation of Mrs Emery told Miss Balfour: 'don't worry, no one would ever think wrong of you in this place'. He added:

'She (Mrs Emery) is at all cost trying to get Miss Balfour out of Mullion and she wants to have her place there and look after the priest'. The suggestion was that Mrs Emery had debts and could not get credit so wanted to be paid to look after the priest, seeing it as a form of income. 'However ... no one would give the support that Miss Balfour has so generously and selflessly'. For a small village, the scale of petty gossip and spite among the women, the dislike of Catholicism and the competition and petty politics was ridiculous; nor could two chapels be sustained.

By 1931, the Bishop replied to a letter from Tozer, Dell & Edwards solicitors in Teignmouth, informing of Miss Balfour of Mullion's wish to transfer the chapel at Mullion and her own property to the diocese subject to her retaining a life interest in the house. Presumably, she had endured enough.

The original Catholic Chapel dedicated to Our Lady of The Lizard contained a beautiful figure with flowers most of the year. The statue, erected with extreme care, was brought over from France, for those wrecked off The Lizard. This is what Pamela tried to grow and enhance. Since her conversion to the Roman Catholic Church in 1911, she remained very active in all the devotions and activities the Catholic Church had to offer, including daily Mass. Not many Catholics build their own chapels and provide occasional free lodging for priests, simply to provide for someone qualified to offer a daily Latin Mass. Of course, with all the other activities within the Church, variety of devotions, rituals, Rosary recitations, and daily Latin Mass (when it happened) she kept herself active. Pamela must have been a very busy, satisfied, and happy individual given the spiritual fulfilment she obtained through her daily activities as a Catholic. Whatever she lost in the art world, she evidently found in the Catholic Church. She may also have been tempted by the landscape, the solitude, and the idea of converting people in this wild and isolated area to the true faith. Pamela was not known for taking easy options.

Most books and articles understandably focus on Pamela's tarot years—her artistic, creative time—but her time in Cornwall was a vital part of her life, which she actively chose. While it did not have the outcome she planned, she sought something more comforting and rewarding than she found in theatrical and artistic circles. Sometime after creating the tarot deck, and sometime after writing to Stieglitz about money (when she lived at York Mansions, Battersea), Pamela made a major life decision: to convert to Catholicism with compunction. Additionally, she approached Catholicism thoroughly, reading the books and developing insight and understanding of its complex principles and rituals, something she never did in the Golden Dawn. She did not marry a Catholic or fall into it because of some family connection. It was sheer agency, personal choice; therefore, it is important to consider what created this choice, and why she died still a Catholic in 1951 if it had made her as miserable as some suggest. Apart from the later practicalities of securing priests and money in the middle of nowhere on The Lizard, there are no indications her faith yielded anything negative.

To become a Catholic, there are many processes that tell us it is not easy, not something taken lightly. First, comes an internal spiritual discussion. Pamela needed to ask herself: Do you believe in God? Do you believe in the Holy Trinity? Do you believe in Jesus as the Messiah? Do you believe in transubstantiation (a big sticking point for many)? Do you pray? Have you read the Bible? What's the catechism? Have you spoken with a priest? Do you have a local church? Have you been to Mass? That was just the start. Then came the process of initiation, which takes time, commitment, and readiness to learn. Pamela did not find learning such specifics easy but she did it. This was not a minor shift in belief for Pamela, nor was it short-lived. She spent forty years as a Catholic. Perhaps she had too many moments when she realised the world seemed to be based on false premises. There are many examples of Pamela finding people unintelligent or unaware—too superficial. She sought meaning and authenticity.

Noted for its strong Methodism and non-conformism, Cornwall was not welcoming for someone on a mission, and a woman at that. Bear in mind women were still trying to get the vote when Pamela moved to Cornwall. They were still not taken seriously in art or in life. Trying to create a Catholic mission was a real job in such circumstances, especially given the distances priests would need to travel and the cost of accommodating them. A trip to The Lizard was not a high priority for any peripatetic priest, given its location and small congregation, so Pamela's enthusiasm was zealous, but also tenacious. Did she feel this was her calling?

People suggest Pamela was naïve. Her confidence had also taken a severe knock. What had happened to the actress, storyteller, and artist touting her trade? The isolation of her mission surely did not help. She had little local support, so running every tiny detail past the bishop, while complaining about priests, much to his irritation, showed how she struggled to understand the pragmatism of the situation.

Sadly, Parc Garland, situated in an Area of Outstanding Natural Beauty, which once had totally open and undeveloped land with views around it, has since been surrounded by eight newer buildings. The house was originally built by a German doctor around 1900, used as a single dwelling, though later as bed and breakfast accommodation (this may be where the priests' holiday accommodation idea stems from). Cornwall Council planning records state there was a change of use to the building in 1966, when it became a guest house and café. By 1971, holiday bungalows were added, and an outbuilding was converted to flats. The building was not listed nor considered by planners to be of particularly high architectural merit but certainly has a presence. It has two storeys and a loft, plus a downhill garden making the house appear more prominent. It also has eight bedrooms, one bathroom, and four reception rooms, which may also be where the priests' retreat idea came from. Parc

Garland, which was (in its time) Britain's most southerly Catholic chapel, sold on 1 October 2007 for £750,000 and was purchased for £400,000 in 2018. In its heyday, it would have had unparalleled views towards Lizard Point. Owner, Hayley White says the views from the attic are still 180-degree panoramic.

The Plymouth Diocesan Record dated May 1933, written by Irene Herniman, describes a beautiful spring day at The Lizard, but winter was very different:

> The cliff walk a mosaic of pink thrift, blue scillas and yellow trefoil and a blue sea lazily lapping the gaunt black rocks. Yet even a superficial glance to sea can detect the long line of rocks, some only showing a wicked tooth along the breakers, others rearing up like sharks waiting for their prey ...
>
> When the wind is in the east no boat can pass Lizard head; in a great storm eighteen months ago, between 80 and 90 boats took shelter in Mullion harbour. It was a Saturday evening, provisions ran short in the little village, the baker had to bake a fresh batch of bread, the butcher scoured the neighbourhood for meat, his own stock having rapidly sold out. And strange though it may seem to those who known [*sic.*] not the Cornish coast, a dense mist descended over the bay, wrapping the fleet of fishing boats and trawlers in a wet blanket ...[15]

Mullion, with its hotels and harbour, even now is a much more attractive proposition, both for holidaymakers and locals. The modern phrase 'location, location, location' comes to mind, for Parc Garland was not in the most attractive tourist spot, though a perfectly good living space. On 25 August 1939, Pamela, listed as a spinster of Parc Garland, assigned the lease of the house and land at Landewednack to Edward William James and his wife, Amelia Mary James, of 309 Romford Road, Forest Gate, Essex. Parc Garland, says the document at Cornwall Record Office, was formerly known as Cross Common House and before that Caerthillian House, together with land and buildings, built on land formerly part of the glebe land, at The Lizard, Landewednack.[16] The term was residue of ninety-nine years, the consideration £1,000. So far as the bishop was concerned, herein probably lay the rub. He was offered an opportunity to spread the faith, whose cost would not be his problem. Sadly, this was not the case.

Curiously, in 1928, Pamela (a Corinne Smith) is listed as a passenger on the White Star Line, Olympia, to New York, departing from Southampton. Her address is given as Claridges Hotel, and her age as fifty. Her occupation is written 'nil'. In addition to Pamela, a Joseph Smith is listed, aged sixty-two, professional artist, who was also staying at the Claridges Hotel. Did they know each other? Were they related? It is hard to tell but Pamela in the register is listed as ditto, which may just be an abbreviation by the list compiler. So, in 1928, Pamela, if this is her, went to New York, perhaps to try to release more funds. However, her ticket number A41789 is listed as the same as Joseph's. She certainly was not exhibiting art. More importantly, who was Joseph?

Was it her faith that led to Pamela's later life obscurity? It would not have helped but it is her direction of a jobbing career illustrator that led Pamela there. Her output was immense but she largely seemed to draw to order, to live, and to make money. Although it is a creative role, it is not the kind of original artwork that leads to posterity. Rather in the way that journalistic writing rarely leads to lasting fame, compared to, for example, novel writing, the work of a jobbing artist was pretty much that—work.

Shortly after the First World War, Pamela's paternal uncle, Theodore, gave her a sizeable legacy with which she purchased the lease of Parc Garland on The Lizard for use as her permanent home. This came after many years of renting. It was an impressively large dwelling for a single lady so, presumably, she had something in mind, buying it for a purpose. She surely had a plan, which probably started the erroneous idea of her running a rest home for priests. She certainly continued a Catholic mission that had previously been established for her faith was obviously vitally important to her.

Of course, although far from London, Parc Garland was not as isolated as we think. It was relatively close to train links to London if needed. The house interior from photographs showed a rather lovely, spacious, light, and characterful period abode, in need of renovation but certainly of its time, with original stone flags in the kitchen, and fireplaces and decor ahead of its time. The house comprised of a 28-foot inner hallway; 23-foot kitchen and breakfast room with Rayburn; 25-foot dining room; three further reception rooms, all with open fires; three bedrooms on the first floor; and an inner landing containing five further bedrooms, many with coastal views. It would have been a beautiful, albeit at times bleak, place to live, and way too large for Pamela to manage entirely on her own, which is where Nora Lake and her husband came in.

Boyd Parsons suggested she moved to Cornwall because she wanted to be as close as she could to America without being on the continent itself; there is credibility in moving to feel closer to her roots.[5] The west of Cornwall was renowned for art, though Newlyn, Lamorna, and St Ives were much more notable than The Lizard itself. Newlyn, for example, was artistically active from the 1880s until the early twentieth century, the '*en plein air*' painting taking advantage of the light. The Lamorna Colony was a post-impressionist offshoot of the Newlyn art scene. Of course, the areas are still reputable today, and the Newlyn School of Art continues. How involved in any of this Pamela would have been is not known but the transport alone would not have been easy. Considering her temperament and the extent of her previous involvement with the art world, however, it seems unlikely she would have severed all connections with art. In all probability, she continued until her death to paint, draw, and work with her toy theatre, both for her own pleasure and for the enjoyment of her circle of friends. This makes some sense, just as a writer never totally stops writing, an artist will continue to draw and paint.

Mr F. Judd, who was town clerk on The Lizard in the 1970s, had, according to Boyd Parsons, heard Pamela was misanthropic and eccentric, and he did not know of any artistic activity on her part, but obviously, he had never met her.[17] This may have stemmed from some of her correspondence with the church at this time. John Garth, a Tolkien researcher, found further background to the Chapel.[18] In 1895, according to the *Royal Cornwall Gazette*, John Roberts, a London lace merchant and manufacturer, and originally a Cornish man, married a Mademoiselle Jodet at Lyon, France, and had returned to his native Lizard with her, to his Maenheere mansion, where she lit a 'monster bonfire' on Lizard Common. According to the OS map Mr Garth also uncovered, Maenheere was a stone's throw from Cross Common, where Pamela moved to Parc Garland. By 1900, the newspaper suggests John Roberts had presented the town with 'handsome fluted cast iron lamp-posts', the first stationed near the Roman Catholic Chapel at the junction of the Penminner cross common roads. By 1901, it seemed the priest in charge at The Lizard was the Rev Charles Julien, who facilitated the performance of a ceremony of the Sacrament of Confirmation at Our Lady of The Lizard by Bishop Graham of Plymouth. He confirmed the Roberts' daughter, Nellie, and others, with Madame Victorine Roberts acting as godmother, followed by a celebration at Maenheere.

By 1904, John Roberts was dead, bequeathing property valued at £3,145, ten guineas each to his male employees of ten years' service, and five guineas to those whose service was of shorter duration. To his wife, Sophie Victorine Roberts, he left a life interest in the use and enjoyment of his house at The Lizard, plus all its effects, but ultimately, this passed to his sons, John Henry Edgar, William and Alfred Roberts. His London property's furniture and effects he left to his sons and his daughter, Kathleen Ellen (Nellie), with his sons having options on purchasing the house and his business. An annuity was to be paid to his wife. Victorine died in Lyon, as a widow, on 4 March 1930.

So, where does the church come in? Well, a local newspaper celebrated the opening of a Roman Catholic Chapel at The Lizard in July 1899.[19] Meanwhile, *The Tablet*, in 1906, promoted The Lizard as a holiday resort of some charm and quietness (though bracing), explaining a small Catholic chapel was open during July, August, and September. It mentioned a devoted benefactress, which was before Pamela's time so probably related to Victorine Roberts. The statue was devoted to wrecks off Lizard head, with an exhortation that Cornish folk should be returned to the Faith that was once theirs.

In 1999, the Sylvanus Trevail (by whom Maenheere was built) Society newsletter mentioned the former Maenheere, explaining how it (now a hotel) faced due south out to sea with a 180-degree view with light flooding in and lawns sloping towards the cliffs.

After John Roberts' death, the house passed to his sister-in-law and then her daughter, Miss Wallis. The chapel remained with a statue of Our Lady of The Lizard shipped in from France, in blue and red, covered in flowers.

23
Testing Times

Pamela's life on The Lizard was much more difficult than we can imagine. The splendid isolation of this beautiful but incredibly remote place would eventually affect anyone, especially someone used to attention and an audience. Money worries were rife from almost the offset, and her grand scheme hit some serious hiccups and opposition.

Helston and The Lizard had not had a Catholic Church until the 1920s, when it offered, in 1925, a tiny church built on private ground by a 'local' parishioner, Miss Balfour. This rather put paid to Pamela's plans for a facility at Parc Garland, which was away from the village. Mullion was and still is a large village, an important centre for the community, services and amenities. It is a hub, unlike Parc Garland's area, Landewednack.

Pamela certainly grew distracted on The Lizard. She obviously struggled to know what to do and from where the money would come to do it. She considered moving, but only towards Penzance, not to east Cornwall. Whether she was later moved to Bude to be as far away as possible within the county is an interesting question. She obviously suffered the impact of the Mullion chapel success, yet it is also possible to see why she may not have received replies to single-minded letters she sent to old friends that add in love and interest to the recipient only at the end—almost an afterthought.

The Bishop of Plymouth, in a letter giving further information about the Catholic chapel near the Lizard Light, said:

> For some years, through the personal devotion and very difficult struggle of two ladies, this chapel (recently renewed) has been kept open. It exists in an out-of-the-world spot, not much known except to summer holiday folk. The rest of the year it has to do with the Coastguard, oddments of military and naval forces, and the Marconi employees of Poldhu. Generally, there are some thirty scattered Catholics as far up as Helston. Anyhow, it is all that is left of Lyonesse on the mainland. The communications on Sunday are impossible and there are no resources for a resident priest. It is my most earnest wish

> at this Western Gateway of the ocean, where even in these poor days nearly one thousand craft of all kinds pass by every month and are signalled at the station, that the men should go and come with a blessing from God over that treacherous sea, so constantly used in the Bible as the symbol of our troubled life. Mass would there be frequently said for them, and with permission, a tower might be visible showing where Our Lord watches.[1]

His Lordship adds:

> There is a deeper purpose to be set out. There are no wayside crosses on the ocean, for all human permanence is therein writ in water. Yet, below the headland, lie crowds of torpedoed ships of all kinds and the bones of those almost forgotten men—of our wonderful Mercantile Marine, the willing helpers of our splendid navy. I have before me a German official return with a map relating to torpedo and mine work from February 1, 1917. Of it, Mr Arnold White said, in the Morning Post, on September 1, 1921, that the return only varies by two ships from our own calculations. The sight is appalling and one wonders how England escaped. But the price has been terrible, and if I can get a hearing the gallant men whose bones strew the floor of the Scilly waters shall have a remembrance. It is proposed as moneys come in: To buy a cottage for a permanent priest; and to establish Foundation Masses so the Holy Sacrifice may regularly be offered by the priest for our poor lost men, and for the living who go to and fro.[2]

The bishop is confident of the generosity of the Royal Navy and Mercantile Marine for this purpose and proposes to establish a fund, to be known as 'Our Lady of The Lizard Fund' as soon as possible.

One of the most interesting announcements in the pastoral is in the statement on 16 December 1922:

> In the extreme south of Cornwall, at the Lizard, a devoted benefactress has for some time kept an open chapel. We have sanctioned a very touching purpose, and it is connected with the little spot just alluded to when speaking of East Dorset. Under that headland lie no less than thirty-six torpedoed vessels, and our commerce and battle-ships continually pass under it. The design is to have a small church there among our people and Mass for those who pass by, and for those whom the sea will one day give up again. In this matter we shall expressly appeal to the Navy, but perhaps there are amongst us those who will have a tender remembrance of the men who kept the dreary four years' watch.[3]

A William Pritchard, writing on paper originally addressed as Catholic Church, 173, Upper Kennington Lane, London, SE11, writes to a Friar Ford a complaint, which perhaps Pamela had put him up to:

> Whilst here, I met a nice young Benedictine who told me that you had instructed him to inform the Priest of Mullion of his presence as it would save the latter 'having to duplicate'. As this seems to confirm what I heard here last year (that the late Bishop made it a tradition of allowing the Priest (I forget his name) going to Mullion, that he should say Mass every Sunday at the Lizard—may I venture to inform you that this condition has not been fulfilled and that from my personal knowledge the small Catholic community is most neglected?
>
> Last year, when I arrived at the end of July I found that no Mass had been said since Pentecost—the previous one being, I think, at Easter. After I left in August, no Mass was said until November. No Mass was said at Christmas! The following masses were on 31st March and 19th May.[4]

He goes on to complain further about the shortage of masses, there regularly being months between events. It seems, by now, Pamela's little church was in a bad way. It would be nice to think the chapel was set up by Pamela but this is not actually the case. Researcher John Garth found confirmation in the 1914 *Kelly's Directory* for Cornwall, Bishop Graham paid a visit to Maenheere in 1900 where there were morning and evening services, six people were confirmed, three young people were given first Communion, and Our Lady of the Wave was blessed.[5] After the departure of *Abbé* Julien, Madame Victorine, on her various visits to Maenheere, secured a priest for The Lizard at least for Sundays, and sometimes one for longer. Conversely, Pamela did receive some money from the Catholic Church to pay for priests, but as time passed, and the Catholic Church grew at more highly-populated Mullion, she struggled more and more and the Church contributed less and less. Pamela clung on to her home at Parc Garland for as long as she could.

Boyd Parsons was fortunate enough to contact Father I. S. Mooney who knew Pamela on The Lizard.[6] Even here, different accounts vary widely. She is described by him as being 'the centre of artistic interest'. Currently, there is a Lizard art group of artists, formed at Cadgwith Cove in 1995. There is no reason to suppose there was no art happening there in the 1920s, but we have no real evidence of it. She was also described as 'a lady of great charm, of old-world courtesy, with a puckish sense of humour and with a very wide understanding of the best values in life'. Her home was described as 'moderately-sized, situated in its own grounds, very tastefully decorated both within and without, showing a display of colour in advance of the custom of those years'. Additionally, he believed (though was not certain) that one of her visiting friends was Monsignor John O'Connor (the original 'Father Brown' in the G. K. Chesterton novels). If so, then Catholicism did not stunt her social circle as much as people think, she merely had friends who reflected her change of focus or interests.

By 1939, Corinne (Pamela) was living at a large mid-terraced residence in a pleasant location at 24 New North Road, Exeter, with Nora Lake and a couple of others, moving to Bude in 1942 and dying in 1951. Archivist Alison Spence says Miss Smith was buried in the churchyard on 20 September 1951.[7] The service was taken by a Roman Catholic priest. Her address is given as 2 Bencoolen House, Bude. There was no municipal cemetery in Bude at that date so the churchyard was used for burials for all local people, regardless of denomination. No plot number is recorded in the register, and no grave plot registers or churchyard plans have been transferred to the Record Office by Bude Church, so there is no other information about the location of the grave.

Pamela's housekeeper and friend, Nora Lake, remains something of a mystery as there is little information about the family. Three Bude residents mentioned a son called Freddie, who does not appear on any documentation so far seen.

Bude local Carole Wakefield mentioned that in 1958 her grandparents divided their home at 20, Flexbury Park Road into two flats, where Freddie Lake and his mother Nora resided (renting the ground floor flat). She said:

> Freddie was a spiritualist, a quiet, unassuming man who worked at Lloyd's Bank. I remember being given a book entitled *Flower Fairies of the Field* by Mrs Lake and she wrote 'Evelyn M Lake' as part of her greeting inside the front cover [creating even more mystery]. My brother and I often used to pop downstairs on Sundays to visit Mrs Lake, who by that time was quite elderly. I remember that her front room smelt of the parma violet sweets she used to enjoy and there was always a rather mystical atmosphere She used to tell us stories and I clearly remember her telling me often that she believed in fairies. They had a cat called Pippity Pops, which my grandfather thought a particularly silly name!

Whether this is the Nora Lake who was friends with Pamela remains open to conjecture.

24
Bude's Miss Smith

Given artists are driven to create, no painter would ditch her drawings and artwork completely, so it is barely surprising Pamela was still offering her drawings to her Bude errand boy, Tony Edwards, in the 1940s when she moved to the town.[1] She surely understood why he, as a young boy, turned them down in preference to money, but what we do not know is whether this was new artwork or old material she had kept. Tony had not, when we first met, seen any books by Miss Smith, such as the *Annancy Stories*, but he described her drawings very clearly, likening them to Germanic fairy tale images. Tony, who spent a lot of time in Germany, commented on the Teutonic nature of Miss Smith's drawings, rather like those of the Brothers Grimm fairy tales.

She continued to draw and paint until the end (providing she could afford materials) both for her own pleasure and for her limited circle of friends. On leaving London, she continued her relentlessly unprofitable work as an artist, illustrator, and writer at The Lizard, while developing her chapel in the grounds of her house. The evidence about the holiday home idea remains unconvincing, not least because very little money was forthcoming from peripatetic priests anyway. Few people journeyed to The Lizard for pleasure, as poor Cornish transport links were and still are, as Tony explained, the stuff of nightmares. Her accumulated debts are also interesting because W. B. Yeats's friend, Masefield, tells us Pamela had unpaid loans from many people, which lost her friends; he also suggests she was partial to alcohol.[2] Is this what changed her life, or spurred her on to change herself? What we do know is Nora Lake was a long-time companion, probably after her husband (who seemed to be handyman and gardener at Parc Garland) died, leaving her with her son, Freddie.

Pamela's chosen locality in her later years in Bude, Cornwall, seems to have been compact, whether by choice or because of ill health. Bude is a small town; her corner of it was smaller still. Pamela's patch would have stretched as far as St Peter's Catholic Church on Bencoolen Road for Mass and to The Strand, then a prime street, for any shopping needs. In the 1940s, the Strand—now a less important street but still the main route into Bude—was a colourful hive of activity. The multitude of surf shops, cafés, and souvenir stores that line the streets of modern Bude were not there then. However, not too long after her arrival, the Americans appeared in town. The 29th Rangers were sent to Bude for amphibious warfare training, much of which occurred around Upton cliffs near where Pamela first lived. Whether this played any part in her moving to the flat at Bencoolen is unknown. We have no record of her talking to the Americans but she always considered herself American so it may have been welcome or not to have a garrison of soldiers nearby. Her flat at Bencoolen was not far from the railway station which was used to bring in the troops so she would have been aware of events.

Author Jack Womer says the Americans largely lived in luxury hotel rooms, yet trained hard and were part of a ration experiment to see what was the optimum nutritional formula for combat.[3] Certainly, while many were located close to the beaches, the sight of American uniforms would have been an everyday one from around Christmas 1943. They were training for what became D-Day, being heavily involved on the Pointe de Hoc and Omaha Beach, Normandy. We cannot say Pamela came to Bude because of the wartime American connection, especially as the dates do not tie up, but she would surely have witnessed the arrival of the American soldiers.

During her Bude residency, along the Strand was a café called Ye Jollye Tea Pot at number twenty-seven, next to Coombe's store.[4] The Life Centre, later to become Oceans, was previously the Conservative Club, the address of the woman (probably her cleaner, though it was strange to have the expense of a cleaner in a small flat unless she and Nora were both very unwell) who reported her death, and before, a sweet shop and tobacconist run by Gerry & Allsop. Nearby was a garage, then Petherick's coal office, with Tremeer's tobacconists at the end, and Tubby Edward's hairdressers at the rear. Next to the old Carriers, the public house, was a gentlemen's outfitters, a small Spencer Thorn jewellers, and the bus garage. There was a solicitor, with Stratton Rural Council office above, the Bude Wine stores, and a haberdasher's shop, then the Globe public house. It is unlikely she used these and even more unlikely they would serve Opal Hush, said to be the claret-based favourite drink of her bohemian youth if she was still keen on red wine and lemonade or soda. The old-fashioned grocers produced aromas of freshly roasting coffee and cheeses. Cooks Stores was another lovely shop. A walk along the Strand then was an assault on the senses but it is unclear how much walking she did, as she was not fit enough by this time. However, she did embark on one final visit to the USA in 1946, probably from Bude railway station, the fastest and easiest way to reach London. The station closed in 1966, after Pamela's death, with the Beeching cuts.

She had errands run for her, with purchases largely made from Belle Vue. Belle Vue inclines uphill, so while not terribly far from Pamela's flat at The Bencoolen, it is probably far enough for someone with a serious heart condition. Symptoms of cardiac problems include chest pain, tightness and shortness of breath, but also numbness and a tendency to feel cold. We know Pamela was chesty as she regularly ordered wadding for her chest, as Tony recalls. Thermogene-medicated wadding contained pink coloured wadding wrapped in paper, within a red box. This fits Tony's memories. Containing capsicum and methyl salicylate, it was used for the relief of rheumatic pain, bronchitis, sciatica, chest colds, lumbago, neuralgia, and similar. Pamela ordered it more than once so obviously, it brought her relief as she believed in its efficacy.

Little is known about Pamela's time in Bude, so, to meet Tony, Miss Smith's errand boy in Bude around 1943, was a wonderful opportunity.[5] Tony attended Bude Secondary School. His parents spotted an advertisement for an errand boy, and as money was tight, he was sent to work. So, he joined Stanley Laurence Miller, high-class fruiterer and greengrocer, next door to the Electricity Board, from where Pamela ordered her deliveries. Coincidentally, Tony's aunt, a cleaner at the theatre in Stratford, lived near Henley-in-Arden (Tony was born during his mother's visit to nearby Ullenhall). She met Pamela while she was at the Royal Shakespeare Memorial Theatre in Stratford. We know Pamela visited Stratford with the Lyceum group so the evidence supports Tony's memories. His aunt told him Pamela was highly respected in theatrical design. She was talented, especially relating to costumes. His aunt knew Pamela had come to Cornwall, which Tony's father had mentioned to her, but she also remembered her being in Stratford for a season.

Pamela was talented enough to work at the seat of Shakespeare. Even then, Stratford had the second greatest theatre in the country. For Pamela to work there meant her talent was in demand or she was cheap labour for the ailing touring theatre company or both. Tony said: 'With hindsight, I wish I'd seen more of her work. I'd become interested in art seeing Mr Branscombe's (Bude local artist) work'.

Tony recalled Pamela's second floor upstairs flat in Bude at the back of The Bencoolen (now an inn) which was once a substantial gentleman's residence. When it was converted into flats, Pamela lived at number two. She shared with Nora Lake (Tony never really met her, saying she 'hovered a lot'). Hovering is an interesting choice of word, implying listening in, eavesdropping, being a little nosy or perhaps protective, maybe not very confident.

Pamela, he says, was 'not exactly slim, and was grey around the temples, with her hair swept back in a bun'. He reckoned Miss Smith was pale, 'in need of Cornish sun', which contradicts most of the photographic and written evidence we have about her. Maybe her pallor reflected her health but it would have been an odd phrase if all the comments about West Indian extraction had any foundation. She was 'pleasant and chatty, but not pretty'. He would not have known her age. 'To a young boy, she was just "old"'.

Every week, she telephoned the shop to give a very modest order; she would also ask Tony to bring a milk loaf (a soft, light sweet style of easily digestible white bread) from the bakery opposite. The chemist was close by, so Tony was also asked to purchase her thermal wadding. Pamela had her aches and pains, quite likely from the bad chest that indicated later heart problems.

In the lobby of the flat where he would deliver the goods, were many sketches of (possibly) tarot cards which to Tony 'looked like gibberish, like the joker in a pack of cards'. Perhaps they were sprite or ballet drawings. We can guess the tarot drawings still existed when Pamela lived in Bude. They were weird drawings, to his eye. She never offered to read his cards, indicating she had left all this behind her or was no tarot reader, even following her own intuitive approach. Maybe it was simply not appropriate to offer a reading to a child, but it was also not really in keeping with her by now Catholic thinking. Children at that time also asked a few questions. If Pamela lost interest in her art as she aged, Tony's account suggests otherwise.

Sometimes, at Christmas, or his birthday, Miss Smith would offer her errand boy the choice of half a crown or one of her little paintings. She was a kind-hearted woman who appreciated his services, but he always took the money. There was no contest. He thinks she was short of money but often wonders now whether she thought he was rejecting her work or whether she was simply trying to save her pennies. Pamela probably found it amusing to tease him, knowing he would opt for the coins. Sometimes, Tony would carry heavy potatoes to the kitchen but usually, he just delivered to the lobby so did not often go inside the apartment. He thinks Pamela still had an outlet for her art products in Bude, which to his mind, made her the purveyor of half-crowns. Certainly, in the 1939 *Kelly's Directory*, Pamela Colman Smith was listed as 'artist'.

She was still zealously Catholic, and in the flat, Tony says: 'Our Lady would be looking at you'. She was very dedicated to Catholicism, enjoying the rituals and devotions. Bude, conversely, was strongly Protestant, with a large dose of non-conformism. Tony explains the church where she is buried (St Michael's, Anglican) was packed on a Sunday but then so was the Methodist Church. Tony attended both churches. In the high Anglican St Michael's, which he felt was about as close to Catholicism as you could get, he carried the incense boat and was an altar boy.

Pamela had an easel in her flat, with a painting on it, again indicating she still enjoyed painting in her later years. His employer, Mr Miller, was also an artist. The art world in Bude was present but small. Tony was used to the artistic crowd floating in and out of the shop but only once went upstairs from the shop, where he found lots of easels and painting materials. There was a good view of the Bude Breakwater (the area is now probably Wroe's café). Another strong woman in control, Mr Miller's wife pretty much ran their business while he painted and enjoyed the company of groups of artists who gathered at his flat. It is uncertain whether Pamela ever joined them but it may be why she used the shop if she felt an artistic affinity. She was a collaborative person in her early years, less so later.

No one truly knows why Pamela came to Bude, but Tony suggests when she became less capable, the paternalistic Catholic Church maybe helped to relocate her. This makes sense. It might be she had become a liability on The Lizard or needed to move on from Exeter. Being next door to St Peter's Church seemed to mean something to her, he felt. Moving to Cornwall took her a long way from London, so he wonders if something happened there. An ex-policeman, Tony hazards it might well relate to a broken romance. Might this have been Edy Craig or a gentleman?

Tony discussed his own upbringing in Bude, useful in painting a picture of Pamela's young errand lad and giving a taste of the town. He was raised on Efford Farm, a paradise for a young boy and not far from Upton where Pamela first lived. From there, he could hear the vicar, Reverend Atkin, at Ebbingford Manor, play the bagpipes with his son. He and his friends were 'up and down the cliffs like monkeys'. They enjoyed recovering things from wrecks, salvaging materials brought in on the first tide (after this they would be ruined). He recalls recovering three enormous boxes of cigarettes hidden in barns by the shore. A Liberty ship went down off Pentire Point with a mixed cargo. Tony remembers it contained 'enough condoms to provide contraception throughout the world'. He found flags of Stars and Stripes, parts for vehicles, and his favourite: ration boxes containing tins of fruit, chopped ham and processed cheese, plus large tins of coffee. Candy and chewing gum were also welcome, along with tins of peanuts from the ever-present Americans.

This driftwood-gathering boy, raised on loot from the beaches, delivering her groceries, was surely a breath of fresh air to Pamela and her companion. For Tony, it was a big delight finding the deck hatch on a ship, much more fun than running errands. A lot of the finds became incorporated into air raid shelters in gardens.

After school finished, Tony was a keen army cadet—understandably as Bude was jam-packed with troops. It also had a 999-seat cinema where there was a queue every night. The train would take the cadets to Dorset via Taunton for training. When he went to his training, Tony promised to return to see Miss Smith but never did as his father found him a new job paying three times the money, two-thirds of which went to his mother as 'keep'. It was his father who told Tony that Miss Smith (he never heard her called by her earlier nickname, Pixie) had died. He recalled she once asked him about his ambitions, then promptly dropped the subject when the army was mentioned. He gained the strong impression she did not approve, implying she was political, maybe a pacifist, but also perhaps adversely affected by the war(s) in some way. Tony was also political, first campaigning for the Liberal Party in 1945 and remaining a party member ever since.

In appearance, Tony Edwards described Pamela as 'sallow', which applies to yellowish or light brown skin, an unhealthy look, but we must bear in mind she was by this time, ageing. However, he also mentioned he only saw her at the top of the stairs inside a building broken up into flats, with artificial light if any, so his view was limited. The only time he ever saw her clearly was if invited in because the shopping was too heavy. She was small in height; he was looking down on her even then.

She had no discernible accent, but to Tony, if someone was not local, they sounded 'funny'. In Bude, a large number of people were escaping the war so were evacuated to the town, resulting in a variety of accents in the locality. Many eastern Europeans were there, unable to return home. Close to the back of the pub at Wainhouse Corner was an Italian POW camp, so miscellaneous people had moved in, all very interesting. Bude was thus a hotchpotch of accents and nationalities, which was no use at all in discerning what Miss Smith's accent was (except it was not Cornish).

Pamela was, according to Tony, kind, and clearly observant. He reminisced:

> She used to pull me up on things occasionally like 'you mustn't say it that way, you say it this way'. She would regularly correct my English. She was interested in where I was going and what was going to happen to me, probably more interested than I was! If she was reclusive at all, it was more for health reasons.
>
> To the best of my knowledge, she never came into the shop. She wouldn't go the length of the Strand to go to the chemist. I used to have to go to the chemist roughly where the Candy Shop was (top of Belle Vue) to collect her thermal wadding and her medications. She would bolt on other items to her grocery delivery.[6]

Was this unwillingness to walk related to weight or health or an increasingly small world mentality as she aged? 'She did walk 100 yards to the Conservative Club. It was the nearest place for her to have a drink if she wanted one'; perhaps, this is an indication that Pamela still enjoyed a drink.

> I can't see her, as a lady, going to the Carriers Inn.
>
> If I'd taken my time, she would say: 'oh, I see you've come the long way, you must have a girl waiting over there'. She often had a little joke. Her companion seemed to float around in the background and only ever stuck her head around the door.[7]

Tony never dealt with Nora, which is surprising if they were a couple. He could not remember speaking with her at all, not once. Yet Jackie Adams, a local lady who had links with the spiritualist church, says Nora was a spiritualist and attended church, so she obviously went out.

His employer, Mrs Miller, thought Miss Smith must have had a broken relationship which had led her to more or less abandon her old life. People seemed to know she had lived on The Lizard. Wherever she had been before that is probably where something went wrong. When in Bude, it is plain Miss Smith did not discuss her earlier exciting, high-achieving life. Although we now think of Bude as geographically out on a limb, Tony explained that then it was much more connected to the world, as it had a station with direct links to London. Bryan Adams, who moved to Bude in 1951 and was also evacuated there during the war, said:

> To come to Bude you'd have to make the effort. Bude was exceptional, almost unique, so far from anywhere else. There was a bus service of sorts but it was nothing serious. The railway was there but expensive. Many people could not afford to use the trains. Pamela presumably, therefore, chose to come to Bude.[8]

Tony's approach differs slightly:

> How you come from the Lizard to Bude, I can only suppose is through a Catholic network which suggested she come here. Then, however, Bude was far more in touch with the world than it is today. You could go to the station and be in London 3.5 hours later.[9]

Of course, she came via Exeter, perhaps wanting somewhere with public transport to visit the city, but away from it.

Tony was no artist but was used to seeing easels. He said the easels in Miss Smith's residence were similar, only smaller, than Mr Branscombe's. This implies she was still actively painting, if only for pleasure, long after her artistic heyday, else why have easels in a small flat? He described her drawings as 'images of fairies and wee folk'. I then showed Tony Miss Smith's *Annancy Stories*. He immediately recognised the drawings as exactly the kind of thing he had seen as a boy. They reminded him of the folklore tales of the Black Forest—figures dancing, fairylike. He mentioned esoteric goblins and sprites, which he now thinks could have been tarot cards in large design but who knows? They were different, so to his mind, they were weird. He saw lots of the style in the *Annancy Stories*—dancing figures, fairylike, he reckoned. Tony grew animated by this. The pictures she drew and painted always struck him as strange. He did not find her art to his taste. They smacked a little of fairyland and were different to anything he would have known, therefore to him they were odd.

Miss Smith accounted for every penny when settling-up. Tony had to buy things with money given to him by the Millers for things like Miss Smith's milk loaf from the bakers. Mrs Miller would give him a shilling or a florin to get these things. Items he collected from the chemist seemed expensive. He explained:

> If it was 2*s* 11*d*, she didn't give me 3*s*. Life was tough in the post-war period, and money was a big issue. The country was bankrupt. Inherited wealth was

seen as one of the ways of getting it back. She obviously would have had her pension but little else because her days on the Lizard would not have put her in touch with money. It was a very austere kind of place. She also had her crucifixes around and a picture of Our Lady in the hallway.

Tony's father called her a papist, and there were very few of them in Bude. Papists were 'held at the end of a long pole', he explained. Bryan Adams knew Father du Moulin-Browne who presided over Pamela's funeral.[6] Bryan attended St Peter's in Bude and married there in 1959, when his wife converted to Catholicism. Bryan described Father Browne as follows:

> A kind and generous man, dedicated to the faith and the community. He paid fees for so many local Bude children to go to St Joseph's school in Launceston.
>
> He turned up at our door when we lived in Burn View in 1951, having just moved to Bude. He quietly made himself known. What was wonderful about the Catholic Church was that it had been the same for hundreds or thousands of years, with the Latin Mass precisely the same everywhere you went. Father Browne lived in Holnicote Road, Bude. He died when hit by a car on a zebra crossing at the bottom of Belle Vue, for he always walked everywhere.
>
> He told us that priests from Launceston would come from time to time to visit, thinking he would take them somewhere nice as he was quite well off. Instead he'd take them to Ye Jollye Teapot which was as 'rough as rats'.[10]

Miss Smith had, by the time she came to Bude, dropped the Colman, Tony believed. He never heard it mentioned and was not aware of it. It is much easier to be forgotten or go incognito with only one part to a surname. Also, he did not ever hear her called Pixie but he felt 'she looked like a pixie, so you could see why she got the name'. His closest description was that she 'resembled a genuine Romany and could have fitted in as a Romany quite easily'. Her skin colour he described as 'like a pale person who came from India'. Tony met many Romanies in Worcestershire in the early 1950s, a big vegetable and fruit growing county. Their mode of dress and sallow skin resembled Miss Smith's. That is what she reminded him of. 'She wore loose clothing. Her dresses were long, longer than the norm at that time, so a little unusual in that respect. She didn't otherwise dress very unusually'. He never once saw her out walking but thinks her world would have been tiny. She lived close to the church, the Conservative Club, and a selection of shops.

> She was not that mobile by the time I knew her. All the stuff she needed was near to her house. The Millers were based at Wroe's, so maybe it helped having me collecting other things. It might have been the painting connection as they tended to hang together and know each other.[11]

Tony never saw her by the beach or sea, so he does not know if she went for a seaside constitutional, given she had taken so many transatlantic voyages during her time.

Where she lived was divided into four flats. Previously a gentleman's residence, it had housed servants and a coach and horses. It was a draughty old place.

> In the old coach house was a man called McGovern who did upholstery. It would have been belted by the wind on that corner. If I was going to Miss Smith's, I'd walk up the steps you immediately come to which currently has a tent there, walk across that paved area, and around this little corner, which is still there, to her front door. Inside, were pictures of goblins and fairies on the walls.[12]

Bear in mind again that Tony did not know what a tarot card was.

> There was a circle of artists in Bude at the time, but whether Miss Smith ever joined them is hard to know, around half a dozen people. Mr Miller was mad keen on painting. I was dropped in this circle of artists, very unusual for most lads of my age but I was friendly with the sons of the Branscombes. We had another artist customer who lived in the old Rocket House on Breakwater Road. He only had one leg, having lost one in World War I. They all bought stuff from the Millers perhaps because they were artists.[13]

Miss Smith never bought art materials from the Millers, whose store she patronised, he thinks, due to artistic links, so Tony's guess is that she bought them by post as he would occasionally collect mail packages to deliver to her.

In terms of her final resting place, cremation then in Cornwall was very uncommon, as were Catholic churches, so St Peter's may have enticed her to Bude. St Michael's was, in Tony's words, Anglo-Catholic, 'more Catholic than Catholic, whereas other places were more low church. The incense servers and boat boys would wear red cassocks there'. It was probably more elaborate at St Michael's than at St Peter's.

> Bude would have been one of the few places that would have had a Catholic church. There would have been some Catholics here because of the War, but not very many, so they might have thought it was a good place for her to go, give her a mission in life to light the fire up at this end.[14]

This confirms the idea of mission without my mentioning it.

To reiterate the scarcity of Catholics in the area, Tony related a tale about being stationed at the garrison in Plymouth where only one or two out of 250–260 recruits were Catholic and would fall out to pray elsewhere other than the garrison church. Launceston had a graveyard for Catholics but Tony assumed, 'she's tucked away up next to the woods at St Michael's'. Brian Adams was an apprentice with the building firm, Pethicks, who were also the town undertakers.

> If there was a death, the boss would take the call, and go to see the family. The foreman would measure up the body, and make an elm coffin (oak if well-off) from scratch. It would be made, lined and polished by three of us in about three hours. The building firm then called in the labourer to dig the grave. He was given a template by the general foreman, a cross of timber with string around it, to ensure the coffin went in without touching the sides. If someone died, they usually stayed at home, often in the front room. It could be difficult getting a coffin out of a tiny cottage, especially if upstairs when we'd have to carry it upright. People were not buried in shrouds, and cremations were rare. For a burial, after making the base, we had to pour liquid pitch to seal the coffin joints, which was quite tricky. If a cremation, candle wax was used instead of this. Transport was arranged by local garages with hearses and taxis.

Times were hard when Tony knew Miss Smith. Money was the big issue, he felt. 'Life would have been quite hard. Money makes life easier for people. If you don't have it, then it is much worse'.

It is curious Pamela was such a mystery in Bude. People who worked for the local undertakers, auction houses, and so on, remember nothing at all about her. John Bate of Bude is the son of Ethel Bate, who was with Pamela when she died. John can remember nothing at all about his mother's involvement with Pamela but says she used to help people out from time to time.

There are rumours that, in the late 1940s, Pamela Colman Smith was so heavy and obese that when she died, her body could not be taken from the second floor flat of The Bencoolen Inn, but instead, it had to be removed through the window. The executors to her estate cite an expense for Peter Peter & Sons for a broken window during removal (at a cost of *9s 6d*). This seems bizarre given she had travelled to New York only a few years earlier. Certainly, from Tony Edwards' testimony, she did not get out much, but was that because of ill health, weight, or general lack of money and sense of privacy? He made no mention of obesity. The broken window possibly related to the removal of furniture.

Solicitors Parnall, Godwin and Chegwin in a letter dated 25 November 1982 stated Miss Colman Smith had since 1946 lived in Bude as a tenant of a flat which she shared with Mrs Nora Lake, which we knew. Curiously, her long-time friend, Mrs Lake, did not seem to hold a memorial service for her friend as one might expect if without family, but if there was no money, that might explain why. Alternatively, perhaps their differing religions played a part.

Miss Colman Smith had been in receipt of remittances of income from Manufacturers Trust Company in New York, but there had not been sufficient to meet her expenditure. She died in considerable debt, including sums owing to the Inland Revenue for income tax. Creditors ultimately accepted just over 25 per cent in full satisfaction of their respective debts (5 shillings and 5 pence).

The will was placed with Bodmin Probate Registry on 13 November 1951. They also imply she may have been cremated. However, Vicar Widdows on 22 December 1982, in a letter to Stuart Kaplan, said:

> Regarding the possibility of a cremation: this is not a very widespread occurrence in Cornwall. There is only one crematorium at Truro, and another at Barnstaple in Devon ... if a cremation did take place, the deposition of cremated remains must have been at the crematorium and not in a churchyard.[15]

If we look at her belongings that were auctioned off, we see cooking bowls, china, casseroles, and a kitchen table. There is also a box of paints among the glassware, books, and furniture. There is mention of a Japanese lacquer box, a trifle more exotic, but also a commode, which is not mentioned. Bamboo seemed to be a favoured material. A trunk and pictures are mentioned.

Brian Adams was raised a Catholic. Discussing Father du Moulin-Brown (priest at St Peter's from 1940–1966), who presided over Pamela's funeral service, he reiterated he was a very kind man. Although there were not many Catholics in Bude, they were very dedicated. He was humorous—'a humour one can imagine Pamela may have enjoyed'.

In *Pamela Colman Smith: The Untold Story*, Kaplan et al (2018) notes that 'Pamela's Bible and hymnal reveal that she frequently perused these texts, copying down key passages and often doodling images of angels as well as both the crucified and risen Christ.' It also mentions that Pamela had 'redoubled her efforts at writing and illustrating books. A 1942 receipt shows that she employed a local (Barnstaple) service to type four manuscripts.' Sadly, they were not accepted for publication. The book strongly suggests, therefore, that Pamela was still trying to work when she moved to Bude and was still very staunchly Catholic. It provides no further information about her companion, Nora Lake.

25

Did Pamela Die a Pauper?

In answer to this chapter's central question, both yes and no. Pamela's last will was written on 23 February 1951, so only seven months before she died of myocardial degeneration (now known as cardiomyopathy, which enlarges the heart muscle, making it rigid). She bequeathed all her real and personal estate to her friend, Nora Lake. Dr Radford, MRCS, certified her death.

There were preferential debts owed for wages (£15) and the Inland Revenue required one year of tax assessment (£688.10) indicating earnings; additionally, she owed Bude and Stratton Unitary District Council £5 13*s* 1*d* for rates.

She had other non-secured debts: utilities and various local companies, including Miller's, where her errand boy, Tony, had worked. Documentation confirmed that Pamela has been a tenant of a flat in Bude shared with Mrs Nora Lake, since 1946. Her will appointed George Lyons Andrew and Richard Hugh Studley Jones as executors.

Her income (for on her death certificate she was a spinster of independent means) had been from Manufacturers Trust Company of New York but her expenditure exceeded her income due to tax owed. In her bank at the time of her death, she had £59 10*s*, a few minor savings, and a balance of income from Brown Shipley & Co of £953 19*s* 9*d*, from American trust funds. The company was originally set up as an import-export investor between Baltimore and Liverpool.

This was a reasonable income. However, after distribution to pay her debts, there were no funds to even pay the rent, so the flat had to be vacated and the contents disposed of by auction. There seems no suggestion that Nora Lake had an income to pay the rent either, so what happened to her at this point? Maybe she returned to family in Exeter. The flat thus had to be cleared and probably quickly. The gross value of Pamela's estate (according to probate) was £1,048, 11*s*, 5*d*, as noted in documentation of 13 November 1951. Payments went to Parkhouse funeral directors, the Cornish & Devon Post for announcements, Notary Public fees, Bodmin Probate Registry, including a certified copy of probate for America, plus other administrative fees. After the sale of her goods, non-preferential creditors accepted a payment of 5 shillings and 5 pence in full satisfaction of their debts.

The items sold on behalf of Miss Coleman (that spelling again) Smith at the Villa Hall, Bude, on Thursday, 15 November 1951, included fairly standard pieces, raising a cheque for £127. Cooking bowls, an enamel roaster, tray, china, mincer, squeezer, box china, dishes, and casseroles suggest that someone in the household was a keen or at least active cook. Also listed were box paints, canvases, easel, and other art materials, as well as other odds and ends. There was an Anglepoise lamp (Pamela always enjoyed artificial light) and a 3-foot 6-inch bed befitting a single person, along with a 3-foot divan, a 2-foot 6-inch iron bed, and a 3-foot iron bed (totalling four beds). That said, there were also four commodes, presumably one for each bed. This indicates that Mrs Lake and Pamela slept separately. Among more exotic items was a Japanese lacquer box selling for 6 shillings and an antique dress chest and shaving stand (an odd item unless part of a collection). There were many books and bookshelves, a tall boy, chairs, carpets, and so on, so it suggests a level of comfort.

As for monies owed, Pamela had preferential debts including wages to J. H. Bickle of 15 shillings, plus a year's tax assessment to the Inland Revenue of £688.10, indicating some reasonable income. A pound in 1951 was worth around £30 now. So her tax bill was the equivalent of £21,300.

There were also advertisement costs for the *Cornish & Devon Post* and the *Western Morning News*, for death announcements or funeral announcements in papers for Bude and The Lizard; thus, we may assume that she was not totally unknown locally. Additionally, a certified copy of probate had to be sent to America. Conversely, she received from A. H. Lake (Alice?) 14 shillings and 7 pence towards the share of an electric light, which again implies friendship not partnership with Nora.

There are many communications from Pamela throughout her life complaining that she was poorly paid, with the state of her bank balance a constant issue. After all, she had no husband so had to support herself. Pamela is commonly known as a pauper at death, but even these assumptions are not right. Certainly, she had unpaid taxes upon her death which took up most of her estate. Without the tax bill, her beneficiary, Nora Lake, would have received something and Pamela would have not been left in an unmarked grave. Maybe it is her naïveté again, for she certainly seemed to imagine that her remaining monies would go to Nora.

Did she fail to pay her taxes during her lifetime because she was financially inept or did she purposefully avoid paying them? Why was her tax bill so high? Generally, people in extremely poor circumstances do not receive large tax bills. Yet, people with little ready cash give low priority to taxes when alive. She was not technically a pauper, as she is often described, though she was certainly very careful with money in her later years, but the Revenue collected their dues diligently. So, the image of poor, unrewarded, underappreciated, and orphaned Pamela, who was taken advantage of by those who should have known better, is one end of the dichotomy.

Another side to her is that mentioned by Kathleen Pyne, which might explain the high tax bill.[1] Pyne suggests Pamela astutely employed incredible productivity levels across a multitude of print and drawing mediums. She says: 'This would make her an extremely energetic businesswoman to have functioned so well for so many years given her circumstances'. As Pyne explains, women then were enormously handicapped in trying to compete with men in the marketplace. Pamela thus used the arts as a medium for the 'enchantment of both children and adults but she made this identity into a theatrical persona which she produced informally for friends and formally in more public venues'. In her younger years, London was a vast melting pot of individuals and groups, a fact which she exploited for personal success. This makes her appear savvy, but also living a life of constant role-playing, theatricality, having to live a persona that did not feel real, but these were her skills, and art was her talent. She had to survive, and survive she did, even if that artistic productivity dropped during her time on The Lizard when she refocused to her religious mission. Most art at that time probably found little demand in Cornwall, and Pamela's was very specific material. It was not the seascapes beloved by tourists. That said, if art had been paramount to her at this time, she would presumably have moved to Newlyn, St Ives, or Lamorna, which developed fine artistic reputations.

Pamela was a talented woman with immense energy, who threw her heart and soul into her many and varied endeavours. She enjoyed a successful yet frustrating career as an illustrator and artist, punctuated by some writing and publishing work, plus storytelling. Masefield suggests she had earlier joined psaltery people and impressed small New York audiences by copying the Florence Farr way of chanting.[2] He also explains why her move to Cornwall may have happened, recalling her as 'blithe Pixie, singing Yeats's songs, or telling West Indian tales with her bright painted dolls. In later life, she took to drink and embarrassed her friends over a series of unpaid loans'. How much later remains a mystery but may have explained some of her alienation from her friends and her desire to leave London.

Additionally, Pamela was the mistress of her own destiny, changing depending upon her audience. Pyne explained this:

> Pamela could change her appearance from bourgeois womanhood to Bohemian, for she grew up among theatrical people and worked with them, so she knew theatrical craft well. Which type of persona she wished to project depended entirely on her socio-economic circumstances, companions, audiences, etc. You have only to look at Gertrude Käsebier's portrait of Pamela made during student days at Pratt to see how she styled herself at that time

and undoubtedly blended in with the middle-class women who attended classes there.[3]

Chameleon-like Pixie—as some liked to (and still) call her, and as she sometimes called herself—was an astute woman, taking full advantage of the more exotic aspects of her life to survive as a single woman and artist. During Pamela's working life, most women needed wealthy parents (Ellen Terry's children were prime examples) or a man to keep them. It was difficult to survive, especially in England's capital city (though there at least was potential income generation there, work, and people prepared to pay something for her skills *vis-à-vis* her later time in Cornwall). Securing a husband was crucial to many women around this time unless they had a reliable source of unearned income, which, of course, Pamela did for many years. For many years, she had no need for a husband.

Her sense of self-direction and autonomy is crucial to any understanding of Pamela the woman. No one is entirely at the mercy of the cultural conditions in which they live. We are all bound by society's structures and norms, but we also all have choices within these constraints; by manipulating these, creating our own personal narrative and impression, we can all develop our own images, which Pamela did large. This is important, for within those limits she worked hard to do things her way. While every historical character uses rational thinking to inform their choices, the ways of the prevailing structures may be difficult to shake off if those choices do not fit contemporary society.

One word often used when describing Pamela Colman Smith is 'strange'. Pyne suggests this, too, was part of her cultivated persona.[4] In her time, Pamela found a way to belong to and play a part in various social circles that benefited her economically, emotionally, and spiritually. She was considered a fish swimming against the tide, but to some extent, she self-promoted this idea of difference to gain an audience. Many other articulate middle-class women were equally disenchanted with traditional notions of femininity. They wanted equality and were prepared to fight hard for it, a battle to be won through social action and political ideology but also propaganda and the war of words and pictures, with which Pamela assisted. Again, there is no intense political purpose to Pamela but she enjoyed using her skills to political ends.

Pyne adds that childlike persona was partly her true nature:

> Also something she could self-consciously amplify when she wished to project herself as a more eccentric personality. It became part of her artistic persona as it is central to the Romantic myth of the artist as a visionary who speaks the truths of children. There is another side of her that comes out, however, in her letters to Stieglitz, asking for money for her work and describing how she made her works—one that is much more savvy about her audiences and the economic side of her art practice. The synaesthetic framing of her work

was a smart way for her to place herself within her London milieu of Irish and English mystics.[5]

She added:

> Her appeal diminished with the change in modernist cultures in New York, right around 1910. Stieglitz abandoned the entire Pictorialist faction of the Photo-Secession at that time ... a faction undergirded by the spiritualism of Whistler and Maeterlinck. He broke, most significantly, with Käsebier at that time ... she had been his figurehead for his modernist movement before 1910, when he begun to showcase European modernists, Matisse, Cézanne, and others who took a more erotic approach to the female body. Neither Pamela Colman Smith nor Käsebier could be re-framed to serve this new agenda. Spiritualism would have been wearing away a bit in London at that time too with the embrace of post-impressionism by tastemakers there. Her fortunes would have been tied to those of Yeats and others of that circle.[6]

Mysticism was also an economic system, and Pamela could see its income-generating possibilities.

> In Pamela's case, we must realise how incredible her productivity was, especially in terms of the different kinds of work she generated across a multitude of print and drawing mediums, in New York and in London... She must have been a very energetic businesswoman to have functioned as well as she did for so many years, given her circumstances ... No one who was genuinely simple or "childlike" could have accomplished and produced the amount and range and quality of what she did for as long as she did. Her 'childlike' nature meant she was crucially engaged with arts as a medium of enchantment for both children and adults. Lots of other artists were as well. Pamela differed from most in the way she made this identity into a theatrical persona which she produced informally for friends and formally in more public venues.[7]

So, not only is it important to investigate the historical setting that shaped Pamela's life, but also the contemporary thinking and events that contributed to her shaping herself, which was an aim of this book. This sense of agency is vital to understanding the woman. There is still so much no one knows about Pamela Colman Smith, but Pamela's public persona was self-created, probably with one aim in mind—selling her work. Lucre, money, financial survival—there is nothing wrong with this. Pamela had every right to be concerned about forging a living, but the cost of being an artist in a capricious world was high. It was probably psychologically very wearing, too, perhaps helping to explain why, in her middle years, Pamela totally changed her life, wholeheartedly embracing

Catholicism where she found some degree of contentment. During her earlier years, Pamela was a bird of passage, rarely settling anywhere for long. Cornwall became, to her, home.

If there is a dichotomous scale, Pamela may sit on either end depending upon who you read and believe. Already we have the makings of a complex character from history, perhaps naïve but also able to exploit this naïveté. Maybe it is this mismatch or incongruence that led to her finding what she later saw as the true faith, with comfort and satisfaction sought within the community that embraced Catholicism. There are few people who would describe Catholicism as "great fun" despite many other positive attributes, but Pamela did. If we take this at face value, she obviously enjoyed her faith and embraced it; conversely, she perhaps led a terribly dull life. In her letters from Parc Garland on The Lizard, there is evidence that she thoroughly enjoyed the symbolism and ritual of Catholicism, going to great pains to get the altar just right, and to ensure that she was playing by the rules.

We leave Pamela on that positive and insightful note, also aware that she received artistic recognition in 1941, when she was granted fellowship and membership of the RSA. There is also a happy ending for Parc Garland.[8] A young couple with children bought the house and are steadily restoring it. The owner, Hayley, is herself an artist. She mentioned the syphoning of Pamela's money by one of her servants (not Nora) who stole from her (perhaps this was the notorious Mrs Emery). She was also surprised by the number of obelisks around the property, indicating a retained occult interest, along with the belief that Pixie read the tarot in the attic, which had a good deal of paint on the floor and windows indicative of continued artwork. Pamela also had the house extended from an L-shape to a square and added slate fireplaces in art deco style covering the Georgian ones.

The chapel (Pixie's 'Cathedral'), previously a coach house, is still there but tumbled down. The couple have discovered a stone pond and an orangery outside. Angie Hodges who visited said she mentioned to Hayley that Pixie would be pleased to have an artist living in the house, relating, 'at that point I felt the hairs on the back of my neck go up and I felt close to tears. It was not a scary feeling'. If it is Pamela's ghost, it seems she was at her happiest in Parc Garland. Finally, for 'secret' reasons she explained to me, Hayley firmly believes Pamela and Nora were friends, not lovers.

This is a project born of my intense desire to know more. It is as accurate as it can be given the constraints of time and money. My assertions come from my wide reading and research. They are meant as discussion points, not academic fact, to help further our understanding and thinking of this remarkable lesser-known woman artist. There is no pot of gold behind this labour of love and no paid research team—there is just me, and I have enjoyed (almost) every minute.

Appendix: Timeline

1878: Corinne Pamela Colman Smith is born to American parents at 27 Belgrave Road, Pimlico, London, on 16 February.

1881: Family moves to Manchester to Oakhurst, Fielden Park, Didsbury.

1888: Relocates to New York in November, on the *Etruria* sailing from Liverpool.

1889: Moves to Jamaica with father's job.

1893: Pamela sails with her mother from Kingston to New York on the SS *Alene*; attends Pratt Institute in Brooklyn, New York, to study art.

1895: Again arrives in New York from Kingston with her mother, sailing on the *Alleghany*; her friendship with Edy Craig cemented on Lyceum theatre company tour of America.

1896: Visits Jamaica for extended stay due to father's work; her mother dies in St Andrew, Jamaica; Pamela has her first article published in *Journal of American Folklore*.

1897: Travels back to New York with her father from Satoon, West Indies, on the *Alleghany*; leaves Pratt Institute without a degree; her studies are interrupted but she sells illustrations and prints through the Macbeth Gallery in New York, specialising in American art; uses William Macbeth as her agent.

1898: Visits Jamaica; writes and illustrates *Chimney Corners* (Irish folk tales by Seamus MacManus), sheet music for *Christmas Carol*, *The Land of Heart's Desire* by W. B. Yeats, *Twelfth Night* and *Merry Makers*, and the cover of a book by Gertrude Käsebier, the photographer who also attended the Pratt Institute; writes and illustrates *Annancy Stories*; fails to get a place at the Drexel Institute of Philadelphia; plans to visit Philadelphia to see Ellen Terry; calls herself Pixie Pamela, a name she says Ellen Terry has given her.

1899: Returns to England (arrived Glasgow, 28 June) with her father, taking up permanent residence; visits Ireland, where they meet W. B. Yeats and his family; her father dies suddenly in New York on 1 December; publishes *Annancy Stories* of twenty-six tales and sixty black and white illustrations; publishes *The Golden Vanity*, *The Green Bed*, and Bram Stoker's souvenir volume, *Sir*

Henry Irving and Miss Ellen Terry in Robespierre; also, illustrations from *The Merchant of Venice*, *Trelawny of Wells*, *Fair Vanity*, and *Widdecombe Fair*; returns to England with Ellen Terry and Henry Irving.

1900: In England, she tours the provinces with the Lyceum, given bit-parts and crowd scenes in plays; receives various commercial publishing rejections; creates several illustrations for souvenir book about actor William Gillette, famous for playing Sherlock Holmes; faculties granted for Stations of the Cross, at Our Lady of The Lizard Church (pertinent to Pamela's later exile in Cornwall); vacations with Jack Yeats and his wife, Cottie, in Devon during the summer.

1901: Tours with the Lyceum, then joins Hermetic Order of Golden Dawn Isis-Urania Temple in November. Has a week at Smallhythe with Edy Craig and Chris St John, followed by several months at Whitstable; lives at 14 Milbourne Grove, South Kensington, London, with Ethel P. F. Fryer-Fortesque; Pamela listed as a 'boarder/visitor' on census; establishes a studio in London; joins Irish Literary Society; designs bookplates; works towards publishing *A Broad Sheet* with Jack Yeats (issue 1 in January 1902); contributes to *The Kensington Magazine,* with illustrations from the Lyceum tour, but for no pay; several sketches of Ellen Terry were later used in *The Craftsman* (1912); moves to a flat of her own to hold weekly 'at homes' in her studio, inviting the London Bohemian set—regulars include: W. B. Yeats, John Masefield, Arthur Ransome, and Alphaeus Cole.

1902: Uncle Theodore E. Smith visits; Pamela stays with the Davis family in Kensington, London, acting cousins (by marriage) of Ellen Terry; interested in mysticism as she grows more involved with the social circles of W. B. Yeats (Celtic Revival), Jack Yeats, Edith and Gordon Craig, Ellen Terry, George Bernard Shaw, and Walter Crane.

1903: Starts *The Green Sheaf* publishing with Jack Yeats for one year (thirteen issues) but this fails to succeed financially. Hand-colouring of *A Broad Sheet* feels too onerous so withdraws; briefly joins the Masquers, organised by Walter Crane, focusing on the beauty of set design; Pamela appears at a Christmas Bazaar in aid of the Girls' Realm of Service, as a storyteller for the children; opens a school for hand-colouring and a shop in Knightsbridge combined with Pamela's office for her freelance designs of menus, Christmas and other cards, book labels, ball programmes, and decorative printing.

1904: Expresses interest in astrology; remains in the Golden Dawn but still in Zelator grade; sets up shop with Mrs Fortesque selling drawings, pictures, hand-coloured prints, and books; resides at 3 Park Mansions, Knightsbridge; foundation of Abbey Theatre, Dublin, with Annie Horniman, part of the Irish cultural Renaissance.

1905–6: Illustrates numerous books, including two by Laurence Alma Tadema.

1906: Arrives in New York from London on board the *Mesaba*; meets Alfred Stieglitz.

1907: Exhibits in New York City, courtesy of Stieglitz of the Photo-Secession; her flat in London is described by Arthur Ransome (listed as 14 Milborne Grove) in Bohemia; also recites for Mark Twain; performs recitals with Florence Farr who taught tarot to initiates of the Golden Dawn; show in Edinburgh in December; Uncle Theodore probably visits to assist with her financial affairs and debts.

1908–9: Stieglitz re-exhibits with Willi Geiger and Donald Shaw MacLaughlin, Pamela does not attend, and it is less popular than the earlier one; in *Strand* magazine, mention of what some call synaesthesia; lives at 84 York Mansions, Prince of Wales Road, London.

1909: Waite commissions tarot art (completed deck April to October) and she works on the *Atelier*, London; stays with Ellen Terry; sails on the *Minnetonka* to New York from London in January as her artwork is again exhibited by Stieglitz, returning May, first class both ways; visits Ellen Terry throughout the summer; while living in Battersea, she writes her famous letter to Alfred Stieglitz saying she just finished a big job for very little cash, assumed to be the tarot deck; gives a lecture on art at Pratt, entitled 'Magic Spectacles'.

1910: Edward VII died; Pamela meets Claude Debussy.

1911: Converts to Catholicism; still lives at York Mansions; illustrates Stoker's *Lair of White Worm*.

1912: Visits New York for her final Stieglitz exhibition, but also still listed as storytelling in London (Palace Theatre) and Eastbourne; exhibits at the Berlin Photographic Company Gallery in New York.

1912–1914: Frequent visitor to Ellen Terry's house at Smallhythe.

1913: Illustrates *The Russian Ballet*, publishes *Bluebeard*.

1914: Still storytelling; works for the Red Cross during the First World War, again contributing poster designs and toys she makes herself for children's aid; works on illustrations in the *Book of Friendly Giants* by Eunice Fuller; first published use of Waite-Smith (Rider-Waite) tarot; says she 'doesn't care for people anymore' in her guest visitors' book on 7 April; gives away her visitors' book.

1915–1918: Produces posters that related to the war effort and various relief funds.

1916: Pamela applies for an American passport, describing her occupation as 'Artist & Illustrator'; her address is Carlyle Place, London.

1917: Illustrates *The Way of the Cross* by Paul Claudel (poet).

1918: Receives a legacy from Uncle Theodore and moves to Parc Garland, Lizard, Cornwall.

1919: Starts Catholic services in Parc Garland, after Madame Victorine Roberts asks if Miss Colman Smith may look after the mission on Our Lady of The Lizard; Pamela offers to maintain the Chapel in a building in the garden of the newly acquired property and also requests permission to erect Stations of the Cross. The recommendation is given by Rev. Henry O'Brien, but she is not allowed to move church furniture, etc., until the deeds of the freehold and land are signed. Miss Smith mentions an elderly priest in Scotland who would come to Cornwall for permanent work.

1920: Pamela reports her little church is coming on well with thirty-one Catholics in The Lizard and the neighbourhood; *Monsignor* Bans stays for the winter.

1922: By now, Pamela is writing to the bishop about money problems, unable to pay Buckfast for peripatetic priests, etc.

1924: Victorine Roberts sends the bishop the lost 'Indulgence' granted in 1901.

1926: Illustrations completed for *The Sinclair Family* by Edith Lyttleton (also known as Edith Balfour).

1927: Financial crisis, with no art sold; seeks advice; bishop writes to Madame Roberts explaining he has had a great deal of trouble about The Lizard, the position of which is 'irregular' and he has been unable to supply a regular priest; Father Dobbeleers writes to the bishop that there is no foundation to the malicious rumours about Miss Balfour.

1928: Death of Ellen Terry; Pamela does not attend Ellen's funeral.

1929: Letter from Father William A. Pritchard of London to Father Ford, saying that the Catholic community at The Lizard has been sorely neglected.

1930: Debt reduced during the year; when cleared will make the Chapel over to the Diocese.

1931: Tozer to the Bishop says Miss Balfour wishes to transfer the Chapel at Mullion and her own property to the diocese, despite legal difficulties.

1934: Pamela still in Parc Garland; Miss Balfour accommodates priests supplied from Penzance.

1939: Heart problems, mentioned in a letter from Nora Lake's sister, Alice.

1941: Pamela granted fellowship/membership of the RSA (Royal Society for the Encouragement of Arts, Manufactures and Commerce).

1942: Caring for Nora Lake and 'nursing her from shock'; hires typing service for four manuscripts; moves to Upton, Bude, and then to 2 Bencoolen House (a flat) previously a gentleman's residence (Reverend J. Allsop) and is currently a public house.

1943: Chapel closes.

1946: Visits USA to New York.

1948: Becomes Fellow of Royal Society of Arts.

1951: Dies in Bude (though listed as Stratton) on 18 September (aged seventy-three) as Corinne Pamela Mary Colman.

Endnotes

Chapter 1

1 Greer, M., marykgreer.com/2017/10/04/tarot-tours-of-scotland-merlins-britain/ accessed 15 July 2018.
2 Wands, S., podcast, biddytarot.com/btp117-secret-life-pamela-coleman-smith/ accessed 23 June 2018.
3 Marson, L., email correspondence globalspiritualstudies.com/ accessed 23 June 2018
4 Colquhoun, I., ithellcolquhoun.co.uk/ accessed 26 June 2018

Chapter 2

1 Pamela Colman Smith, Special Collections Dept, Bryn Mawr College Library. Letters to Mary B, Reed, Pamela's cousin.
2 House valuation zoopla.co.uk/property/27-belgrave-road/london/sw1v-1rb/23090563, accessed 8 July 2018
3 Yeo, E., *Women's History Review*, 8 (2) (1999), pp. 201–218.
4 *The Economist*, 'The Servant Problem' (17 December 2017).
5 Jordan, E., 'Making Good Wives and Mothers', *History of Education Quarterly*, 31(4) (1991), p. 439.
6 Widdowson, F., 'Review of Dyhouse, C., *Girls Growing Up in Late Victorian and Edwardian England*', History Workshop, No. 15 (1983), pp. 176–180.
7 Cogan, F., 'All-American Girl: The Ideal of Real Womanhood in Mid-Nineteenth-Century America', *Journal of American Studies*, 24 (3) (1989), pp. 464–465.
8 Wands, S., *Magician and Fool* (2017), a novel.

Chapter 3

1 Biography of Pamela Colman Smith website pcs2051.tripod.com/ accessed various dates.
2 *Ibid.*
3 *Ibid.*
4 *Ibid.*
5 Colman, S., *The Mother's Present* (1847).
6 Colman, S., *Stories for Corinne* (1848).

7 Biography of Pamela Colman Smith pcs2051.tripod.com/yeats.htm accessed various dates.
8 Author interview material with Tony Edwards, Bude, 2017.

Chapter 4

1 Albert Bigelow Paine Letters, The Huntingdon Library, San Marino, California, huntington.org, accessed various dates
2 McCoy, M., 'The Lie is Eternal: A Novelist's Take on Portraying Twain in Fiction', esirc.emporia.edu/bitstream/handle/123456789/3553/Great%20Plains%201.pdf?sequence=1 accessed 25 June 2018.
3 Albert Bigelow Paine Letters, The Huntingdon Library, California, huntingdon.org, accessed various dates.
4 *Ibid.*
5 *Ibid.*
6 *Ibid.*
7 *Ibid.*
8 *Ibid.*
9 *Ibid.*
10 *Ibid.*
11 *Ibid.*
12 *Ibid.*
13 *Ibid.*
14 *Ibid.*
15 *Ibid.*
16 *Ibid.*
17 *Ibid.*
18 *Ibid.*

Chapter 5

1 Craig, E., *Ellen Terry and Her Secret Self* (1932).
2 Colour pictures from the archives shown to the author by Susannah Mayor, curator, Smallhythe, Kent.

Chapter 6

1 Albert Bigelow Paine Letters, The Huntingdon Library, San Marino, California, huntington.org, accessed various dates.
2 Coldwell, J., 'Pamela Colman Smith and the Yeats Family', *The Canadian Journal of Irish Studies*, Vol. 3, No. 2 (1977), pp. 27–34.
3 Greer, M., *Women of the Golden Dawn* (1995).
4 Harper, G. M., *Yeats's Golden Dawn* (2013).

Chapter 7

1 Craig, E., *Ellen Terry and Her Secret Self* (1932).
2 *Ibid.*
3 *Ibid.*
4 Shearer, M., *Ellen Terry* (2011).
5 *Ibid.*

6 Auerbach, N., *Ellen Terry, Player in Her Time* (1997), quoting Charles Reade.
7 Craig, *op. cit.*
8 *Ibid.*
9 Auerbach, N., *op. cit.*
10 Craig, E., *op. cit.*
11 Albert Bigelow Paine Letters, The Huntingdon Library, San Marino, California, huntington.org, accessed various dates.
12 Edith Craig in spartacus-educational.com/WcraigE.htm accessed 27 June 2018.
13 Adlard, E., *Edy: Recollections of Edith Craig* (1949), biographical note by Christopher St John.
14 Terry, E., *Memoirs* (1974 reproduction).
15 Letters to Bobby (Mary) Reed, Special Collection, Pamela Colman Smith Letters, 1896–1900, Archives of American Art, Smithsonian Institute.
16 *Ibid.*
17 Cockin, K., *Edith Craig and the Theatres of Art* (2017).
18 *Ibid.*
19 Holroyd, M., *A Strange and Eventful History* (2008).
20 Terry, E., *Memoirs* (1974 reproduction)
21 The Irving Society, theirvingsociety.org.uk/ accessed 23 June 2018.
22 Holroyd, M., *op. cit.*
23 Cockin, K., *Edith Craig and the Theatres of Art* (2017).
24 Letter from Ellen Terry to Gordon Craig.
25 Laneri, R., 'This Book Belongs To—The Lost Art of Bookplates', forbes.com/forbes/welcome/?toURL=https://www.forbes.com/sites/booked/2011/10/21/this-book-belongs-to-___-the-lost-art-of-bookplates/&refURL=&referrer= accessed 23 June 2018.
26 Melville, J., *Ellen and Edy* (1987).
27 Terry, E., *The Story of My Life* (1908).

Chapter 8

1 Craig, E., *Ellen Terry and Her Secret Self* (1932).
2 Toy Theatres, V&A, vam.ac.uk/moc/collections/toy-theatres/ accessed 23 June 2018.
3 Pollock's Toyshop, pollocks-coventgarden.co.uk/ accessed 8 July 2018.
4 Colman Smith, *The Craftsman* (July 1908), pp. 417–419.
5 Greer, M., marykgreer.com/2015/02/06/pamela-colman-smith-heart-of-the-heights/ accessed various dates.

Chapter 9

1 Diaghilev and the Ballet Russes, vam.ac.uk/articles/diaghilev-and-the-ballets-russes?gclid=CjwKCAjw7IbaBRBqEiwA6AyZgnQuSUAKJBA-mMYlxgj6tJcRjlvQIUyMtmAGQwnWHdRL1MQKidgAkBoCRS0QAvD_BwE accessed 26 June 2018.
2 Nicholson, V., *Among the Bohemians* (2005).
3 *Ibid.*
4 Ransome, A., *Bohemia in London* (1907).
5 *Ibid.*
6 *Ibid.*
7 Nicholson, *op. cit.*
8 Boyd Parsons, M., *To All Believers* (1975).

Chapter 10

1 Embassy of Japan in Ireland (Ie.emb-japan.go.jp, 2018)
2 MacDonald, Marianne, (5 November 1995) Yeat's Debt to the Sisters he Chose to Forget, The Independent https://www.independent.co.uk/news/uk/home-news/yeatss-debt-to-sisters-he-chose-to-forget-1538544.html, accessed 9 July 2018.
3 Foster, R. F., *W. B. Yeats* (1997)
4 Mikhail, E. H. (ed.), *W. B. Yeats*, pp. 372–380.
5 Coldwell, J., 'Pamela Colman Smith and the Yeats Family', *The Canadian Journal of Irish Studies*, Vol. 3, No. 2 (1977), pp. 27-34
6 *Ibid.*
7 Schuchard, R., *The Last Minstrels* (2010).
8 Albert Bigelow Paine Letters, The Huntingdon Library, San Marino, California, huntington.org, accessed various dates
9 Greer, M., marykgreer.com/2015/02/06/pamela-colman-smith-heart-of-the-heights/ accessed various dates.
10 Murphy, W., *Family Secrets* (1995).
11 *Ibid.*
12 Pyle, H., *Jack B. Yeats* (1989).
13 John Burns Library blog https://johnjburnslibrary.wordpress.com/2018/03/26/the-many-business-endeavors-of-pamela-colman-smith/ accessed 15 July 2018.
14 O'Connor, E. F., '"We Disgruntled Devils Don't Please Anybody": Pamela Colman Smith, The Green Sheaf, and Female Literary Networks', *South Carolina Review*, 48(2) (2016), pp. 72–89.

Chapter 11

1 Nunn, P., 'The Mid-Victorian Woman Artist' (1982), PhD thesis.
2 *Ibid.*
3 *Ibid.*
4 *Ibid.*
5 Colman Smith, P., *Should the Art Student Think?* (1908)
6 Hannah Rose Shaw blog: theartofhannahroseshaw.co.uk/art-theatre-and-tarot-the-extraordinary-life-of-pamela-colman-smith/—no longer accessible.
7 Brooklyn Daily Eagle, 1 November 1904, bklyn.newspapers.com/image/53435816/ accessed 9 July 2018.
8 Guardian articletheguardian.com/uk/2004/jun/02/arts.guardianhayfestival2004 accessed 9 July 2018.
9 Pyne, K., *Modernism and the Feminine Voice* (2007).
10 Mary Greer's Tarot blog, marykgreer.com accessed various dates
11 Coale, D., Georgia O'Keeffe and the Rider-Waite Tarot Deck, arthistory.us/display.php?eid=55 accessed 23 June 2018
12 Reily, N., *Georgia O'Keeffe, A Private Friendship, Part I* (2007).
13 Whelan, R., *Alfred Stieglitz* (1997).
14 New York Sun review marykgreer.com/2015/02/10/pamela-colman-smith-1912-correspondences/ accessed various dates.
15 Whelan, R., *op. cit.*
16 Greer, M., marykgreer.com/2015/02/09/pamela-colman-smith-1909-magic-spectacles/, accessed various dates.
17 Casseres, B. de, library.brown.edu/pdfs/1427132497992436.pdf accessed 9 July 2018.

18 Review in *Brooklyn Life*, marykgreer.com/ accessed various dates.
19 Mary Greer's Tarot blog marykgreer.com/ accessed various dates.
20 *Ibid.*
21 *The Columbus Journal* (Columbus, Neb.) 187401911, 26 October 1904, Image 6.

Chapter 12

1 Illustration art blog, illustrationart.blogspot.com/2011/10/old-question-finally-answered.html accessed 9 July 2018.
2 Mary Greer's Tarot blog, accessed various dates.
3 *Ibid.*
4 *Ibid.*
5 *Ibid.*
6 *Ibid.*
7 O'Connor, E. F., '"We Disgruntled Devils Don't Please Anybody": Pamela Colman Smith, The Green Sheaf, and Female Literary Networks', *South Carolina Review*, 48(2) (2016), pp. 72–89.
8 Albert Bigelow Paine Letters, The Huntingdon Library, San Marino, California, huntington.org.
9 Katz, M., and Goodwin, T., *Secrets of the Waite Smith Tarot* (2015).
10 Pamela Colman Smith letters to Alfred Stieglitz Yale University Library, Beinecke Rare Book and Manuscript Library, Alfred Stieglitz/Georgia O'Keeffe archive.
11 *Ibid.*
12 *Ibid.*
13 *Ibid.*
14 *Ibid.*
15 *Ibid.*
16 *Ibid.*
17 *Ibid.*
18 *Ibid.*
19 *Ibid.*
20 *Ibid.*
21 Boyd Parsons, M., *To All Believers* (1975).

Chapter 13

1 Synaesthesia Association UK, uksynaesthesia.com/ accessed 23 June 2018.
2 MacDonald, M., 'Fairy Faith' article online, accessed 30 June 2018.
3 *Ibid.*
4 *Ibid.*
5 Heyrman, H., doctorhugo.org/synaesthesia/art/index.html accessed 10 July 2018.
6 *Ibid.*
7 Author's interview with synaesthete London artist, Jane Mackay, 2017.
8 Boyd Parsons, M., *To All Believers* (1975).
9 *Ibid.*
10 *Ibid.*
11 Forbes-Sempill, 'Music Made Visible', *Illustrated London News* (12 February 1927), p. 260.
12 *Ibid.*
13 *Ibid.*
14 Author's interview with synaesthete London artist, Jane Mackay, 2017.

15 Mary Greer's Tarot Blog accessed various times.
16 Vance, J., Goldendawnpedia website no longer available.
17 Forbes-Sempill, *op. cit.*
18 Hartmann, E., and Kunzendorf, R. G., *Boundaries and Dreams* (2006)
19 *Ibid.*
20 *Ibid.*
21 Author's interview with synaesthete London artist, Jane Mackay.
22 *Ibid.*
23 *Ibid.*
24 *Ibid.*
25 Tripod website pcs2051.tripod.com/synesthesia.htm accessed various dates.
26 MacDonald, M., *op. cit.*
27 Hoffman, A., lab notes (1943)
28 Ward *et al*, *Synaesthesia, Creativity and Art* (2008).

Chapter 14

1 Kaplan, S., *The Encyclopaedia of the Tarot* (1979)
2 'Why Rituals Work', *Scientific American* (2013) accessed 11 July 2018, scientificamerican.com/article/why-rituals-work/
3 Waite, A., *The Occult Review* (1909).
4 Decker, R. and Dummett, M., *A History of the Occult Tarot 1870–1970* (2002).
5 *Ibid.*
6 Waite, A., *Shadows of Life and Thought* (1938).
7 Pamela used many variants of her name: Colman, Coleman, Corinne, Corine, and so on.
8 Farley, H., *The Occult World*, Chapter 57 (Routledge, 2016), pp. 571–579.
9 Puritan Board Blog, puritanboard.com/threads/the-occult-in-the-late-19th-early-20th-centuries.34386/ accessed 23 June 2018.
10 Gertrude Moakley was a librarian who, in 1938, suggested that Pamela had drawn heavily from the Sola Busca cards in illustrating the minor arcana/pip cards.
11 *Ibid.*
12 Boyd Parsons, M., *To All Believers* (1975).
13 Coldwell, J., 'Pamela Colman Smith and the Yeats Family', *The Canadian Journal of Irish Studies*, Vol. 3, No. 2 (1977).
14 Traditional tarot deck dating from 1856 containing four suits: batons, épées (swords), cups, and coins.
15 Delistrary, C., article, delistraty.com/2016/10/29/the-surprising-historical-significance-of-fortune-telling/ accessed 2018.
16 *Ibid.*
17 Boyd Parsons, *op. cit.*
18 Hardwick, J., *The Yeats Sisters* (1996).
19 *Ibid.*
20 Gilbert, R. A., *A. E. Waite* (1987).
21 Beattie, R., *Nature Mystics* (2015).
22 Pyne, K., *Modernism and the Feminine Voice* (2007).
23 Stieglitz, A., *Is Photography a Failure?* (1922).
24 *Ibid.*
25 Colman Smith, P., pcs2051.tripod.com/arts_and_crafts.htm accessed various dates.

Chapter 15

1 Colman Smith, P., *The Green Sheaf* (1903).
2 *Ibid.*
3 Pamela Colman Smith letters to Alfred Stieglitz Yale University Library, Beinecke Rare Book and Manuscript Library, Alfred Stieglitz/Georgia O'Keeffe archive.
4 O'Connor, E. F., '"We Disgruntled Devils Don't Please Anybody": Pamela Colman Smith, The Green Sheaf, and Female Literary Networks', *South Carolina Review*, 48(2) (2016), pp. 72–89.
5 *Ibid.*
6 Cariann Colman contacted me; we enjoyed an exchange about Pamela's ethnicity.
7 Pyne, K., *Modernism and the Feminine Voice* (2007).
8 Tripod website, pcs2051.tripod.com/accessed various dates.
9 Terry, E., *The Russian Ballet.*
10 *Ibid.*
11 Rachlin, A., *Edy Was a Lady* (2011).
12 Bebergal, 'Making the Tarot Literary Again', *New Yorker* (2016).
13 Crispin, J., *The Creative Tarot* (2016).
14 I asked a small group of people to read Alone by Pamela Colman Smith and give their individual impressions.
15 O'Connor, E. F., *op. cit.*
16 Tonnies, thoughtco.com/gemeinschaft-3026337 accessed 14 July 2018.

Chapter 16

1 Reason, A. and Eakins, T., *Thomas Eakins and the Uses of History* (2010).
2 Greer, M., *Women of the Golden Dawn* (1995).
3 Katz, M. and Goodwin, T., *Secrets of the Waite-Smith Tarot* (2015).

Chapter 17

1 Boisseau, R., *The Women of the Abbey Theatre* (2004).
2 *Ibid.*
3 Morton, T., *Changing Spaces* (2012).
4 Cockcroft, I. and Croft, S., *Art, Theatre and Women's Suffrage* (2010).
5 Farley, H., *Lost Envoy* (2016).
6 Cockin, K., *Edith Craig and the Theatres of Art* (2017).
7 O'Connor, E. F., '"We Disgruntled Devils Don't Please Anybody": Pamela Colman Smith, The Green Sheaf, and Female Literary Networks', *South Carolina Review*, 48(2) (2016), pp. 72–89.

Chapter 18

1 Bland, L., *Banishing the Beast* (2002).
2 Pateman, C., *The Sexual Contract* (1988).
3 Surplus Women ww1centenary.oucs.ox.ac.uk/unconventionalsoldiers/%E2%80%98 surplus-women%E2%80%99-a-legacy-of-world-war-one/ accessed 23 June 2018.
4 *Ibid.*
5 *Ibid.*
6 Email communication with Melinda Boyd Parsons, 2017.

7 Smith-Rosenberg, C., *Disorderly Conduct* (1985).
8 *Ibid.*
9 Evans, M., *Feminism and Modernity* (2007).
10 Hicok, B., *Degrees of Freedom* (2008).

Chapter 19

1 Hall, R., *The Well of Loneliness* (1928), a book banned on publication.
2 Shearer, M., *Ellen Terry* (2011).
3 Melville, J., *Ellen and Edy* (1987).
4 *Ibid.*
5 *Ibid.*
6 St John, C., *Hungerheart* (1915).
7 Melville, *op. cit.*
8 Craig, E., *Ellen Terry and Her Secret Self* (1932).
9 Holroyd, M., *A Strange Eventful History* (2008).
10 Visit to Smallhythe (2017); Susannah Mayor, curator.
11 Glasgow, J., *Lesbian Texts and Contexts* (1990).
12 Visit to Smallhythe (2017); Susannah Mayor, curator.
13 Auerbach, N., *Ellen Terry* (1997).
14 Glendinning, V., *The Life of Vita Sackville-West* (2005).
15 Hamer, E. *et al*, *Gender Studies* (2016).
16 Auerbach, N., *op. cit.*
17 *Ibid.*
18 Hamer, E., *Britannia's Glory: A History of Twentieth-Century Lesbians* (1996)
19 Auerbach, N., *op. cit.*
20 *Ibid.*
21 *Ibid.*
22 *Ibid.*
23 *Ibid.*
24 Interview with Jackie Adams, Bude, 2017.

Chapter 20

1 Frontain, R. J., *Reclaiming the Sacred* (2013).
2 Emsley, C., *Crime and Society in England 1750–1900* (1996).
3 Woollacott, A., *Khaki Fever* (1994).
4 Whitehead, A., *100 Years in Cornwall* (1993).
5 *Ibid.*
6 *Ibid.*
7 *Ibid*, Cornish Magazine cited in the book.
8 *Ibid.*
9 Email correspondence with Angie Hodges of the English Catholic History Association.
10 Mullen, L., *The Chance of Salvation* (2017).
11 Nicholson, V., *Among the Bohemians* (2005).
12 *Ibid.*
13 Ransome, A., *Bohemia in London* (1907).
14 Mullen, L., *op. cit.*
15 Newsome, D., *The Convert Cardinals* (1993).

16 Coldwell, J., 'Pamela Colman Smith and the Yeats Family', *The Canadian Journal of Irish Studies*, Vol. 3, No. 2 (1977).
17 Boyd Parsons, M., *To All Believers* (1975).
18 Atkins, B., *Yeats* (2010).
19 Underhill, E., *Mysticism* (1911).
20 Letters held by Plymouth Diocesan Archive.
21 English Catholic History Association, echa.org.uk/ accessed 29 June 2018.
22 Kaplan, S., *Encyclopedia of the Tarot* (1979).
23 Ross, D., *Critical Companion to W. B. Yeats* (2009).
24 Burdett, C., bl.uk/romantics-and-victorians/articles/aestheticism-and-decadence accessed 12 July 2018.

Chapter 21

1 Sister Benignus is the Plymouth Diocese Archivist in Exeter.
2 Tribute to Brian Torode, btsarnia.org/ accessed 15 July 2018.
3 Kaplan, S., from folder of information given to Bude locals.

Chapter 22

1 Letters held at Plymouth Diocesan Archive, Exeter.
2 *Ibid.* Coleman is one of the many variants of Pamela's name.
3 Document held at Plymouth Diocesan Archive, May 1933.
4 *Ibid.*
5 *Ibid.*
6 *Ibid.*
7 *Ibid.*
8 *Ibid.*
9 *Ibid.*
10 *Ibid.*
11 *Ibid.*
12 *Ibid.*
13 *Ibid.*
14 *Ibid.*
15 crocat.cornwall.gov.uk/DServe/searchpage.htm document reference P105/2/22.
16 Email communication with Melinda Boyd Parsons, 2017.
17 *Ibid.*
18 Correspondence with John Garth, 2017.
19 *The Cornishman*, July, 1899

Chapter 23

1 Letters from Plymouth Diocesan Archives.
2 *Ibid.*
3 *Ibid.*
4 *Ibid.*
5 Email communication with Tolkien researcher, John Garth, 2017.
6 Letter from I. S. Mooney to Williams Innes Homer.
7 Alison Spence, Principal Archivist, Cornwall Council

Chapter 24

1 Recorded interview material by author with Tony Edwards in Bude, 2017.
2 Masefield, J., *Some Memories of W. B. Yeats* (1940).
3 Womer, J., *Fighting with the Filthy Thirteen* (2012).
4 Information on old Bude from Ray Boyd.
5 Recorded interview material by author with Tony Edwards in Bude, 2017.
6 *Ibid.*
7 *Ibid.*
8 Interview with Jackie and Brian Adams, Bude.
9 Recorded interview material by author with Tony Edwards in Bude, 2017.
10 Interview with Jackie and Brian Adams, Bude.
11 Recorded interview material by author with Tony Edwards in Bude, 2017.
12 *Ibid.*
13 *Ibid.*
14 *Ibid.*
15 Information in folder gathered by Stuart Kaplan, shared with local people in Bude.

Chapter 25

1 Pyne, K., *Modernism and the Feminine Voice* (2007).
2 Masefield, J., *Some Memories of W. B. Yeats* (1940).
3 Pyne, K., *op. cit.*
4 *Ibid.*
5 Email communication with Kathleen Pyne.
6 *Ibid.*
7 *Ibid.*
8 Parc Garland, Pamela's home is now owned as a family home. Conversation with owner, Hayley White.

Bibliography

Hungerheart: The Loves of Christopher St John—A Sketch Of The Past (2018), asketchofthepast.com/2013/03/04/hungerheart-the-loves-of-christopher-st-john/ [Accessed 27 Jun. 2018].

Adlard, E., *Recollections of Edith Craig* (London: Frederick Muller, 1949)

Allitt, P., *Catholic converts* (Ithaca: Cornell University Press, 2000)

Anon, *The Plymouth Diocesan Record*, 3(8) (1923).

Anon, *Journal of the Royal Society of Arts © 1942 Royal Society for the Encouragement of Arts, Manufactures and Commerce*, jstor.org/publisher/thersa [Accessed 24 Jun. 2018].

Apatoff, D., *The Old Question Finally Answered: 'What is the Difference Between Illustration and Fine Art?'* (2011), illustrationart.blogspot.com/2011/10/old-question-finally-answered.html [Accessed 9 Jul. 2018].

Arkins, B., *The thought of W.B. Yeats* (Oxford: Peter Lang, 2010), p. 77.

Arthistory.us, *ArtHistory.us—Georgia O'Keeffe and the Rider-Waite Tarot Deck* (2018), arthistory.us/display.php?eid=55 [Accessed 23 Jun. 2018].

Auerbach, N., *Ellen Terry* (Philadelphia: University of Pennsylvania Press, 1997)

Beattie, R., *Pagan portals, nature mystics:The Literary Gateway to Modern Paganism* (Lanham: John Hunt Publishing, 2015)

Bebergal, P., Phillips, B., Daloz, K., Finnegan, W., Sorkin, A., Entous, A., Bebergal, P., Bebergal, P., Slattery, L., and Phillips, B., 'Making the Tarot Literary Again', *The New Yorker* (2016), newyorker.com/books/page-turner/making-the-tarot-literary-again [Accessed 11 Jul. 2018].

Benjamin Pollock's Toyshop, *Our History—Benjamin Pollock's Toyshop* (2018), pollocks-coventgarden.co.uk/about-us/our-history/ [Accessed 8 Jul. 2018].

Biddy Tarot, *BTP117: The Secret Life of Pamela Colman-Smith with Susan Wands*, (2018), biddytarot.com/btp117-secret-life-pamela-coleman-smith/ [Accessed 23 Jun. 2018].

Bland, L., *Banishing the Beast* (England: I. B. Tauris and Co. Ltd, 2002)

Boisseau, R., *The Women of the Abbey Theatre, 1897–1925* (College Park, Md.: University of Maryland, 2004)

Brooklyn Public Library, *4 Nov 1904, Page 1—The Brooklyn Daily Eagle at Newspapers.com*, bklyn.newspapers.com/image/53435816/ [Accessed 9 Jul. 2018].

Brooks, R., *History of the Massachusetts Bay Colony* (2018), historyofmassachusetts.org/history-of-the-massachusetts-bay-colony/ [Accessed 23 Jun. 2018].

Brown, R., *Khaki fever* (2018), richardjohnbr.blogspot.com/2014/08/khaki-fever.html [Accessed 23 Jun. 2018].

btsarnia, *A Catholic Treasury—Jottings from the Late Donald Halliday of North Hinksey*, btsarnia.org/2017/09/20/a-catholic-treasury-jottings-from-the-late-donald-halliday-of-north-hinksey/ [Accessed 27 Jun. 2018]; btsarnia.org/ [Accessed 15 Jul. 2018].

Catholic Straight Answers, *What does the Church teach about fortunetellers, psychic counselors, and witches?* (2018), catholicstraightanswers.com/what-does-the-church-teach-about-fortunetellers-psychic-counselors-and-witches/ [Accessed 27 Jun. 2018].

Chroniclingamerica.loc.gov. *Deseret evening news. (Great Salt Lake City [Utah]) 1867–1920, November 25, 1899, Part 3, Image 23*, chroniclingamerica.loc.gov/lccn/sn83045555/1899-11-25/ed-1/seq-23/#date1=1789&index=19&rows=20&words=Colman+ColmanSmiths+Pamela+Smith&searchType=basic&sequence=0&state=&date2=1963&proxtext=pamela+colman+smith&y=9&x=12&dateFilterType=yearRange&page=1 [Accessed 14 Jul. 2018]; *The Columbus journal. (Columbus, Neb.) 1874–1911, October 26, 1904, Image 6*, chroniclingamerica.loc.gov/lccn/sn95073194/1904-10-26/ed-1/seq-6/#date1=1789&index=17&rows=20&words=Colman+Pamela+Smith&searchType=basic&sequence=0&state=&date2=1963&proxtext=pamela+colman+smith&y=9&x=12&dateFilterType=yearRange&page=1 [Accessed 14 Jul. 2018]; *The Evening Statesman (Walla Walla, Wash.) 1903–1910, February 27, 1907, Image 5*, chroniclingamerica.loc.gov/lccn/sn88085421/1907-02-27/ed-1/seq-5/#date1=1789&index=2&rows=20&words=Colman+Pamela+Smith&searchType=basic&sequence=0&state=&date2=1963&proxtext=pamela+colman+smith&y=9&x=12&dateFilterType=yearRange&page=1 [Accessed 14 Jul. 2018]; *The sun. (New York [N.Y.]) 1833–1916, March 17, 1912, FOURTH SECTION, Image 55*, chroniclingamerica.loc.gov/lccn/sn83030272/1912-03-17/ed-1/seq-55/#date1=1789&index=10&rows=20&words=Colman+Pamela+Smith&searchType=basic&sequence=0&state=&date2=1963&proxtext=pamela+colman+smith&y=9&x=12&dateFilterType=yearRange&page=1 [Accessed 14 Jul. 2018].

Cockin, K., *Ellen Terry* (London: Routledge, 2016); *Edith Craig and the Theatres of Art* (London: Bloomsbury Academic, 2017)

Cockin, K. and Campling, J., *Women and Theatre in the Age of Suffrage* (Houndmills, Basingstoke, Hampshire: Palgrave, 2001)

Cockroft, I. and Croft, S., *Art, Theatre and Women's Suffrage* (London: Aurora Metro, 2010)

Coldwell, J., 'Pamela Colman Smith and the Yeats Family', *The Canadian Journal of Irish Studies* 3(2) (1977), pp. 27–34.

Coldwell, J. and Lenoski, D., 'The Irish Tradition in Literature', *The Canadian Journal of Irish Studies*, 6(2) (1980), p. 62.

College, J., *pamela colman smith | Search Results | John J. Burns Library's Blog* johnjburnslibrary.wordpress.com/?s=pamela+colman+smith [Accessed 23 Jun. 2018]

Colman, *The Mother's Present* (Boston: S. Colman, 1847); *Stories for Corinne* (New York: Samuel Raynor, 1848)

Colman Smith, P. *The Green Sheaf* (1903); 'Should the art student think?', *The Craftsman* XIV(4) (1908), pp. 417–419, digicoll.library.wisc.edu/cgi-bin/DLDecArts/DLDecArts-idx?type=article&did=DLDecArts.hdv14n04.i0016&id=DLDecArts.hdv14n04&isize=text [Accessed 8 Jul. 2018].

Confraternity.org.uk., *Confraternity of the Blessed Sacrement*. [online] Available at: https://www.confraternity.org.uk/ [Accessed 29 Jun. 2018].

Contentdm.okeeffemuseum.org, *Letter from I.S. Mooney O.S. B. to William Innes Homer: William Innes Homer Papers* (2018), contentdm.okeeffemuseum.org/cdm/compoundobject/collection/wih/id/2061/rec/11 [Accessed 29 Jun. 2018].
Craig, E., *Ellen Terry and Her Secret Self* (New York: E.P. Dutton & Co., 1923)
Crispin, J., *The Creative Tarot* (n.d.)
de Casseres, B., *Modernist Journals Project* (1909) modjourn.org/render.php?id=1427131865473723&view=mjp_object [Accessed 9 Jul. 2018].
Decker, R. and Dummett, M., *A History of the Occult Tarot* (n.d.)
Delistraty, C., *The Surprising Historical Significance of Fortune-Telling* (2016) delistraty.com/2016/10/29/the-surprising-historical-significance-of-fortune-telling/ [Accessed 11 Jul. 2018].
Hugo, D., *Art & Synesthesia—Dr. Hugo Heyrman (motions of the mind)* (2018), doctorhugo.org/synaesthesia/ [Accessed 23 Jun. 2018]; *'Art and Synesthesia: in search of the synesthetic experience' by Dr. Hugo Heyrman,* doctorhugo.org/synaesthesia/art/index.html [Accessed 10 Jul. 2018].
Dyhouse, C.,*Girls Growing up in Late Victorian and Edwardian England* (London: Routledge, 2016)
Ellenterryarchive.hull.ac.uk, *Ellen Terry and Edith Craig Database* (2018), ellenterryarchive.hull.ac.uk/ [Accessed 23 Jun. 2018].
English Catholic History Association, *English Catholic History Association* (2018), echa.org.uk/ [Accessed 29 Jun. 2018].
Evans, M., *Feminism and Modernity* (London [u.a.]: Routledge, 2002)
Ezard, J., Bohemian Culture 'is now the norm', *The Guardian* (2018), theguardian.com/uk/2004/jun/02/arts.guardianhayfestival2004 [Accessed 9 Jul. 2018].
Faderman, L., *Surpassing the Love of Men* (London: Women's, 1997)
Ferguson, C. and Radford, A., *The Occult Imagination in Britain, 1875–1947* (2016)
fineartviews.com, *Fine Artist vs. Illustrator* (2018) faso.com/fineartviews/18678/fine-artist-vs-illustrator [Accessed 26 Jun. 2018].
Foley O'Connor, E., 'We Disgruntled Devils Don't Please Anybody':Pamela Colman Smith, The Green Sheaf, and Female Literary Networks'. *South Carolina Review*, 48(2) (2016), pp. 72–89.
Forbes-Sempill, M., 'Music Made Visible', *Illustrated London News* (Feb. 12 1927), p. 260.
Foster, R., *W. B. Yeats* (Oxford: Oxford University Press, 1997)
Francesca Gino, M. and Francesca Gino, M., *Why Rituals Work*, Scientific American (2013), scientificamerican.com/article/why-rituals-work/ [Accessed 11 Jul. 2018].
Frontain, R., *Reclaiming the Sacred* (Routledge, 2013)
Genuki.org.uk, *GENUKI: Cornwall Towns and Parishes, Cornwall* (2018), genuki.org.uk/big/eng/CON/indexpars [Accessed 23 Jun. 2018].
Gilbert, R., *A. E. Waite* (Wellingborough, Northhamptonshire: Crucible, 1987)
Glendinning, V., *The Life of V. Sackville-West* (London: Phoenix, 2005)
Globalspiritualstudies.com, *Welcome to Global Spiritual Studies!* (2018), globalspiritualstudies.com [Accessed 23 Jun. 2018].
Greer, M., *Women of the Golden Dawn* (Park Street, 1998); *Tarot Tours of Scotland & Merlin's Britain* (2018), marykgreer.com/2017/10/04/tarot-tours-of-scotland-merlins-britain/ [Accessed 15 Jul. 2018].
Hall, R. and Duffy, M., *The Well of Loneliness* (n.d.)
Hamer, E., Money, J., Meyers, J., Norton, R., Collis, R., More, K., Whittlem S., Thadani, G., Smith, R., and Ainley, R., *Gender Studies* (London: Bloomsbury, 2016)
Hansard.millbanksystems.com, *INCOME TAX (Hansard, 10 April 1951)* (2018), hansard.millbanksystems.com/commons/1951/apr/10/income-tax-1 [Accessed 24 Jun. 2018].
Hardwick, J., *The Yeats Sisters* (Hammersmith, London: Pandora, 1996)

Harper, G., *Yeats's Golden Dawn* (New York: Palgrave Macmillan, 2013)
Herniman, I., 'Our Lady of the Lizard', *Plymouth Diocesan Record*, 8(10) (1933).
Hicok, B., *Degrees of Freedom* (Lewisburg: Bucknell University Press, 2003)
Hoffman, A., *LSD: Completely Personal* (1943), maps.org/news-letters/v06n3/06346hof.html [Accessed 10 Jul. 2018].
Holroyd, M., *A Strange Eventful History* (n.d.)
Ie.emb-japan.go.jp, *Press Release: Embassy of Japan in Ireland* (2018), ie.emb-japan.go.jp/itpr_en/00_000224.html [Accessed 23 Jun. 2018].
Ithellcolquhoun.co.uk, *Ithell Colquhoun, artist, writer, occultist—homepage* (2018), ithellcolquhoun.co.uk/ [Accessed 26 Jun. 2018].
Jay, K. and Glasgow, J., *Lesbian Texts and Contexts* (London: Only Women Press, 1992), p. 242.
Jefferson, M., 'The Real New York in 1910', *Bulletin of the American Geographical Society*, 43(10) (1911), pp. 737–740.
John J. Burns Library's Blog, *The Many Business Endeavors of Pamela Colman Smith* (2018), johnjburnslibrary.wordpress.com/2018/03/26/the-many-business-endeavors-of-pamela-colman-smith/ [Accessed 15 Jul. 2018].
Jordan, E., '"Making Good Wives and Mothers?" The Transformation of Middle-Class Girls' Education in Nineteenth-Century Britain', *History of Education Quarterly*, 31(4) (1991), p. 439.
Journals.sagepub.com, *Boundaries and Dreams—Ernest Hartmann, Robert G. Kunzendorf, 2006* (2018), journals.sagepub.com/doi/abs/10.2190/HK76-038K-407M-8670 [Accessed 10 Jul. 2018].
JSTOR Daily, *Synesthesia for Beginners | JSTOR Daily* (2018), daily.jstor.org/synesthesia-for-beginners/?utm_term=SYNESTHESIA%20FOR%20BEGINNERS&utm_campaign=jstordaily_04262018&utm_content=email&utm_source=Act-On_Internal&utm_medium=email [Accessed 14 Jul. 2018]; *The Surprising Historical Significance of Fortune-Telling | JSTOR Daily* (2018), daily.jstor.org/surprising-historical-significance-fortune-telling/ [Accessed 23 Jun. 2018]; *Pamela Colman Smith and the Yeats Family on JSTOR* (2018), jstor.org/stable/25512406 [Accessed 23 Jun. 2018].
Kaplan, S., *The Encyclopedia of Tarot* (New York: US Games Systems, 1979)
Katz, M. and Goodwin, T., *Secrets of the Waite-Smith Tarot* (2015).
Kelly, J. and Schuchard, R. *The Collected Letters of W.B. Yeats*. Oxford University Press.
Laneri, R. (2011). *This Book Belongs To ___: The Lost Art Of Bookplates* (2005), forbes.com/forbes/welcome/?toURL=https://www.forbes.com/sites/booked/2011/10/21/this-book-belongs-to-___-the-lost-art-of-bookplates/&refURL=https://www.google.co.uk/&referrer=https://www.google.co.uk/ [Accessed 23 Jun. 2018].
MacDonald, M., *The Fairy Faith and Pictured Music of Pamela Colman Smith* (1912), digicoll.library.wisc.edu/cgi-bin/DLDecArts/DLDecArts-idx?type=article&did=DLDecArts.hdv23n01.i0008&id=DLDecArts.hdv23n01&isize=M [Accessed 23 Jun. 2018].
Marianne, M., 'Yeats's Debt to Sisters He Chose to Forget', *The Independent* (1995), independent.co.uk/news/uk/home-news/yeatss-debt-to-sisters-he-chose-to-forget-1538544.html [Accessed 9 Jul. 2018].
Mary K. Greer's Tarot Blog, marykgreer.com [Accessed 23 Jun. 2018].
Masefield, J., *Some Memories of W. B. Yeats* (1940)
Mastermason.com, *Waite* (2018), mastermason.com/luxocculta/waite.htm [Accessed 27 Jun. 2018].
McCoy, M.,*The Lie is Eternal: A Novelist's Take on Portraying Twain in Fiction* (2016) esirc.emporia.edu/bitstream/handle/123456789/3553/Great%20Plains%201.pdf?sequence=1 [Accessed 25 Jun. 2018].

Melville, J., *Ellen and Edy* (London: Pandora, 1987)

Mikhail, E., *W. B. Yeats* ([S.l.]: Macmillan Publishers Limited, 1977)

Morton, T., 'Changing Spaces: art, politics, and identity in the home studios of the Suffrage Atelier', *Women's History Review*, 21(4) (2012), pp. 623–637.

Mullen, L., *The Chance of Salvation: A History of Conversion in America* (Cambridge: Harvard University Press, 2017), p. 240; *The Chance of Salvation: An Interview with Lincoln Mullen* (2017), thegospelcoalition.org/blogs/evangelical-history/the-chance-of-salvation-an-interview-with-lincoln-mullen/ [Accessed 12 Jul. 2018].

Murphy, W., *Family Secrets* (Syracuse, NY [u.a.]: Syracuse Univ. Press, 1995)

Nationaltrustcollections.org.uk, *Results, Maker: 'Pamela Colman Smith (Pimlico 1877–Bude 1925)'* (2018), nationaltrustcollections.org.uk/results?Maker=Pamela+Colman+Smith+(Pimlico+1877+-+Bude+1925) [Accessed 9 Jul. 2018].

New England Historical Society, *Mary Webster, the Witch of Hadley, Survives a Hanging - New England Historical Society* (2018), newenglandhistoricalsociety.com/mary-webster-witch-hadley-survives-hanging/ [Accessed 23 Jun. 2018].

Newsome, D., *The Convert Cardinals* (London: J. Murray, 1993)

Newton, E., 'The Mythic Mannish Lesbian: Radclyffe Hall and the New Woman', *Signs*, 9(4) (1984), pp. 557–575.

Nicholson, V., *Among the Bohemians* (New York: Perennial, 2005)

Nunn, P., discovery.ucl.ac.uk/1348998/1/438297.pdf [Accessed 14 Jul. 2018].

Parsons, M. and Smith, P., *To All Believers* (Newark: University of Delaware, 1975)

Pateman, C., *The Sexual Contract* (New York, NY: John Wiley & Sons, 2014)

Petry, A., *Frances B. Cogan, All-American Girl: The Ideal of Real Womanhood in Mid-Nineteenth-Century America* (Athens & London: The University of Georgia Press, 1989), pp. 298; *Journal of American Studies*, 24(03), p. 464.

Photocriticism.com, *Archive Texts: Stieglitz's 'Is Photography a Failure?'* (1922), photocriticism.com/members/archivetexts/photocredos/pf/stieglitzfailurepf.html [Accessed 11 Jul. 2018].

Pyle, H., *Jack B. Yeats* (London: A. Deutsch, 1989)

Pyne, K., *Modernism and the Feminine Voice* (Berkeley: University of California, 2007)

Rachlin, A., *Edy was a Lady* (Leicester: Matador, 2011)

Ransome, A., *Bohemia in London* ([S.l.]: Wentworth Press, 2016)

Reason, A. and Eakins, T., *Thomas Eakins and the Uses of History* (Philadelphia: University of Pennsylvania Press, 2010)

Reily, N., *Georgia O'Keeffe, A Private Friendship, Part I* (La Vergne: Sunstone Press, 2007)

Robinson, D., *Secret Bude* (Amblerley, 2016)

Ross, D., *Critical companion to William Butler Yeats* (New York: Facts On File, 2009)

Schuchard, R., *The Last Minstrels* (Oxford [u.a.]: Oxford University Press, 2010)

Shakespeare Birthplace Trust, *Bram and the Guv'nor: 'Who knew archives could be so much fun?'* (2018), shakespeare.org.uk/explore-shakespeare/blogs/bram-and-guvnor-who-knew-archives-could-be-so-much-fun/ [Accessed 24 Jun. 2018].

Shakespeare.org, *Shakespeare & Company* (2018), shakespeare.org/ [Accessed 23 Jun. 2018].

Shearer, M., *Ellen Terry* (Stroud, Gloucestershire: Sutton, 1998)

Smith, P., *Annancy Stories* (Nabu Press, 2010)

Smith-Rosenberg, C., *Disorderly Conduct* (New York, NY: Oxford Univ. Press, 1986)

SOLA-BUSCA TAROT MAYER, *Sola-Busca & Waite-Smith Tarot*, solabuscatarot1998mayer.wordpress.com/sola-busca-waite-smith-tarot/ [Accessed 26 Jun. 2018].

Spare, A. and Allen, J., *Lost Envoy* (London: Strange Attractor Press, 2016)

Spartacus Educational, *Edith Craig* (2018), spartacus-educational.com/WcraigE.htm [Accessed 27 Jun. 2018].

Spielvogel, J., *Western Civilization* (Boston: Cengage Learning, 2017)

Stamberg, S., *Modern Movement: How The Ballets Russes Revolutionized Dance* (2013), npr.org/2013/05/30/187066946/modern-movement-how-the-ballets-russes-revolutionized-dance?t=1530007783313&t=1531674594995 [Accessed 15 Jul. 2018].

Stieglitz, A., *Camera Work No 27* (1909), library.brown.edu/pdfs/1427132497992436.pdf [Accessed 23 Jun. 2018].

Stiles, H., *A History of the City of Brooklyn* (Ann Arbor, MI: University of Michigan Libraries, 2012)

Stoker, B., *Dracula; and the Lair of the White Worm* (London: Foulsham, 1986)

Tarot Heritage, *Tarot for the Masses, Mid-20th Century* (2018), tarot-heritage.com/history-4/tarot-for-the-masses-mid-20th-century/ [Accessed 26 Jun. 2018].

Telegraph.co.uk, *Wales: A Tale of Two Ladies Ahead of Their Time* (2018), telegraph.co.uk/travel/destinations/europe/uk/wales/724170/Wales-A-tale-of-two-ladies-ahead-of-their-time.html [Accessed 27 Jun. 2018].

Terry, E., *The Story of My Life—With Illustrations (Limited Edition of 1,000)* (London: Hutchison & Co., 1908); *Ellen Terry's Memoirs* (Ayer Co Pub, 1974); *The Russian ballet* (USA: Nabu Press, n.d.)

Terry, E. and Cockin, K., *The Collected Letters of Ellen Terry* (London: Pickering & Chatto, 2011)

Terry, E. and St John, C., *Ellen Terry and Bernard Shaw* (London: Max Reinhardt, 1952)

The British Library, *Aestheticism and decadence* (2014), bl.uk/romantics-and-victorians/articles/aestheticism-and-decadence [Accessed 12 Jul. 2018]; *Gender Roles in the 19th Century* (2018), bl.uk/romantics-and-victorians/articles/gender-roles-in-the-19th-century [Accessed 23 Jun. 2018].

The Economist, 'The Servant Problem' (2018), economist.com/christmas-specials/2011/12/17/the-servant-problem [Accessed 25 Jun. 2018].

The Guardian, 'First World War: How British Society Changed at Home' (2018), theguardian.com/world/2008/nov/11/first-world-war-changing-british-society [Accessed 27 Jun. 2018].

The Irving Society, *Henry Irving & Bram Stoker: A Working Relationship by Michael Kilgarriff* (2018), theirvingsociety.org.uk/henry-irving-bram-stoker-a-working-relationship/ [Accessed 23 Jun. 2018].

The Puritan Board, puritanboard.com/ [Accessed 23 Jun. 2018].

ThoughtCo, *What Gemeinschaft and Gesellschaft Mean in Sociology* (2018), thoughtco.com/gemeinschaft-3026337 [Accessed 14 Jul. 2018].

Uksynaesthesia.com, *UK Synaesthesia Association: What is Synaesthesia?* (2018), uksynaesthesia.com/whatis.html [Accessed 23 Jun. 2018].

Underhill, E., *Mysticism* (n.d.)

User, D., *The Yeats Society* (2018), yeatssociety.com/ [Accessed 23 Jun. 2018].

V & A Museum, *V & A Diaghilev and the Ballets Russes* (2018), npr.org/2013/05/30/187066946/modern-movement-how-the-ballets-russes-revolutionized-dance?t=1530007783313 [Accessed 26 Jun. 2018].

V&A Museum of Childhood, *Toy Theatres—V&A Museum of Childhood* (2018), vam.ac.uk/moc/collections/toy-theatres/ [Accessed 23 Jun. 2018].

Waite, A., *Shadows of Life and Thought* (Montana: Kessinger Pub. Co., 1997); *The Pictorial Key to the Tarot; being fragments of a secret tradition under the veil of divination ... With 78 plates, illustrating the greater and lesser Arcana, from designs by Pamela Colman Smith* (William Rider & Son: London, 1911), pp. xii and 340

Wands, S., *Magician and Fool* (n.d.)

Ward, J., Thompson-Lake, D., Ely, R., and Kaminski, F. 'Synaesthesia, creativity and art: What is the link?' *British Journal of Psychology*, 99(1) (2008)., pp. 127–141.

Whelan, R., *Alfred Stieglitz* (New York: Da Capo, 1997)

Whitehead, A., *100 Years in Cornwall: The History of a Canon Regular Ministry* (1993)

Wiener, M. *Clive Emsley, Crime and Society in England 1750–1900* (London and New York, Longman, 2018), journals.openedition.org/chs/944?lang=en [Accessed 23 Jun. 2018].

Womer, J., *Fighting with the Filthy Thirteen* (Grub Street, 2017)

Woollacott, A., 'Khaki Fever' and Its Control: Gender, Class, Age and Sexual Morality on the British Homefront in the First World War', *Journal of Contemporary History* 29(2) (1994), pp. 325–347, jstor.org/stable/260893 [Accessed 27 Jun. 2018].

Ww1centenary.oucs.ox.ac.uk. (2018). 'Surplus Women': a legacy of World War One? World War I Centenary, ww1centenary.oucs.ox.ac.uk/unconventionalsoldiers/%E2%80%98surplus-women%E2%80%99-a-legacy-of-world-war-one/ [Accessed 23 Jun. 2018].

Yeats, W., Kelly, J., Domville, E., and Schuchard, R., *The collected letters of W. B. Yeats* (2005)

Yeo, E., 'The creation of "motherhood" and Women's responses in Britain and France, 1750–1914', *Women's History Review*, 8(2) (1999), pp. 201–218; 'Labour History and Culture: A Postscript', *Labour History* 79 (2000), p. 117.

Zealand, N., *Papers Past | WEEKLY-WHISPERS* (Nelson Evening Mail, 1907-05-04) Paperspast.natlib.govt.nz, paperspast.natlib.govt.nz/newspapers/NEM19070504.2.30 [Accessed 14 Jul. 2018].